EUROPEANISED POLITICS?

BOOKS OF RELATED INTEREST

Recasting European Welfare States
edited by Maurizio Ferrera and Martin Rhodes

The Changing French Political System
edited by Robert Elgie

Compounded Representation in West European Federations
edited by Joanne B. Brzinski, Thomas D. Lancaster and Christian Tuschhoff

Politics and Policy in Democratic Spain: No Longer Different?
edited by Paul Heywood

Britain in the Nineties: The Politics of Paradox
edited by Hugh Berrington

Crisis and Transition in Italian Politics
edited by Martin Bull and Martin Rhodes

Southern European Welfare States: Between Crisis and Reform
edited by Martin Rhodes

The Euro-Mediterranean Partnership: Political and Economic Perspectives
edited by Richard Gillespie

The State in Western Europe: Retreat or Redefinition?
edited by Wolfgang C. Müller and Vincent Wright

The Regions and the European Community
edited by Robert Leonardi

The Regional Dimension of the European Union
edited by Charlie Jeffery

National Parliaments and the European Union
edited by Philip Norton (new in paperback)

The Crisis of Representation in Europe
edited by Jack Hayward

The Politics of Immigration in Western Europe
edited by Martin Baldwin-Edwards and Martin A. Schain

EUROPEANISED POLITICS?
European Integration and National Political Systems

Editors

KLAUS H. GOETZ
SIMON HIX

FRANK CASS
LONDON • PORTLAND, OR

First Published in 2001 in Great Britain by
FRANK CASS PUBLISHERS
Newbury House, 900 Eastern Avenue
London, IG2 7HH

and in the United States of America by
FRANK CASS PUBLISHERS
c/o ISBS, 5804 N.E. Hassalo Street
Portland, Oregon, 97213-3644

Website: www.frankcass.com

British Library Cataloguing in Publication Data

Europeanised politics?: European integration and national
political systems
1. European Union 2. European Union countries –Politics
and government
I. Goetz, Klaus H. II. Hix, Simon
320.9'4

ISBN 0 7146 5141 9 (hb)
ISBN 0 7146 8166 0 (pb)

Library of Congress Cataloging-in-Publication Data

Europeanised politics? : European integration and national political
systems / editors, Klaus H. Goetz, Simon Hix.
    p. cm.
Based on two workshops held at Nuffield College in Oxford in 1999.
Includes index.
ISBN 0-7146-5141-9 (hardbound) – ISBN 0-7146-8166-0 (pbk.)
    1. European Union. 2. European Union countries – Politics and
government. I. Goetz, Klaus H., 1961– II. Hix, Simon.

JN30 .E9424 2000
341.242'2–dc21   00-046592

This group of studies first appeared in a Special Issue of *West European Politics*
(ISSN 0140-2382) Vol.23, No.4 [Europeanised Politics? European Integration and
National Political Systems]

Printed in Great Britain by Antony Rowe Ltd., Chippenham, Wiltshire

Contents

Preface   vii

Introduction: European Integration and   **Simon Hix and**
National Political Systems   **Klaus H. Goetz**   1

The Limited Impact of Europe on National
Party Systems   **Peter Mair**   27

European Integration, Voters and
National Politics   **Matthew Gabel**   52

Political Contention in a Europeanising Polity   **Doug Imig and**
    Sidney Tarrow   73

Policy Networks in a Multi-Level System:
Convergence Towards Moderate Diversity?   **Gerda Falkner**   94

Europeanised Politics – Europeanised Media?   **Holli A. Semetko,**
European Integration and Political   **Claes H. de Vreese and**
Communication   **Jochen Peter**   121

Backbenchers Learn to Fight Back: European   **Tapio Raunio**
Integration and Parliamentary Government   **and Simon Hix**   142

The Positioning of EU Judicial Politics within
the United Kingdom   **Damlan Chalmers**   169

European Integration and National Executives:
A Cause in Search of an Effect?   **Klaus H. Goetz**   211

Abstracts   232

About the Contributors   237

Index   239

Preface

The papers collected in this volume arise out of two workshops, held at Nuffield College Oxford. We would like to thank the Warden and Fellows of Nuffield for allowing us use of the College's splendid facilities. The workshops were sponsored by the London Office of the Friedrich Ebert Foundation and the Suntory and Toyota International Centres for Economics and Related Disciplines (STICERD) at the LSE. Without their generous assistance, this volume could not have been published. The second workshop benefited greatly from the comments of the discussants of the papers, and we would like to thank Geoff Evans, David Farrell, Hussein Kassim, Anand Menon, Roger Scully, Alec Stone Sweet and Paul Taggart for their perceptive remarks. Special thanks are due to Stephanie Wright of Nuffield College, who did most of the work involved in organising and running the workshops and, importantly, made sure that bills were paid promptly.

Like so many other collaborative efforts in comparative European politics, this project was inspired by the late Vincent Wright. He provided the initial impetus, opened his College to us, chaired the first workshop and was to take part in the second, but had already become too ill to attend. He was a wonderful man, and we would like to dedicate this volume to his memory.

Klaus H. Goetz
Simon Hix

Introduction: European Integration and National Political Systems

SIMON HIX and KLAUS H. GOETZ

EUROPEAN INTEGRATION AND DOMESTIC POLITICAL CHANGE

The process of European integration has been studied and analysed at great length in a variety of academic disciplines. The main focus of this endeavour is usually to try to explain institution-building, policy integration or policy outputs at the European level. In the main theories of integration, domestic politics is a central explanatory factor of the integration process. For example, in the early 'neo-functionalist' theory of Ernst Haas and his followers, one of the driving forces of the delegation of policy functions to the European level was the battle between domestic interest groups, political parties and rival groups of elites. In the contemporary 'liberal-intergovernmental' approach of Andrew Moravcsik, the integration process is driven by competition and bargaining between the European nation-states, but 'national' preferences emerge from the on-going processes of domestic politics, where rival interests compete for control of the policy agenda.

Much less effort has gone into thinking about the reverse effect: European integration as an explanatory factor in domestic political continuity or change. The study of national political systems has evolved largely in isolation from the study of European integration for three main reasons. First, the separation has been a natural product of a division of labour in the discipline of political science: between comparative politics, with its focus on domestic political institutions and processes, and international relations, with its focus on international regimes and regional integration. Second, many scholars of comparative European politics have taken a healthily sceptical attitude to the study of European integration – as either a normative project or as not contributing much to generalisable political science knowledge. Third, as long as the empirical impact of European integration on national polities and politics was seemingly small, it could be ignored as a relevant variable. In other words, either the study of European integration was someone else's job, or it was not very interesting, or it was largely irrelevant.

This position is no longer sustainable. With the growing development of the 'multi-level' European polity, the disciplinary boundary between comparative politics and international relations is increasingly porous.[1] With the growing sophistication of the study of European integration and the EU, by understanding developments at the European level we can now begin to think about how this might help explain changes in domestic political systems. Finally, with the establishment of the Single Market and Economic and Monetary Union and the delegation of competences to the European level in many areas of domestic politics, the impact of European-level decisions on the choices available in national political systems is now too evident to ignore.

The present volume seeks to contribute to the now fairly rapidly growing literature that intends to direct attention to the domestic political consequences of European integration. The key question asked is what has been the impact of European integration on government and politics in domestic political systems. Put in more formal terms, the dependent variable is continuity and change in domestic political systems. Whereas the dependent variable in this collection of essays is, of course, the staple diet of comparative European politics, European integration as an explanatory variable of domestic institutional and political development has only recently begun to be analysed in systematic comparative fashion. The present collection covers some of the central fields in the comparative study of European political systems. Thus, five chapters deal with the European impact on what might loosely be termed the input side of domestic politics, including party systems (Mair), voting behaviour (Gabel), unconventional forms of political protest (Imig and Tarrow), public–private networks (Falkner) and political communication (Semetko, de Vreese and Peter). The remaining contributions focus on domestic governing institutions, including parliaments (Raunio and Hix), courts (Chalmers), and, finally, central executives (Goetz).[2] As the systematic and theory-oriented inquiry into domestic European effects is still at an early stage, in particular as far as domestic politics as opposed to government is concerned, our aspirations have been reasonably modest. First, the collection reviews and discusses the state of debate about the impact of European integration in specific areas and on the general development of domestic political systems. Second, where possible, the contributions present new findings or at least collate and structure existing evidence. Third, we have aimed to develop some tentative

explanations about how European integration affects domestic institutions
and processes. Finally, the contributors were invited to discuss avenues for
further research.

In this introductory chapter, we start by specifying the explanatory
variable a little more clearly, by discussing what we mean by 'European
integration'. This serves two purposes: to introduce the subject for students
of domestic politics who may be unfamiliar with the specific policy
competences and institutional design of the EU, but also to set the context
for subsequent theoretical analysis. Based on these definitions, we develop
some tentative propositions about how European integration might affect
domestic political systems, and briefly review some of the main
contributions to existing knowledge on the incidence and intensity of the
European effect. Much of the writing on Europeanisation approaches the
subject from an institutionalist perspective. While such an approach helps to
clarify the links between pressures for change and patterns of national
adaptation, European integration as a source of change cannot be considered
in isolation from other (potential) sources of domestic institutional and
political change.

WHAT IS EUROPEAN INTEGRATION?

European integration comprises two inter-related processes: the delegation
of policy competences to the supranational level to achieve particular policy
outcomes; and the establishment of a new set of political institutions, with
executive, legislative and judicial powers.

National Policy Delegation and European-Level Political Outcomes

Within domestic systems, policy competences are divided between different
levels of government and are delegated from majoritarian institutions, such
as legislatures and governments, to non-majoritarian institutions, such as
central banks and independent regulators. In much the same way, European
governments have delegated policy powers to the supranational level.[3] For
present purposes, the reasons behind this delegation – a subject of
contention between rival theories of European integration – are less
important than the outcomes that result from the establishment of policy
competences at the European level. To understand the impact of European
integration on domestic systems it is not decisive whether delegation is
determined by domestic government preferences, driven by transnational
economic actors, or 'cultivated' by supranational agents. What matters for
domestic actors and institutions is how the delegation to the European level

affects policy outcomes in the domestic arena. Put another way, who are the winners and losers from the EU?

The main policy competence of the European Union (EU) is in the area of *market regulation*. The European level is responsible for almost 80 per cent of all rules governing the production, distribution and exchange of goods, services, capital and labour in the European market. On the one hand, the EU is a deregulatory project. The removal of technical, fiscal and physical barriers to the 'free movement' of goods, services, capital and labour in the single market programme; the use of the principle of 'mutual recognition' (whereby any product or service legally sold in one member state can be sold throughout the EU); the restrictions on state aids, and EU competition policies have all contributed to the considerable deregulation and liberalisation of domestic markets and the privatisation of many national monopolies. On the other hand, domestic regulations have been replaced by a new 're-regulatory' regime at the European level. The main instrument of this regime is the 'harmonisation' of existing national standards. This normally means the establishment of a common minimum level, rather than a single uniform standard throughout the EU. This is the case with rules for health and safety at work and 'product standards', such as environmental standards and consumer protection standards. However, where the EU regulates 'process standards', such as workers' rights, European directives usually allow a high degree of freedom for member states to interpret the rules in the process of transposing EU law into domestic legislation.[4]

As in the domestic arena, the main justification for European re-regulation is the correction of 'market failures'.[5] For example, consumer standards reduce information asymmetries in market contracts, environment standards limit negative externalities of market transactions, and competition policies prevent monopolistic and anti-competitive practices. In this interpretation, the impact of the EU is relatively benign: EU policies are deliberately pareto-efficient and so everyone gains. However, regulations also have some 'indirect' redistributional or value allocative affects.[6] Common standards, adopted by a qualified majority of national governments, are inevitably lower than the standards in some member states and higher than in others. As a result, from the perspective of a member state with a relatively liberalised economy and low levels of welfare and environmental protection, such as Britain, the EU regulatory regime is 'socialism through the back door', as Margaret Thatcher famously put it. Alternatively, from the perspective of a member state with a highly regulated economy and high levels of welfare and environmental protection, such as Denmark, the EU regulatory regime is 'Anglo-Saxon capitalism through the back door'.

In contrast to regulation, the direct *redistributional* capacity of the EU is small. The EU budget is only 1.27 per cent of the total GDP of the EU member states and less than four per cent of total government expenditure in the EU. Nevertheless, the EU budget has had a significant indirect redistributional impact. This is particularly the case in the area of the Common Agricultural Policy (CAP), which consumes over 50 per cent of the EU budget. Whereas the cost of CAP to individual consumers and tax-payers may be less than £5 per week, the average European farmer receives a considerable proportion of his annual income from the EU purse. Similarly, the cost of EU regional funds may be small compared to the sum of national expenditure on regional development. But, for the beneficiary regions – particularly with Objective 1 status (with less than 75 per cent of average GDP) – these funds can account for as much as ten per cent of annual GDP. Basically, as with most welfare expenditure programmes, the costs of EU redistributional policies are diffuse (shared between all European taxpayers), whereas the benefits are concentrated (on farmers, backward regions, scientists, or European-level NGOs).

With Economic and Monetary Union (EMU), the EU also has a powerful role in *macro-economic stabilisation*. This operates through three main mechanisms. First, the independent European Central Bank is responsible for setting interest rates, with the main goal of securing 'price stability'. Second, the rules governing national budget deficits – as set out in the EU Treaty and the Growth and Stability Pact – force the member states to pursue fiscally conservative budgetary policies. Third, this is reinforced in the process of 'macro-economic policy surveillance' in the Council of Economic and Finance Ministers (EcoFin), where national governments have to justify their macro-economic policies and strategies in light of the European interest.

Perhaps more than in any other policy area, EMU's implications for domestic politics are considerable. Basically, macro-economic policy debates can no longer be resolved at the national level. On the one hand, the primary goal of price stability and the independence of the ECB have locked in a 'monetarist' policy agenda in this field. Giving up sovereignty over monetary and exchange-rate policy also entails major constraints on other macro-economic policies: expansionary welfare policies must be financed through commensurate increases in taxation, and EMU forces member states to use supply-side labour market policies to reduce unemployment. Nevertheless, EMU also offers the opportunity of pursuing neo-Keynesian demand-management policies at the European level. With a single currency, a similar proportion of EMU GDP is traded in a foreign currency as in the United States. As a result, devaluation of the Euro will not have such a long-term inflationary effect on the European economy as it did for the individual member states prior to EMU.

Finally, in addition to these economic policy competences, the member states have begun to delegate competences to the European level in more explicitly 'politicised' areas: justice and interior affairs, and foreign and defence policies. In the area of justice and interior affairs, the EU is committed to removing internal borders and developing common policies towards the movement of persons across the EU's external borders (such as immigration, refugee and asylum policies, and common rights for third-country nationals in the EU) and to co-operation in tackling cross-border crime. In time, the direct impact of these policies will be considerable, as they will redefine what it means to be a citizen of one of the EU member states. At the present time, however, these policies have only affected domestic policy choices at the margins. Similarly, in the area of common foreign and defence policies, the EU has begun to co-ordinate member states' foreign policy agendas and strategies. However, more than any other EU policy competence, foreign policy co-operation remains the preserve of national sovereignty, where all the key decisions are made unanimously and the powers of the supranational institutions are severely curtailed.

As result, the delegation of policy competences in the areas of interior and foreign affairs has had a limited impact on domestic policy choices. Nevertheless, these competences provide executive officials from different member states with an arena for sharing expertise and information, away from domestic interest groups, the media, parliaments and courts. This consequently brings us to the second major element of European integration: supranational institution-building.

Supranational Institution-Building

In addition to a new policy environment, European integration has led to the creation of a new level of political institutions, on top of the existing institutional structures of domestic polities. First, executive powers at the European level are divided between the EU governments and the European Commission. The EU governments set the long-term policy agenda by requesting the Commission or the Council (of national ministers) to undertake certain tasks or policy initiatives. They also control the delegation of powers to the European level and between the EU institutions, through treaty reforms in the now frequent intergovernmental conferences. They scrutinise the implementation of EU legislation by the Commission in the comitology system. And they are responsible for the transposition of EU law into domestic law.

As for the agenda-setting aspect of executive power, the European Commission has a monopoly on legislative initiative in the areas of regulation and budgetary expenditure. Concerning the administrative aspect of executive power, the Commission is responsible for ensuring the implementation of primary EU law (from the EU Treaty) and of secondary legislation (which must be transposed by the member states). In so doing, the Commission can use tertiary legislative instruments (just as executives do in the domestic arena). For example, in the area of competition policy, the Commission is responsible for implementing the EU Treaty articles on state aids and anti-cartel practices, and makes rulings about cross-border mergers under the Merger Regulation.

Second, executive power is shared between the EU governments and the European Parliament (EP). The main legislative procedure remains the so-called 'consultation procedure', where the EU governments must receive an opinion from the EP about a piece of legislation, which they can duly ignore. This does, however, give the EP a power of delay if the legislation is urgent. Also, with the Single European Act, the Maastricht Treaty and the Amsterdam Treaty, the powers of the EP have been progressively strengthened. So much so that in most areas of economic and social policy, EU legislation must receive the positive assent of both the Council and the EP, in the so-called 'co-decision procedure'. Also, the Council increasingly takes decisions by a qualified majority of votes (where the votes are weighted according to the size of the member states and an oversized majority is required for legislation to be adopted). However, the norm of consensus in the Council is strong, as member states have no incentive to implement decisions if they opposed the legislation in the adoption stage.

Third, judicial power is exercised by the European Court of Justice in Luxembourg and the courts of the EU member states. There are two basic doctrines of EU law. First, 'direct effect' means that the subjects of EU law are individual citizens rather than the EU states, and that the EU Treaty and secondary legislation are part of the domestic law of the member states. Together, this means that private citizens have access to EU law in their domestic courts. In other words, EU law is 'the law of the land' in all the member states. Second, 'supremacy' means that if there is a conflict between domestic law and EU law, then EU law is sovereign. In other words, EU law is also 'the *higher* law of the land'.[7]

Finally, mention needs to be made of the richness, complexity, pluralism and openness of the 'policy community' that exists at the European level. Brussels is more like Washington, DC than any national capital in Europe. Over 1,000 lobby groups have offices in Brussels with the specific aim of trying to influence the EU policy process. The fact that the Commission is understaffed, requires policy expertise in the highly technical process of harmonising the diverse European market, and needs the support of certain constituencies for legislation to pass the Council and the EP, ensures relatively open access for private interests at a very early stage of the policy process. Some see this as naïve American-style pluralism, which inevitably favours concentrated capitalist interests at the expense of diffuse public interests.[8] Nevertheless, there are elements of corporatism and neo-pluralism in the EU process. For example, the Commission has been instrumental in establishing a 'social dialogue' between the European-level employers' and trade union associations. Some national groups have privileged access in certain policy areas, such as French and German farmers in the making and reform of the CAP. And numerous public interest groups and non-governmental organisations receive substantial funds from the EU budget to guarantee their representation in the Brussels policy community.

Overall, this structure of governance institutions at the European level provides a particular environment for domestic political actors, the effect of which will be discussed below. Suffice it to say at this stage that the complexity of the EU policy process can lead to final policy outcomes that are different from the original intentions of governments and private interests that supported the delegation of powers to the European level.[9] This is particularly true in policy areas where the supranational institutions have been able to shape policy outcomes. First, in the legislative stage, a particular strategic environment in the Council can sometimes allow the Commission or the Parliament to propose legislation or legislative amendments that a qualified majority of member states prefer to the original status quo. This was often the case in the completion of the single market and in the setting of common environmental standards. Second, in the post-legislative stage, the requirement of unanimity to reform the Treaties gives the Commission and the Court of Justice a high degree of discretion in legislative implementation and interpretation. There is always one member state that would veto a move to reign in their powers.

The problem is that governments and private interests do not have perfect information in the policy process, and often have relatively short time-horizons (such as winning the next domestic general election) and so cannot always predict the ultimate policy outcomes. European integration provides the opportunity for delegation of powers to the European level and a new institutional arena for the pursuit of domestic policy goals. However, this strategy is not without risk.

THE DOMESTIC IMPACT: FROM IMPLICIT PROPOSITIONS TO AN ANALYTICAL FRAMEWORK

While theories of European integration have tended to treat domestic political systems as an explanatory variable in the process of integration, they do yield propositions about the likely repercussions of integration on domestic politics and government. But because these propositions are typically side-products of the main aim of explaining the dynamics of the integration process, they tend to be implicit rather than explicit and remain largely untested. For example, Andrew Moravcsik has pointed out that the logical conclusion of intergovernmentalist theories of integration, which see European integration as the product of the collective interests of the nation states, is that European integration 'strengthens the state' against society.[10] Yet, if integration is driven by governing elites, as is claimed, only certain state interests should be strengthened, such as executives at the expense of parliaments; senior public officials who are involved in the EU policy process at the expense of middle-ranking officials; or governing parties at the expense of opposition parties and private interest groups.

In contrast, one logical extension of the neo-functionalist assumption that European integration is promoted by certain private interests, such as transnational capital, could be that these interests will be strengthened in the domestic arena. But if these interests can achieve their desired policy outcomes at the European level, they may choose to exit the domestic policy arena altogether. If this happens, then their influence in domestic policy communities may in fact be weakened rather than strengthened.

Advocates of understanding the EU as a 'regulatory state' implicitly see the EU as being central in the transformation of the style of governance in the domestic arena. Through the EU, the old style of domestic political competition through majoritarian institutions, which leads to redistributive policy outcomes, is gradually being replaced by a new style of consensual problem-solving through independent regulatory agencies, which aims to achieve pareto-efficient policy outcomes.[11] However, these theorists do not tend to discuss what this means for traditional domestic actors or institutions, such as parties, parliaments and the process of electoral competition, which are wedded to the old style of majoritarian redistributionalism.

Although these propositions have largely remained under-formalised and under-tested, they may serve as a useful basis on which to develop broader analytical frameworks for understanding the impact of integration on domestic political systems. From these propositions, and from our definition of the process of European integration, the latter can be expected to have two types of impact on domestic actors and institutions:

(1) the delegation of policy competences to the European level and the resulting political outcomes constrain domestic choices, reinforce certain policy and institutional developments, and provide a catalyst for change in others; and

(2) the establishment of a higher level of governance institutions provides new opportunities to exit from domestic constraints, either to promote certain policies, or to veto others, or to secure informational advantages.

Moreover, these two processes are inherently inter-related. For example, losers from the policy impact of the EU may attempt to change this situation by pursuing new strategies through the European level institutions.

European Outcomes: New Constraints, Reinforcements and Catalysts

Political outcomes at the European level have both direct and indirect impacts on domestic political systems. *Direct* impacts are outcomes that require domestic policies to be changed to conform to new European-wide norms. For example, the EU regulatory regime has forced the liberalisation of domestic markets. Similarly, EMU severely limits the macro-economic policy choices available to national decision-makers. Essentially, in the 'social market economy' of the EU single market, a fully neo-liberal deregulatory strategy is impossible. At the same time, however, the single market regime restricts public ownership and the protection of national champions, and EMU prevents Keynesian demand-management policies or expansionary welfare policies.

These types of impacts have been discussed at length in the literature.[12] What is more interesting for the present study is the *indirect* impact of European governance outcomes on domestic political institutions and input processes in domestic political systems. First, European governance outcomes have a significant indirect impact on institutional processes. In the area of public administration, for example, European integration propels member states to introduce new regulatory policy styles: through privatisation of national monopolies, and the creation of a host of new independent regulatory agencies, as part of the enforcement of EU rules. More specifically, EU regional policies encourage member states to establish planning authorities at the regional level, which in turn produce demands for a democratisation of these structures, and hence the creation of elected regional assemblies and governments. Similarly, in the area of legislative–executive relations, the fact that a whole host of policy issues are passed up to the European level restricts the ability of parliaments to scrutinise executives in a number of important policy areas. And in the field of judicial politics, the institutional design of the EU legal system, which allows national courts to apply EU law, strengthens the judicial review powers of national courts *vis-à-vis* domestic executives.

In some member states and institutional areas, European governance outcomes may *reinforce* existing trends. For example, in member states with existing regional authorities, such as Italy and Spain, EU regional policies have reinforced the demands of regional bodies for further delegation of policy competences away from central government. In contrast, in other member states and other institutional areas, European governance outcomes act as a *catalyst* in producing new institutional forms. For example, in member states with 'statist' public administrations, such as France and Italy, EU policies may act as catalysts in the creation of relatively alien non-majoritarian regulatory agencies. Similarly, in the area of judicial politics the EU has encouraged the creation of new judicial review powers, which might not have existed without the establishment of the EU legal system and the doctrine of direct effect.

Second, European governance outcomes have a significant indirect impact on input processes. For example, it has been suggested that European integration is now a salient issue amongst the electorates of most member states, cutting across the traditional left–right divide. This produces new political forces, divisions in traditional parties, and new electoral alignments. Moreover, direct elections to the European Parliament have indirect implications for domestic electoral processes, parties and party systems. The creation of a new and nation-wide (rather than regional) 'second-order' contest gives opposition and protest parties the opportunity to undermine support for governing parties, and gives voters the chance to punish the parties they support or signal their genuine policy preferences. European governance outcomes also influence the structure of interest representation and intermediation. The delegation of regulatory policy competences to the European level reduces the incentives for private firms and employers' associations to co-operate with trade unions and governments in corporatist policy arrangements.

Again, in some member states and in some input processes, these indirect effects appear to reinforce existing changes. For example, in member states where corporatist structures are already under threat, such as Britain, European policy outcomes appear to hasten their decline. In contrast, in other member states and other input process, these indirect effects are a catalyst for new developments. For example, in member states where Green parties were weak, such as Italy, Britain and Spain, European environmental policies and European-wide policy ideas have been a catalyst in raising the profile of environmental issues and boosting the electoral success of these parties. Similarly, in all member states, the introduction of European elections has been a catalyst for growing concerns about voter apathy.

The European Institutional Arena: New Exit, Veto and Information Opportunities

But this is only half of the story. The direct and indirect changes produced by European governance outcomes, or the potential changes that European integration could produce, provide incentives for domestic actors to mobilise at the European level either to promote certain effects or to undermine others. As a result, the other half of the story is how a new institutional arena at the European level impacts on domestic political systems by providing a new 'structure of opportunities' for domestic actors.

With another level of institutions at a higher political level, politics at the domestic level is inherently a 'nested game'.[13] This is a metaphor for situations where actors participate in two different games at the same time, and individual strategies and collective outcomes in one game (political arena) are inherently linked to individual strategies and collective outcomes in the other game (political arena). As a result, a strategy that might appear sub-optimal in one game (such as at the domestic level in the EU system) may in fact be optimal if political outcomes in the other game (at the European level) are also taken into account when deciding what actions to take. In such a situation, the existence of a new arena at the European level provides three different types of opportunities for domestic actors.

First, the European level offers the advantage for domestic actors to *exit* the domestic arena. This will occur if an actor is blocked from achieving a desirable policy or institutional outcome at the domestic level, but can predict that the direct or indirect impact of European-level outcomes will facilitate the ultimate end goal in the domestic arena. Although these actors may be powerful in the domestic system, actions can be blocked by public opinion, veto players in the policy process (as a result of such corporatist policy styles) or institutional mechanisms that prevent action without an oversized political majority (such as proportional representation, coalition government, strong bi-cameralism, federalism, and powerful independent courts). In this situation, even powerful actors in the domestic system – such as a governing political party and the interests they represent – have an incentive to promote actions at the European level. For example, multi-national firms lobbied for the single market programme, with the conscious expectation that this would force domestic governments to accept market and trade liberalisation. Similarly, centre-right governments in continental consensual systems, such as Germany and Italy, used EU policy outcomes to promote deregulatory policies in the domestic arena against strong domestic opposition.

Second, and sometimes in direct opposition to the *exit* opportunity, domestic actors can use the European level to seek a *veto* on domestic actions. This can occur if an actor is a loser in the domestic arena, but can reasonably predict that the direct or indirect impact of European-level outcomes will promote their cause in the domestic arena. This is particularly an opportunity to actors that might be weak in the domestic arena, such as interest groups who are excluded from the domestic policy process, or institutional players with access to the European-level arena, such as courts, central banks and regulatory agencies. For example, in the late 1980s, the British trade union movement used the European level to try to establish re-regulations at the European level to moderate the excesses of Thatcher's neo-liberal agenda in the domestic arena. Similarly, national judges can use the procedure for making 'preliminary references' to the European Court of Justice to promote their own policy agendas and powers against the competing interests of domestic parliamentary majorities.

Third, actors who are formally and informally part of the process of European-level governance can also use this position to gain *informational advantage* in the domestic arena. Information is a vital resource in policy battles. Actors with greater knowledge of likely policy outcomes, or who have a monopoly on technical expertise in a particular policy area, can often 'frame' policy debates to their advantage. The technical nature of much EU policy creates information asymmetries in domestic systems. Those who participate at the European level tend to be advantaged in the domestic arena. For example, government ministers (who sit in the EU Council) have more information about EU policies than their own backbenchers or opposition spokespersons. Similarly, senior bureaucrats, who spend much of their time in Brussels, have more information about EU policies than middle-level administrators.

This opportunity structure is likely to have particular effects on the institutional and input processes in domestic political systems. For example, on the institutional side, executives (governing parties) are more able to pursue exit strategies and have informational advantages than parliaments (backbench politicians and opposition parties). But, opposition parties in the larger member states (who are likely to have a Commissioner and significant representation in the European Parliament) may be able to pursue veto strategies to balance the comparative advantage of governing forces. Similarly, central public administrations are more able to pursue exit strategies than regional levels of governments. But, regional administrations, particularly in federal systems, may be able to use their access to the EU policy process and the Commission to pursue veto strategies against the advantage of central administrations.

On the input side, political elites could be argued to be better able to use the EU level to their own advantage than rank-and-file party members or the mass electorate. European integration, after all, is an elite-led project. For example, party leaders, who attend party leaders' summits and have access to their party representatives in the Council, the Commission and the Parliament, can pursue exit and informational advantage strategies to strengthen their positions within their party organisations. Similarly, private interests (such as multi-national firms), which are likely to secure concentrated redistributive benefits from EU policies, have a greater incentive to pursue exit, veto or informational advantage strategies than public interests (such as trade unions and environmentalists), where the costs of EU policies may be diffuse. Nevertheless, the openness of the EU policy process and the pursuit of neo-pluralist strategies by the Commission (such as subsidising under-represented groups) ensure that both diffuse and concentrated interests tend to be able to pursue exit and veto opportunities and have access to key information.

DETERMINING THE EUROPEAN EFFECT: INCIDENCE AND INTENSITY

The preceding remarks have sketched out a basic logic behind the national Europeanisation effect and have provided some illustrative examples. Of course, these substantive effects have not gone unnoticed, and the last few years have seen a growing academic interest in examining both the material consequences of European integration and, to a lesser extent, the modalities and processes by which integration affects national polities and governments. But the existing literature is still fairly inchoate. There are, as yet, no received wisdoms that could be challenged, no readily recognisable rival schools of thought, and no 'classic' accounts. In other words, the study of domestic Europeanisation has all the hallmarks of an emergent field of inquiry. As noted at the outset, some aspects of domestic government and politics have thus far received considerably more attention than others. While there are notable contributions dealing with the European impact on governmental-administrative aspects (and the substance and processes of public policy making), the effects on domestic politics – notably political cleavages, voters, elections, parties, party competition, party systems and patterns of democratic legitimation – are only beginning to be researched and are still little understood, especially within a comparative framework. In other words, the polity and policy dimensions of the problem have received more attention than politics. This bias may well have to do with the visibility of the incidence of the European effect. Whereas institutional and policy innovations, such as the setting up of special national co-ordinating committees for EU affairs or adjustments in national agricultural policy following EU accession, are quite easy to trace, the EU effect on cleavages or electoral behaviour is more difficult to ascertain, especially in a short-term perspective. But it may also be the case that domestic polities and policies have been affected earlier and more profoundly by European integration than domestic politics.

Amongst the Europeanisation literature with a strong orientation towards formal organisations, it is worth highlighting at least four main emphases: governmental-administrative institutions; national parliaments; the judiciary; and interest associations. Of these four, the institutions of national government and public administration have perhaps received the earliest and most sustained attention. This is scarcely surprising, given the pivotal role of national executives in the integration project. The integration effects on national central administrations have been the subject of scholarly interest at least since the early 1970s,[14] and the topic has since developed into a recognised area of inquiry amongst students of comparative government and comparative public administration.[15] Particular emphasis is often laid on the national co-ordination of EU-related policy-making[16] and the manner in which national executives seek to shape policy development at the EU level.

A second major focus in the study of national organisational adaptation has been legislative bodies.[17] Again, two closely related concerns dominate in this literature: How can national parliaments adapt their traditional working methods to deal effectively with EU-related business, notably as it relates to the transposition of EU legislation into national law? And how can they influence supranational decision-making processes? Third, the role of national courts in the integration project and the domestic impact of European legislation and the European Court of Justice feature quite prominently in the Europeanisation debate.[18] In studies of the judiciary, institutional and substantive concerns are closely intertwined, for the role played by national courts in domestic politics is, of course, determined not just by the definition of their formal powers *vis-à-vis* other organs of state or supranational power, but also by the substance of the law they are asked to interpret and its place in the hierarchy of norms. For example, the contextualisation of the German Basic Law within a wider European setting and progressive constitutionalisation at EU level require the Federal Constitutional Court to clarify its relations with the ECJ, but also suggest a gradual decline of the Court's role in domestic political life, as the Basic Law itself degenerates into a 'partial order'.[19]

Finally, outside the range of state institutions, the Europeanisation of interest associations and changes in national patterns of interest representation in the wake of European integration have been studied systematically. Interestingly, it is perhaps with reference to non-state political institutions that arguments about the effects of changing opportunity structures on domestic interinstitutional relations have so far been explored most systematically.

If one seeks to characterise organisation-centred contributions to the Europeanisation debate in terms of their substantive emphases, a linkage or co-operation perspective predominates. That is to say, they focus on institutional arrangements that link national and EU structures and the institutional practices that have evolved at the national level to support domestic–EU connections. In common with much writing in the comparative study of institutions, the Europeanisation debate tends to focus on short time horizons and offers 'snapshots' or 'state of the art' reports rather than detailed longitudinal analysis, though they are important exceptions to this general observation, such as Bulmer and Burch's recent study of Whitehall and Europe, tracing the European effect to well before the UK's accession to the EC.[20] This concentration on the recent past and current developments has two critical consequences. First, the early periods of Europeanisation, in particular amongst the original founder members of the European Communities, are little understood and, to the extent that they are examined, are relegated to the province of 'institutional history', somewhat outside the mainstream of comparative politics.[21] Second, Europeanisation tends to be discussed in substantive terms, while the procedural characteristics, which can only be adequately grasped from a longer-term perspective, are often neglected, a point to which we return below.

It is an indication of the growing awareness of the potential importance of European integration for domestic political systems that polity-centred accounts exist for both the founding members of the communities and the most recent accession countries, including Austria, Sweden and Finland.[22] And although the impact on member states is at the heart of the discussion, current non-member states seem not immune to the European effect, as the cases of Norway[23] and Switzerland[24] would appear to bear out. Most recently, a great deal of work has started to be done on the adaptation of the post-Communist applicant states of central and eastern Europe, in particular the measures required to improve their institutional capacities to cope with the *acquis communautaire* in advance of their eventual accession to the EU.[25] As one would expect, there is a clear sectoral institutional concentration in most studies. For example, work on the Europeanisation of legislatures tends to proceed with little or no reference to studies on public administration. But there have also been attempts to provide surveys of the Europeanisation of national political systems as a whole, such as Bulmer and Paterson's early studies on the Federal Republic of Germany and Europe,[26] the 12 edited country-specific volumes of the 'EC Membership Evaluated Series', published by Pinter in the early 1990s, or Guyomarch *et al.*'s recent survey of France in the European Union.[27]

Turning from polity-centred analyses to Europeanised politics, the state of current knowledge is much patchier, and the systematic study of Europeanisation effects is still in its infancy. This observation may seem surprising, given the long-standing interest in how the alleged 'democratic deficit' of the European project might be overcome. But until fairly recently, this discussion has centred predominantly on how the EU itself might be 'democratised' rather than on the effects of integration on the defining features of domestic political systems. There is, however, at least one major exception to the general neglect of the politics dimension in Europeanisation studies. This concerns the impact of European integration on public opinion and, in particular, the perception of the EU by the member states' populations.[28] Supported by the EU, systematic research into this issue has been undertaken for several decades, allowing for sophisticated time-series analysis.

EXPLAINING THE EUROPEAN EFFECT: VARIETIES OF INSTITUTIONALISM

Given the substantive, analytical and methodological diversity of the Europeanisation literature and the breadth of topics covered, generalisations about its substantive findings are necessarily a hazardous undertaking, especially if they are formulated at the level of the political system, rather than its individual components, and supposed to apply to all member states. What seems more interesting, at the present stage of the debate, is how, in cross-national and cross-sectoral terms, commonalties and differences in Europeanisation experiences are explained.

Like much empirical political science, the study of European integration and its effects, from both the perspectives of international relations and comparative politics, bears the signs of the 'institutionalist' turn of the last decade or so,[29] and many recent contributions to the Europeanisation debate are explicitly basing their arguments on neo-institutionalist thinking. This is not the place to rehearse the debate about the – seemingly ever more numerous – varieties of neo-institutionalism in political science.[30] Certainly, the old dichotomy between institution and actor-centred approaches seems to have been fundamentally eroded. What remains, however, are differences not just in the *relative* weight given to institution or actor-centred explanations, but also in how institutions are defined and how the behaviour of actors in institutions is understood to be motivated. In surveying institutionalist explanatory accounts of Europeanisation, one may, accordingly, distinguish four main categories: (i) explanations that operate principally at a macro-institutional level and conceive of both European integration and, in particular, the national effect primarily in institutional terms; (ii) accounts that adopt a broad understanding of institutions, but again understand the European effect primarily in institutional terms; (iii) studies that stress individual utility calculations (a 'logic of consequentiality') in explaining Europeanisation effects; and (iv) analyses that likewise emphasise individual behaviour, but refer to a 'logic of appropriateness' in explaining patterns of national reaction to European integration.

Until recently, macro-institutional accounts were perhaps most influential in the study of the polity and politics effects of European integration. For example, in macro-institutional terms, different 'national democratic formulas'[31] have been seen to account for differences in the strength and incidence of adjustment pressures in member states and the ease with which member states respond to these pressures. Relevant components of such formulas refer to well-established typological distinctions in comparative politics between majoritarian and consensus democracies; (semi-)presidential and parliamentary systems; unitary versus federalised states; common law versus Roman law-inspired legal systems; or, perhaps more contentiously, Anglo-Saxon versus 'Rhenish' capitalism. The underlying idea here is that some configurations of national political systems are more easily compatible with the integration project than others. Institutional congruence or 'closeness of fit' is certainly an important element in trying to explain different trajectories of Europeanisation. For example, in respect of Germany, Bulmer has argued convincingly that EU–German congruence in 'constitutional order', 'norms and conventions', 'patterns of mesolevel governance' and 'policy goals' has not only facilitated domestic adaptation, but also allowed Germany to play a leading role in shaping the integration project.[32] Similarly, Katzenstein has highlighted the institutional similarities between 'Europe's associated sovereignty' and 'Germany's semi-sovereignty', both of which are 'distinguished by overlapping competencies, not by their concentration or division'.[33] By contrast, 'Britain and France concentrate rather than divide power in their polities'[34] and 'British and French political elites must make far greater adjustments to the organization of power in the European polity than their German counterparts'.[35]

Bulmer's congruent 'norms and conventions' are part of an understanding of institutions that goes beyond the organisational and formal and stresses the cultural aspects of institutions. Such a view has become closely associated with March and Olson's 'rediscovery' of institutions, although it does, of course, have a very long pedigree in the social sciences. In the field of Europeanisation studies, the impact of national institutional 'traditions' that go beyond formal rules and regulations has moved centre-stage in many recent analyses, notably in polity-oriented studies. Examples include Bulmer and Burch's work on the Europeanisation of central government;[36] or Harmsen's recent account of the Europeanisation of central administrations in France and the Netherlands.[37] In all cases, the manner in which broadly defined national institutions may clash with, or conform to, European integration and, in particular, their capacity to accommodate, refract or resist pressure for change are key to understanding distinct national and sectoral trajectories of Europeanisation.

A third category of explanatory accounts is closely related to the rational choice variant of the new institutionalism. As in our brief sketch offered above, such accounts tend to emphasise changes in domestic opportunity structures associated with European integration and explain national adaptive reactions by reference to the actions of utility-maximising domestic actors. It is probably no surprise that such an analytical perspective has found particular resonance in the study of interest representation and intermediation, which would appear to have a 'natural' affinity to actor and interest-centred explanations; but, as Mair's contribution to this volume underlines, it may, likewise, be made fruitful for understanding domestic reaction (or the lack of it) in other parts of the political system.

Finally, actor-centred (or at least actor-sensitive) explanations on domestic patterns of Europeanisation also come in neo-institutionalist variants that understand actor's behaviour in terms of a 'logic of appropiateness' that is seen to underlie it. In this case, too, actors have interests and preferences and institutions shape the manner in which these are likely to be pursued. But the perception of these interests and preferences is understood to be profoundly shaped by the institutions themselves rather than as an external given. Put differently, interests and preferences are endogenous rather than exogenous. An example of Europeanisation research that adopts such an analytical perspective is the work by Knill and Lenschow on national administrative traditions and their impact on the implementation of European policies.

CONTEXTUALISING THE EUROPEAN EFFECT

If there is a common theme to emerge in the Europeanisation literature, it is that national institutions and actors matter, in the sense that they have a profound, if not determining, effect on how European integration as a force of polity and politics change plays out in the domestic context. Thus, it is generally acknowledged that there is no direct translation of adaptive pressures resulting from the lack of fit between EU-level institutional and policy arrangements into adaptive reactions. Rather, diverse national and sectoral traditions act as decisive 'intervening variables'. It is because of the diversity of these traditions across the member states that most commentators caution against the expectation of growing convergence amongst European political systems; this even appears to apply to the field of linkage structures and processes, that is, institutional arrangements at the national level explicitly designed to deal with EU-related business.[38]

As is argued elsewhere in this volume, such a stress on the path-shaping and path-constraining power of domestic factors may lead sceptical observers to question whether European integration is really as powerful a force in the development of domestic political systems as much of the Europeanisation literature appears to assume. By paying closer attention to the procedural characteristics of Europeanisation, notably the time dimension,[39] and its modal features, or mechanisms of change,[40] the explanatory power of research into the effects of integration can certainly be enhanced. This will go at least some way towards answering a chief criticism raised against the Europeanisation theme, namely that it fails to

consider counterfactuals. This point has been expressed fairly trenchantly
by Schmitter,[41] who contends that

> no realistic or compelling assessment of the impact of the EU on
> domestic democracy can afford to ignore taking *counterfactuals*
> into account. One has to begin with some plausible scenario of
> what national democracies might have looked like today if they had
> not benefited and suffered from several decades of European
> integration ... The impact of the EU on domestic democracy is a
> process, not (yet) an outcome ... Even reflecting retrospectively, it is
> difficult to separate out a distinctive, much less a definitive,
> contribution since *the net effect of the EU seems to be to complement*
> *(and, probably, to enhance) trends that were already affecting*
> *domestic democracies.*[42]

Certainly, as far as the domestic political institutions and politics of late
west European entrants to the EU and of Norway and Switzerland (as the
two remaining larger western non-member states) are concerned, it would
seem difficult to argue that late or non-membership resulted in trajectories
of domestic political development that have differed dramatically from
those of neighbouring member states. But it could rightly be put against this
line of argument that the effects of integration also make themselves felt in
non-member countries, especially if Europeanisation is associated with
voluntaristic patterns on policy and institutional transfer, learning and
imitation rather than coercive adaptation.

Counterfactuals might be desirable, but, in this case at least, they can be
no more than interesting, though ultimately inconclusive, thought
experiments. If the Europeanisation literature is to escape the charge of
overestimating the explanatory value of its independent variable, then it will
need to consider more systematically than has hitherto tended to be the case
the interaction between European integration and other (potential)
explanations of domestic institutional and political development. Both
European integration as a source of change and Europeanisation as an effect
are likely to interact strongly with other economic, political, legal and social
developments. This is, perhaps, most evident when we look at the countries
of post-Communist central and eastern Europe, where institutional and
policy adjustment to the EU is closely intertwined with the 'triple transition'
of democratisation, liberalisation and privatisation.[43] Similarly, European
integration and post-authoritarian political and social modernisation were
closely allied in the cases of Spain, Portugal and Greece, and, at least during
the first post-war decade, Italy and the Federal Republic of Germany. In the

case of the latter, political consolidation could not have taken pace without embedding the new state firmly within the European Communities.[44]

The chapters contained in this volume provide many hints as to how European integration, as a source of change, and Europeanisation, as an effect, interact with other oft-told stories of change in comparative politics. What is of special interest in the present context is whether there is a common thread that runs through these change stories. As regards affinities in sources of change, there are obvious connections between the discussion of European integration and the literature on globalisation.[45] The globalisation thesis comes in many different versions, stressing, alternatively, its economic, technological, cultural, political or legal dimensions. The European integration project often features prominently in the globalisation debate, from a dual perspective: in its economic dimension it is seen as a major contributor towards the creation of a globalised economy, whereas in its political dimension, through the establishment of a new set of political institutions, it is often interpreted as an attempt to retain or regain a degree of political control over economic development. In this scenario, European integration is then a driving force and a symptom of a broader transformation process.[46]

As regards Europeanisation as a domestic effect, there is a close affinity between many of the indications of change discussed in this volume, principally from a comparative politics perspective, and the debate on the (re)conceptualisation and (re)foundation of nation state centred democracy, as it is conducted in political and social theory. With the danger of over-simplification, it may be said that while the present volume concentrates on dissecting the concrete manifestations of change in European democratic orders, contributions from the angle of political and social theory focus on elucidating the normative implications of the changes observed or predicted. The affinity of interests is, to some extent, masked by the lack of a common idiom: while the language of postmodernisation has been highly influential in theoretical debates on the future of the nation state and democracy, it has not (yet?) entered the mainstream of the comparative politics discourse.[47] Yet, many of the key themes in the postmodern debate on the future of the democratic nation state[48] – such as 'deterritorialisation', the external and internal 'delimitation' of the state, the 'de-hierarchisation' of the relations between state and society – are also central concerns in the Europeanisation debate, although the terminology employed might be different.[49]

To summarise, in order to advance beyond the present state of the analysis of the domestic impacts of European integration – as documented in this volume – the analytical and theoretical reach of this emergent field of comparative research needs to be broadened in several directions. First, the present emphasis on policy and institutional aspects needs to be complemented by more sustained efforts at examining the domestic *political* effects of integration. It may, of course, emerge that there is a disjuncture between a 'Europeanised statehood' and a 'non-Europeanised politics' – but at present such a hypotheses cannot be confirmed or disconfirmed. Second, in studying the European impact, substantive effects can only be properly understood if more systematic attention is paid to the modes and processes of domestic Europeanisation. Third, while it is necessary to disentangle European integration as an explanatory variable and the European effect as a dependent variable, both will need to be 're-entangled' if we wish to do justice to the real-life interdependency of forces of economic, political and cultural change. In this respect, analyses of globalisation and postmodernisation offer promising avenues for enriching the Europeanisation debate.

NOTES

1. See, for example, R.O. Keohane and H.V. Milner (eds.), *Internationalization and Domestic Politics* (Cambridge: Cambridge University Press 1996).
2. We have consciously excluded policy outputs from this study, as the impact of European integration on public policy has recently been analysed in some detail by other projects. See, for example, H. Kassim and A. Menon (eds.), *The European Union and National Industrial Policy* (London: Routledge 1996); D. Hine and H. Kassim (eds.), *Beyond the Market: The EU and National Social Policy* (London: Routledge 1998).
3. See, for example, P. Dunleavy, 'Explaining the Centralization of the European Union: A Public Choice Analysis', *Aussenwirtschaft* 52 (1997), pp.183–212.
4. F.W. Scharpf, 'Negative and Positive Integration in the Political Economy of European Welfare States', in G. Marks *et al.* (eds.), *Governance in the European Union* (London: Sage 1996).
5. See K. Gatsios and P. Seabright, 'Regulation in the European Community', *Oxford Review of Economic Policy* 5 (1989), pp.37–60.
6. For example, W. Streeck, 'From Market Making to State Building? Reflections on the Political Economy of European Social Policy', in S. Leibfried and P. Pierson (eds.), *European Social Policy: Between Fragmentation and Integration* (Washington, DC: The Brookings Institution 1995); and W. Streeck, 'Neo-Voluntarism: A European Social Policy Regime?', in G. Marks *et al.* (eds.), *Governance in the European Union* (London: Sage 1996).
7. J.H.H. Weiler, 'The Transformation of Europe', *Yale Law Journal* 100 (1991), pp.2403–83.
8. W. Streeck and P.C. Schmitter, 'From National Corporatism to Transnational Pluralism: Organized Interests in the Single European Market', *Politics and Society* 19 (1991), pp.133–64.
9. P. Pierson, 'The Path to European Integration: A Historical Institutionalist Analysis', *Comparative Political Studies* 29 (1996), pp.123–63.

10. Andrew Moravcsik, 'Why the European Community Strengthens the State: International Cooperation and Domestic Politics' (Centre for European Studies Working Paper Series 52, Harvard University, 1994).

11. For example, G. Majone, *Regulating Europe* (London: Routledge 1996); B. Kohler-Koch, 'Catching Up with Change: The Transformation of Governance in Europe', *Journal of European Public Policy* 3 (1996), pp.359–80; and C. Joerges and J. Neyer, 'From Intergovernmental Bargaining to Deliberative Political Process: The Constitutionalisation of Comitology', *European Law Journal* 3 (1997), pp.273–99.

12. For example, F.W. Scharpf, *Governing in Europe: Effective and Democratic?* (Oxford: Oxford University Press 1999); and S. Leibfried and P. Pierson, 'Semisovereign Welfare States: Social Policy in a Multitiered Europe', in idem (eds.), *European Social Policy.*

13. G. Tsebelis, *Nested Games: Rational Choice in Comparative Politics* (Berkeley: University of California Press 1990).

14. H. Wallace, *National Government and the European Communities* (London: Chatham House 1973).

15. See recently, e.g., K. Hanf and B. Soetendorp (eds.), *Adapting to European Integration: Small States and the European Union* (London: Longman 1998); Y. Mény et al. (eds.), *Adjusting to Europe: The Impact of the EU on National Institutions and Policy* (London: Routledge 1996); W. Wessels and D. Rometsch (eds.), *The European Union and the Member States: Towards Institutional Fusion?* (Manchester: Manchester University Press 1996).

16. V. Wright, 'The National Co-ordination of European Policy-Making', in J. Richardson (ed.), *European Union: Power and Policy-Making* (London: Routledge, 1996), pp.148–69, with further references.

17. More recently, for example, R.S. Katz and B. Wessels (eds.), *The European Parliament, the National Parliaments and European Integration* (Oxford: Oxford University Press 1999); F. Laursen and S.A. Pappas (eds.), *The Changing Role of Parliaments in the European Union* (Maastricht: European Institute of Public Administration 1995); P. Norton (ed.), *National Parliaments and the European Union* (London: Frank Cass 1996); E. Smith (ed.), *National Parliaments as Cornerstones of European Integration* (London: Kluwer Law International 1996).

18. See only A.-M. Slaughter et al. (eds.), *The European Court and National Courts, Doctrine and Jurisprudence* (Oxford: Hart 1998), with further references.

19. D. Grimm, 'Die Zukunft der Verfassung', *Staatswissenschaften und Staatspraxis* 1 (1990), pp.5–33 at 28; see more generally K.H. Goetz and P. Cullen, 'The Basic Law After Unification: Continued Centrality or Declining Force?', in idem (eds.), *Constitutional Policy in Unified Germany* (London: Cass 1996), pp.5–46.

20. S. Bulmer and M. Burch, 'Organizing for Europe: Whitehall, the British State and European Union', *Public Administration* 76 (1998), pp.601–28.

21. See, for example, the special issue of the *Yearbook of European Administrative History*, Vol.4 (1992), on the 'Early European Community Administration'.

22. See, for example, G. Falkner, 'How Pervasive are Euro-Politics? Effects of EU Membership on a New Member State', *Journal of Common Market Studies* 38 (2000), pp.223–50; G. Falkner and W. Müller (eds.), *Österreich im europäischen Mehrebenensystem: Konsequenzen der EU-Mitgliedschaft für Politiknetzwerke und Entscheidungsprozesse* (Vienna: Signum 1998); M. Ekengren and B. Sundelius, 'Sweden: The State Joins the European Union', in Hanf and Soetendorp (eds.), *Adapting to European Integration*, pp.131–48, with further references.

23. J. Trondal, *Europeisering av sentraladministrative organer. Om tilknytningsformer til EU og departmentale koordineringsformer* (Oslo: ARENA Working papers WP 97/27 1997).

24. A. Epiney, *Schweizerische Demokratie und Europäische Union* (Berne: Stämpfli 1998); S. Kux, 'Switzerland: Adjustment Despite Deadlock', in Hanf and Soetendorp (eds.), *Adapting to European Integration*, pp.167–85.

25. SIGMA (ed.), *Preparing Public Administrations for the European Administrative Space* (Paris: SIGMA Papers No 23, 1998).
26. S. Bulmer, *The Domestic Structure of European Community Policy-Making in West Germany* (New York/London: Garland 1986); S. Bulmer and W. Paterson, *The Federal Republic of Germany and the European Union* (London: Allen & Unwin 1986).
27. A. Guyomarch *et al.*, *France in the European Union* (Basingstoke: Macmillan 1998).
28. For a comprehensive survey, see S. Niedermayer and R. Sinnott (eds.), *Public Opinion and Internationalized Governance* (Oxford: Oxford University Press 1995).
29. See, for example, M.D. Aspinwall and G. Schneider, 'Same Menu, Separate Tables: The Institutionalist Turn in Political Science and the Study of European Integration' (2000); J. Jupille and J. Caporaso, 'Institutionalism and the European Union: Beyond International Relations and Comparative Politics', *Annual Review of Political Science* 2 (1999), pp.129–41.
30. For a recent review see B.G. Peters, *Institutional Theory in Political Science: The 'New Institutionalism'* (London: Pinter 1999).
31. V. Schmidt, 'European Integration and Democracy: The Differences Among Member States', *Journal of European Public Policy* 4 (1997), pp.128–45; idem, 'European Integration and Institutional Change: The Transformation of National Patterns of Policy-Making', in G. Göhler (ed.), *Institutionenwandel* (Opladen: Westdeutscher Verlag 1997), pp.143–80.
32. S. Bulmer, 'Shaping the Rules? The Constitutive Politics of the European Union and German Power', in P.J. Katzenstein (ed.), *Tamed Power: Germany in Europe* (Ithaca: Cornell University Press 1997), pp.49–79.
33. P.J. Katzenstein, 'United Germany in an Integrating Europe', in idem (ed.), *Tamed Power*, pp.1–48.
34. Ibid., p.41.
35. Ibid., pp.42–3. Similarly, for example, J.J. Anderson, 'Germany: Between Unification and Union', in idem (ed.), *Regional Integration and Democracy: Expanding on the European Experience* (Lanham: Rowman & Littlefield 1999), pp.171–92.
36. Bulmer and Burch, 'Organizing for Europe'.
37. R. Harmsen, 'The Europeanization of National Administrations: A Comparative Study of France and the Netherlands', *Governance* 12 (1999), pp.81–113.
38. H. Kassim *et al.* (eds.), *EU Policy Coordination: The National Dimension* (Oxford: Oxford University Press forthcoming).
39. See Goetz in this volume.
40. C.M. Radaelli, *Whither Europeanization? Concept Stretching and Substantive Change* (Paper presented at the PSA Annual Conference, London, 10–13 April).
41. P.C. Schmitter, 'Reflections on the Impact of the European Union upon "Domestic" Democracy in its Member States', in M. Egeberg and P Laegreid (eds.), *Organizing Political Institutions. Essays for Johan P. Olsen* (Olso: Scandinavian University Press 1999), pp.289–98.
42. Ibid., pp.296–7 (emphasis original).
43. See, for example, A. Ágh, *The Politics of Central Europe* (London: Sage 1998), pp.24ff.
44. K.H. Goetz, 'Integration Policy in a Europeanized State: Germany and the Intergovernmental Conference', *Journal of European Public Policy* 3 (1996), pp.23–44.
45. See, for example, D. Held, *Democracy and the Global Order* (Cambridge: Polity Press 1995); P. Hirst and G. Thompson, *Globalization in Question* (Cambridge: Polity Press, 2nd edn. 1999).
46. For a recent attempt to link the Europeanisation and globalisation theme analytically and empirically see Anderson (ed.), *Regional Integration and Democracy*.
47. The exception proving the rule is R. Inglehart, *Modernization and Postmodernization: Cultural, Economic, and Political Change in 43 Societies* (Princeton: Princeton University Press 1997).

48. For a first overview see S. Crook *et al.*, *Postmodernization in Advanced Society* (London: Sage 1992).
49. For an attempt to combine Europeanisation and postmodernisation theory in the study of domestic institutional change, see K.H. Goetz, 'Verwaltungswandel – ein analytisches Gerüst', in E. Grande and R. Prätorius (eds.), *Modernisierung des Staates?* (Baden-Baden: Nomos Verlagsgesellschaft 1997), pp.177–206.

The Limited Impact of Europe on National Party Systems

PETER MAIR

This study is intended to offer a brief assessment of the impact of Europeanisation on the national party systems of the member states of the European Union (EU). This implies quite serious limitations in the focus of the analysis. In the first place, the primary concern is with the impact of Europeanisation on the party *systems* of the member states, as opposed to its effects on the individual parties that constitute those systems. As such, virtually no attention is paid to the question of how Europe may have provoked fissures within parties, or to the extent to which it may have encouraged the formation of internal party factions that align themselves on either side of the European debate. Second, the discussion is primarily concerned with the impact of Europeanisation within the *national* political arena. Hence, little consideration is given to the effects that Europe may have wrought on forms of inter-party competition within the European political arena as such. In other words, those modifications to national party systems that emerge only within the context of competition that ensues during elections to the European Parliament are more or less consistently excluded from this analysis. This is not to deny the importance of either of these topics. Indeed, both merit more serious and systematic treatment than is currently the case even within the now expanding literature on the Europeanisation of party politics. To do these topics justice, however, would clearly require more than a single paper. There is a third limitation in that, for reasons of manageability, this study concentrates on evidence of the *direct* impact of Europe on national party systems. This is perhaps the gravest limitation of all, since the most telling impact may well be expressed indirectly, in the sense that Europe increasingly imposes severe constraints on the policy manoeuvrability of governments and on the parties that make up those governments. As such, Europe also constrains the capacity of these parties to engage in competition, and it thereby affects the workings of party systems in practice. But although this question is addressed briefly in the concluding section, it is largely excluded from the analysis below.

The discussion begins with a brief assessment of the direct impact of European integration on the two defining features of national party systems: their format and their mechanics. On the basis of a necessarily cursory assessment, it is suggested that there is very little evidence of any direct impact on these features of party systems. Indeed, of the many areas of domestic politics that may have experienced an impact from Europe, party systems have perhaps proved to be most impervious to change. The second section suggests that one possible explanation for this imperviousness is the absence of any major spillover effects from the European to the national electoral arena. Although the Europarties themselves might play an important representative role, the absence of a genuine European party system serves to inhibit any restructuring of domestic party competition that might result from competition at the European level. Moreover, as long as party competition at the European level remains undefined by competition for a European executive office, it is unlikely that a European-level party system will develop. And this, in turn, serves to protect national party systems from spillover effects. The third section explores another potential explanation for the capacity of national party systems to resist the impact of Europeanisation. In this case, the focus is on the misplaced division of competences associated with the national and European electoral arenas. In brief, it is argued that the national electoral arena is best suited to the contestation of key European issues, whereas the European arena is best suited to debate about more everyday policy questions. More often than not, however, the debates are actually pursued the other way around, with the result that elections in each arena fail to prove decisive. The voters have a voice, of course, but it tends to be on matters that sometimes cannot be decided in the particular arena in question. Two different arguments are advanced to account for this misplacement, the more sceptical of which holds that electoral disempowerment actually serves the interests of the parties in competition. It is also suggested that even if the key questions of European integration were to be debated within the national electoral arena, the mainstream consensus is such that voters would still find themselves unable to make any meaningful choices. Finally, the discussion concludes with a brief assessment of the potential indirect effects of Europe within a wider process of depoliticisation. The main point here is that decision-making at the European level constitutes a major area in which decisions are seen to be a matter for the governing politicians and their bureaucracies, rather than as something that necessarily requires the active engagement of, or consultation with, the electorate at large. In this sense, the European dimension enhances an already existing tendency within modern democracies to separate the world of politics from that of the wider society, and hence helps to accentuate the popular turning away from traditional politics.

EUROPE AND NATIONAL PARTY SYSTEMS: FORMAT AND MECHANICS

Any assessment of the impact of European integration on national party systems will almost inevitably begin with the contrast between the periods before and after the introduction of direct elections to the European Parliament. These first direct elections opened up a wholly new electoral arena for the expression of political preferences in the member states, and they offered the first opportunity for parties to attempt to establish formal cross-national links as part of their direct efforts to appeal to voters. These elections also marked the first occasion on which parties could be seen to take public responsibility for the bonds that they had forged with other like-minded parties within the European Parliament, and on which they had to defend their record as part of a European parliamentary grouping to their own electorates. Although many of the parties that competed in these elections had been active on the European stage for many years, it was with direct elections that this first became a specifically electoral arena. Hence, it is likely to be from that point onwards that we might find the most important of the direct changes that Europeanisation could have occasioned. The stretch since the introduction of direct elections is also a relatively long one in the life of most political parties and party systems. Indeed, for the majority of the member states of the current EU, the European electoral arena has been now been functioning for more than two decades, that is, since 1979.[1] Any comparison between the state of parties and party systems before and after the introduction of direct European elections is, therefore, almost certainly likely to reveal substantial change.

What remains to be seen, of course, is whether the change thus revealed might reasonably be associated with Europeanisation. If we restrict the focus to national party systems, which is the core concern of this analysis, then there are two obvious ways in which Europe might be seen to have had an impact. In the first place, Europeanisation might have affected the *format* of these systems, that is, the number of relevant parties in contention in national electoral arenas. In other words, as a direct consequence of Europeanisation, new parties might have been established that either add to, or substitute for, the number already in contention. Second, Europe might have influenced the *mechanics* of party systems, that is, the way in which parties interact with one another in the national electoral arenas, either by modifying the ideological distance separating the relevant parties, or by encouraging the emergence of wholly new European-centred dimensions of competition. Although there is much more to be said about party systems than can easily be encapsulated by these two features, format and mechanics nevertheless constitute the key defining elements of any party system;[2] accordingly, it is here that any direct impact of Europeanisation could and should first be seen. Europe might also have had an indirect impact on both of these features, of course, but since indirect effects are much more difficult to specify, it is perhaps best to begin with an assessment of the direct impact, if any.

Format

Let us first turn to the question of format. The most important point to note here is that the party systems of the European member states, and in the Western democracies more generally, have become substantially more fragmented over the past two decades. In other words, since 1979, and indeed as part of a longer-term process that can be dated back to at least the 1960s, European countries have witnessed the formation of a plethora of new political parties. As such, they have also undergone some quite substantial changes in the format of their party systems. Between 1960 and 1998, for example, across 12 of the current member states (excluding the more recently democratised polities of Greece, Portugal and Spain), more than 140 new political parties emerged to contest domestic parliamentary elections for the first time.[3] Moreover, among these new parties, more than 120 post-date the lead-up to, and first experience with, direct European elections in the countries concerned. In this sense, and considering only temporal coincidences, one may associate Europeanisation with a major enlargement in the number of parties contesting domestic elections and with a quite pervasive change in the formats of national party systems.

On the other hand, and this is by far the more striking figure, of these new parties, only three may, as far as can be ascertained, be linked *directly* to the issue of European integration. That is, among the many parties that have newly emerged since 1979 to compete in the national political arena in these 12 member states, only three appear to have been established with the explicit and primary intention of mobilising support for or against the EU. Moreover, these three parties have proved among the least successful of any new parties to have emerged in the same period, polling an average of just 1.5 per cent of the votes in domestic elections to date.[4] As far as domestic competition is concerned, therefore, we may conclude, at least initially, that Europe has had virtually no direct or even demonstrable effect on the format of the national party systems. To be a little more precise here: Europe has clearly generated new parties, particularly within that segment of opinion that is hostile or sceptical towards (further) European integration. But while such new parties have emerged, they have tended to remain confined to the European electoral arena. Thus, they have typically confined themselves to contesting only the elections to the European Parliament, and have eschewed strictly domestic competition. Examples would include the People's Movement Against the EU in Denmark, and the Free Citizen's Alliance in Germany.[5] Strictly speaking, therefore, their impact on the format of domestic party systems has been almost non-existent. It is certainly much less than that of the new Green parties, for example, or the new extreme right parties, or even the more sporadic, but also newly emergent pensioners' parties. In sum, to the simple question of whether Europe has had a direct impact on the format of national party systems, the equally simple answer must be an unequivocal 'no'.

Mechanics

A comparably simple question on the mechanics of party systems is less easily posed or answered. The mechanics of a party system concern the modes of interaction between the (relevant) parties. Accordingly, any evidence of the direct impact of Europeanisation might first be sought by attempting to align the various parties competing in domestic elections on a pro- *vs.* anti-European integration dimension. This would allow us to observe the extent to which there is any new clustering of party blocs or camps between which competition might be anticipated. Any such clustering could then be taken to indicate either an impact on the level of polarisation in the system or the onset of a new – pro- *vs.* anti-European – dimension of party competition.

For this purpose, some recent data derived from an expert study of party positions conducted by Leonard Ray[6] offer perhaps the most reliable and up-to-date guide. Ray carried out his survey in 1996, polling 135 experts on 18 European countries, each of whom located his/her country's parties on a scale running from 1, recording strong opposition to European integration, to 7, recording strong support for European integration. The results are quite revealing, if not wholly surprising. Of the 122 parties in the EU member states for which locations are provided for 1996, 63 (51.6 per cent) were deemed by the experts who were surveyed to be strongly in favour of

TABLE 1

SUPPORT FOR PARTIES IN RECENT NATIONAL ELECTIONS, BY POSITION ON
EUROPEAN INTEGRATION

Country (election year)	Percentage Votes for Strongly Pro-European Integration Parties (N parties)	Percentage Votes for Strongly Anti-European Integration Parties (N parties)	Percentage Votes for Parties Neither Strongly Pro nor Strongly Anti European Integration (N parties)
Austria (1995)	71.9 (3)	22.2 (2)	4.8 (1)
Belgium (1995)	72.8 (7)	0 (0)	21.0 (5)
Denmark (1998)	77.1 (5)	12.5 (3)	10.0 (2)
Finland (1999)	49.0 (3)	6.0 (2)	40.6 (3)
France (1997)	49.3 (4)	16.1 (2)	20.2 (2)
Germany (1998)	75.5 (3)	1.8 (1)	18.5 (3)
Greece (1996)	92.0 (4)	5.6 (1)	0 (0)
Ireland (1997)	32.7 (2)	0 (0)	58.0 (6)
Italy (1996)	39.9 (4)	24.3 (2)	28.9 (3)
Luxembourg (1994)	75.0 (3)	2.6 (1)	19.9 (3)
Netherlands (1997)	56.4 (3)	0.6 (1)	37.1 (5)
Portugal (1995)	79.6 (3)	9.9 (3)	9.3 (2)
Spain (1996)	85.9 (10)	0 (0)	10.7 (1)
Sweden (1998)	75.8 (4)	16.5 (2)	5.1 (1)
UK (1997)	63.3 (5)	2.6 (1)	30.7 (1)
National Mean (N = 15)	66.4	8.0	21.0

Note: Party positions with regard to European Integration refer to 1996 and are derived from the positions identified by Ray in his expert survey: see Leonard Ray, 'Measuring Party Orientations Towards European Integration: results from an expert survey, *European Journal of Political Research* 36/2 (1999), pp.283–306. Ray uses a scale ranging from 1 (strongly opposed to European integration) to 7 (strongly in favour of European integration). For the purposes of this table, parties scoring 1 or 2 on this scale (rounded figures) are categorised as strongly anti-European integration; parties scoring 6 or 7 (rounded figures) are categorised as strongly pro-European integration; and parties scoring 3, 4, or 5 (rounded figures) are classified as being neither strongly pro- nor strongly anti-European Integration. Since not all parties are included in Ray's survey, the vote percentages do not necessarily add up to 100 per cent.

Sources: Electoral data are drawn from Thomas T. Mackie and Richard Rose, *The International Almanac of Electoral History* (Basingstoke: Macmillan, 3rd edn. 1991), and their *A Decade of Election Results: Updating the International Almanac* (Glasgow: CSSP 1997), as well as from the *Political Data Yearbook*, published as part of the *European Journal of Political Research*.

European integration, scoring 6 or 7 on the 7-point scale (my categorisation); 21 (17.2 per cent) were considered to be strongly opposed to European integration, scoring 1 or 2; the remaining 38 (31.1 per cent) were regarded as being neither strongly pro- nor strongly anti-, scoring 3, 4 or 5. This last group, incidentally, includes Fianna Fáil and Labour in the Irish case, as well as Forza Italia in Italy and the Liberal Party in the Netherlands. All of these parties have proved willing in practice to endorse or even advocate most of the panoply of recent pro-integrationist measures, including the establishment of EMU, the increasing powers of the European Parliament, and the greater use of majority voting in the Council of Ministers. In any event, what matters more here is the group that is strongly opposed to European integration. It is largely through the division between this bloc and the rest that the basis for a pro- *vs.* anti-European alignment might be sought, and, hence, albeit in a roundabout manner, any evidence for the direct impact of Europeanisation on the patterns of competition within party systems at the national level.

The first point to note here is that while it counts for some 17 per cent of the parties' in competition, the anti-Europe bloc gains a remarkably low percentage of popular votes. This can be seen in Table 1, which groups the various parties in the three European integration categories and then records their percentage vote by country in the most recent national elections. On average, the anti-Europe parties receive just eight per cent of the national vote, as against an average of 66 per cent for the strongly pro-European parties and an average of 21 per cent for those located in the middle of the scale. To be sure, there is quite substantial variation between the countries, ranging from highs of 24, 22 and 17 per cent for the anti-Europe 'bloc' in Italy, Austria and Sweden, respectively, with Denmark and France also reaching double figures, to lows of 0 or close to 0 per cent in Belgium, Ireland, the Netherlands and Spain. At first sight, then, we have a cluster of countries in which the vote for anti-European parties in the most recent national elections reaches a 'substantial' level of ten per cent or more, and in which we might, therefore, anticipate that the European divide might impact upon the mechanics of competition and on the character of the party system itself.

The second point to note, however, is that additional factors are also at play in establishing this potential alignment. As can be seen from Table 2, the parties which might be defined as anti-European, and particularly those which record reasonably high levels of electoral support, are those which also have other powerful strings to their bows. Thus, it is striking to see that the parties within this group that are far and away the most successful vote-

TABLE 2

ANTI-EUROPEAN PARTIES IN NATIONAL ELECTIONS

Country	Strongly Anti-European Parties (score on Ray Index)	Percentage Vote (most recent national election)
Austria	Freedom Party (1.80)	21.9
	Communist Party (1.00)	0.3
Belgium	na	na
Denmark	Progress Party (2.44)	2.4
	Red-Green Unity List (1.33)	2.7
	Danish People's Party (na)*	7.4
Finland	Christian League (1.38)	4.2
	Rural Party [+ True Finns] (1.29)	1.8
France	National Front (1.22)	15.2
	Communist Party (2.00)	9.9
Germany	Republican Party (1.29)	1.8
Greece	Communist Party [Int] (1.20)	5.6
Ireland	na	na
Italy	National Alliance (2.25)	15.7
	Communist Refoundation (2.14)	8.6
Luxembourg	National Movement (1.13 [1992])	2.6
Netherlands	Centre Democrats (2.13)	0.6
Portugal	Communist Party (1.75)	8.7
	Revolutionary Soc. Party (1.83)	0.6
	Popular Democratic Union (2.17)	0.6
Spain	na	na
Sweden	Green Ecology Party (1.00)	4.5
	Left Party (1.71)	12.0
United Kingdom	Referendum Party (na)*	2.6

Notes: * Parties that are not included in Ray's survey but which are clearly and strongly anti-European. For details of calculations and sources, see Table 1.

catchers – the Austrian Freedom Party (21.9 per cent of the vote), the French National Front (15.2 per cent), the Italian National Alliance (15.7 per cent) and the Swedish Left Party (12.0 per cent) – are also parties with quite strong and extreme domestic ideological identities. Under no circumstances could they be interpreted as being primarily dependent on an anti-European appeal. Indeed, the parties that emerge more generally as being strongly opposed to European integration are those which in any case lie well outside the mainstreams of their respective party systems, and are, in the main, parties of the extreme right or of the extreme left. This pattern is already well known by now, and has recently been explored very effectively by Paul Taggart. His work reveals a strong link between the adoption of strong Eurosceptic positions, on the one hand, and the status of a party as a protest or 'outsider' party, on the other.[7] Whether the adoption of an anti-European position by such parties is opportunistic or genuine is perhaps beside the point, and is certainly not something that can be dealt with here. What is important, however, is the congruence between opposition to European integration and many of the other facets of these parties' ideologies, since, as Taggart notes, opposition to Europe is one of the most evident means through which 'they can set themselves apart from the 'centre' of politics.'[8]

For this reason alone, it is hard to accept that Europeanisation as such has had a significant direct impact on the mechanics of the party systems of the member states. To be sure, a pro- *vs.* anti-European divide can sometimes be discerned; but given the character of the parties involved, Europe as such appears as neither a necessary nor sufficient condition for that divide. There are simply too many other factors at work, and were the European issue to disappear in its entirety, this would be unlikely to have any significant impact on the overall structure of competition in these systems. Regardless of Europe, in other words, these parties would still remain outside the mainstream. Europe has not made for significant new alliances or enmities, and in this sense it does not appear to have directly affected the level of polarisation in the national systems, or to have encouraged the emergence of a new dimension of competition.

There are, of course, some possible exceptions to this pattern. Principal among them is the British Conservative Party. In Ray's data for 1996, it was coded precisely in the centre (3.5) of the European integration scale, but, especially since its defeat in the British general election of 1997, it has come to adopt quite a strong anti-European position. On the one hand, this anti-Europeanness might well be disregarded. Despite its current rhetorical claims, and despite its evident and sometimes quite lasting internal divisions,[9] the Conservative Party has a long history of pro-Europeanism, stretching from its endorsement of Britain's initial entry into the then Common Market, through the referendum in 1975, to the agreement on, and signing of, the Maastricht Treaty in 1991–92. Moreover, the party's current opposition is partly partisan and contingent – it offers a means of distinguishing itself from an increasingly centrist Labour government. It is also quite limited, in that it is focused mainly on opposition to joining the single currency. In this sense, anti-European sentiment can be seen as one more stick with which the opposition Conservatives can attempt to beat the incumbent Labour government, and, as such, it is simply an additional weapon in an already established armoury. On the other hand, this remains a particularly interesting case, since the UK is currently the only one of 15 member states in which a substantial pro- *vs.* anti-Europe divide coincides with the major partisan divide within the party system, separating traditional centre-left from traditional centre-right. Elsewhere, and despite the electoral support for parties which have taken up the anti-European cause (see Table 2), the party mainstream, or what Gordon Smith has referred to as the 'core' of the party system, is characterised by a more or less robust pro-European consensus.[10] In this sense, the UK is also singular in offering voters the potential to take Europe as a cue in choosing between governing alternatives. Moreover, during a period in which other sources of identity prove insufficiently robust in challenging for Labour's centre ground, anti-Europeanness is a theme that increasingly comes to define the Conservative identity more generally, at least in the shorter term.

A second exception might well be the French Gaullists. Their forces have already split along pro- and anti-European lines in the European electoral arena, a development that raises the possibility that they might also experience considerable difficulties in maintaining programmatic and party cohesion in future national electoral contests. This also typifies a more general phenomenon, whereby Europe forces fissures inside parties which may then eventually be released in further fractionalisation within national parliaments and national electoral arenas. As in the British case, it is certainly possible to conceive of scenarios in which the gradual settlement or downgrading of alternative sources of division creates the space in which a nascent European divide emerges into greater prominence.

Even allowing for these exceptions and speculations, however, it seems reasonable to conclude that neither the format nor the mechanics of the large majority of the party systems of the member states have been directly effected in any significant way by Europeanisation – at least insofar as these pertain to the national arena. To be sure, there have been occasions when, at a pinch, changes in the internal balance of a party system might be *indirectly* associated with European influences. One may mention, in particular, the case of the Italian Communist Party, which attempted within its domestic competition to build from the fact that it finally out-polled the Christian Democrats in the European elections of 1984; that of the Dutch Christian parties, whose eventual merger into the pan-Christian CDA was helped along by the co-operation between the three parties involved within the European Parliament;[11] or that of the various Green parties, the diffusion of whose electoral credibility throughout the member states was clearly enhanced by their effective showing in the various direct elections to the European Parliament. But these are essentially secondary examples, which fail to belie the conclusion that among all of the various themes considered by the contributors to the present volume, it appears to be party systems at the domestic level that have proved most resilient to any direct impact of Europe.

This is not to suggest that we have witnessed no change whatsoever, of course. On the contrary, the systems themselves as well as the individual parties have proved extraordinarily flexible in adapting to changes that derive both internally and externally. Indeed, to draw up a catalogue of the changes that have involved the parties, the party systems and the electorates of the 15 member states, even with reference only to the obvious watershed marked by the first direct European elections, would prove a daunting task. As far as the parties are concerned, we have seen in the last quarter-century a growing shift away from engagement with the wider society and towards closer engagement with the state. This process has been helped along by the parties' growing financial dependence on public subsidies, their progressive subjection to the regulations of new party laws, and their own increasing emphasis on gaining access to government office. We have also seen evidence of shrinking party memberships and even a declining sense of popular identification with parties, a change to which the parties have responded by increasingly taking on the role of campaign organisations. At the level of party systems, one observes not only increased fragmentation, but also a shift in balance, with a general decline in electoral support for the non-socialist left (compensated only in part through the growth in support for Green parties), and an increase in the appeal of the far right. Within the mainstream of many party systems, there is evidence of ideological convergence and consensus, as well as growing signs of a new promiscuity in coalition formation. The latter may yet serve to undermine the traditional structures of competition on which these systems have been built. Finally, at the level of the electorates, there is evidence of an individualisation and particularisation of voting choice, the fragmentation of traditional social-structural identities, and a growing sense of indifference with, and disengagement from, the political world. These are all major changes by any standards, and few would seek to deny their import. Yet none of these changes, and particularly none of those associated with the party systems, can be traced directly or exclusively to the impact of Europeanisation as such – even though, as is suggested below, they may well be associated with more indirect effects.

THE LIMITS OF SPILLOVER AND THE ABSENCE OF A EUROPEAN PARTY SYSTEM

Much of the speculation surrounding the potential impact of European integration on the party systems of the national states has focused on the possible spillover from party competition in the European electoral arena and from the transnational party alignments within the European Parliament itself. By drawing attention to the building of Europarties and the increased salience of legislative coalition formation in Strasbourg, it becomes possible to sketch out a scenario whereby national party systems are seen to suffer contagion from a nascent European party system and/or become transformed by the emergence of a Europeanised cleavage system.[12]

There are two important arguments that may be cited against this scenario, however. The first, which can be summarised very briefly, underlines how national political parties, consciously operating within the terms of reference of their national party systems, serve as the principal gatekeepers within the European electoral arena, and hence seek to monopolise access and to dominate the agenda.[13] In other words, European elections become simply a stage on which national politics is rehearsed once again, and in which the alignments that derive from the domestic arena are reproduced in more or less identical form. To be sure, the parties are not always wholly successful in translating their traditional domestic role onto this European stage. As noted above, the opportunity structure offered by the European electoral arena can sometimes enhance the prospects for parties that are effectively marginalised in domestic politics, while the differing agenda that is often associated with European elections can also help provoke new patterns of alignment. In general, however, the national parties function quite effectively as gatekeepers within this arena, and they also work to ensure that the representatives who win election to the European Parliament remain bound to their domestic party organisations. For this reason, it is unlikely that the opportunities for contestation in themselves might provide the basis for a significant challenge to the dominance of domestic actors, any more than the opportunities for contestation in the local arena have impacted significantly on the alternatives available at the national political level (see also below). It is in this sense that Reif and Schmitt's emphasis on the second-order character of European elections is particularly important.[14]

The second argument concerns the nature of the European-level party system itself. In fact, there is – at least as yet – no European party system as such. Rather, what we have, at most, is a collection of proto-Europarties, which, in many respects, may even best be disaggregated into collections of national parties that enjoy loosely defined cross-national links. But whatever the status of the Europarties may be,[15] there is certainly no real sense in which one can speak of a distinct and autonomous European party *system*. Party systems are defined by reference to a given structure of competition, in which the patterned interactions between the parties enjoy a pronounced degree of predictability and stability.[16] It follows from this that it is perfectly possible to conceive both in theory and practice of a collection or 'basket' of parties which does not at the same time constitute a system as such.[17] In other words, while a plurality of parties may exist, their interactions need not necessarily constitute an identifiable structure. To be sure, the national party components of the proto-Europarties will often be constitutive of a national party system within their own national territories. Indeed, this is part of the process by which the alignments within national party systems become translated into the European arena. At the European level, however, there is no such system in operation, and hence the Europarties that emerge in the European Parliament are much more akin to the notion of the basket of parties, being juxtaposed to one another rather than competing with one another in any predictable or patterned sense. In this sense, the Europarties should not be seen as components of some larger and self-perpetuating system. At the European level, at any rate, such a system does not exist.

Nor can such a system exist as long as competition fails to be structured at the European level itself. The only way in which such a structure could emerge is through competition for executive office at that higher level. What is of crucial importance here, at least insofar as we are concerned with party systems, and hence with the structures of competition that define those systems, is whether the parties control executive office and whether they compete with one another for the exercise of such control. Should they lack such control, then they will also lack a focus for competition; and, lacking a focus for competition, they will then lack the capacity to develop into a party system. This is not to deny that these parties may serve an important representative function. Regardless of whether they control executive office, they clearly are in a position to give voice to their constituents' demands. Nor is it to deny their capacity or willingness to form alliances with other parties with a view to promoting particular policy alternatives, and even to control the allocation of parliamentary positions. But as long as they are prevented from forming a government at the European level, they will remain mutually autonomous legislative parties whose primary terms of reference derive from the national electoral environments from which they have emerged. In a recent assessment of the state of Europarties, Mogens Pedersen[18] suggested that these were

> not genuine parties, if by this we mean organisations that span and control the electoral linkage. First, these new parties do not have an

electorate. In elections to the European Parliament the voters within each nation vote for their own parties. Second, these 'parties' do not have an internal organisation to carry out the policies of the leadership ... Third, the cohesion of such groups is not comparable to the cohesion of most national parliamentary groups.

This view might now be qualified by evidence about the ever-increasing partyness of the Europarties.[19] But it is worth emphasising that what Pedersen might just as well be depicting here are the two congressional parties in the United States. There also, at least at the congressional level, no national electorate exists, and there is effectively no national party organisation. Likewise, at least on issues other than the recent partisan impeachment of the President, there has always been a marked lack of legislative partisan cohesion.[20] In sum, at the level of the American Congress, and precisely because the Congress does not involve the contest for government, there is no real party system to speak of. Rather, the representatives in Congress reflect the politics of 50 different state-level party systems. Their terms of reference, even at the federal level, remain primarily tied to the parameters of the individual and sometimes quite unique state-level contests from which they have emerged.[21] American parliamentarism in this sense may be characterised by what Sartori defines as 'assembly government'.[22]

It is necessary to emphasise that the preceding remarks refer only to the parties in the American Congress. At another level in the American polity it is, of course, possible to speak of a 'single' national or federal party system – that is, that which emerges every four years through the competition for the office of President. This is the party system that belongs to the *executive electoral arena* and it is necessarily structured by the race for the White House. Yet, this presidential party system is quite different from the collection of state-level congressional party systems, and it overlaps only to a limited extent with these latter party systems. In the American case, then, there is a 'single' national party system that may be associated with the competition for national executive office. Beyond that particular system, parties traditionally emerged only to give voice to voters at the federal/national level rather than constituting a separate and self-standing party system. The American case, therefore, differs from most systems of parliamentary (as opposed to assembly) government in the co-existence and complete separation of an executive electoral arena and a legislative electoral arena. This fact has enabled the polity to maintain both a national party system at presidential level, and a collection of state parties and party systems at the legislative level.

The relevance of the comparison with the European electoral arena should now be obvious. The European electoral arena is an exclusively legislative electoral arena. There is, as yet, no executive electoral arena, notwithstanding the small gains made by the European Parliament with respect to its capacity to control the executive (in the form of the European Commission). Nor, putting it very briefly, will there ever be an executive electoral arena at the European level, unless either the President of the Commission becomes subject to popular election (thus following the US example) or the Commission is deemed to be wholly accountable to the Parliament (thus following the conventional European national pattern of parliamentary government). In the absence of such fundamental constitutional change, the European Parliament will remain an essentially representative body in which competition at the European level cannot be structured by the competition for executive office. In the absence of such a change, therefore, there will be no European party system. On the contrary, and as has long been the case in the US Congress, the parties in the European Parliament will derive their primary identity and terms of reference from within their own individual national environments; and they will have little or nothing to differentiate their pattern of competition from that in the national political arena. For this reason, the scope for spillover from the European to the national electoral arena will always remain limited; and for this reason also, national party systems are likely to remain relatively impervious to any direct impact of European integration.

DIFFERENT ARENAS, DIFFERENT COMPETENCES

Since the advent of mass democracy in Europe, voters have enjoyed access to a variety of different electoral arenas within which politics may be contested. With some variation, two of these arenas were common to all states. The first was the local or sub-national arena, in which voters could participate in more or less decisive contests for elections to local, provincial or sometimes even regional authorities. The second was the national arena, in which the universal contest for election to the national parliament was sometimes supplemented by contests for an elected presidency or, even more rarely, for a directly elected upper chamber. The third arena in which voters traditionally won a voice in politics was by means of direct democracy, although here again states varied in terms of the opportunities that were offered as well as in terms of the decisiveness that was accorded to the outcomes. More recently, of course, voters in the EU member states have also enjoyed access to a major new electoral arena, the European electoral arena.

Looking at this now extended variety of electoral arenas in which national citizenries may become involved, and in which some or all national parties necessarily compete, we might anticipate two key features of their inter-relationships. First, we might expect that the parties competing in each national system are likely to seek 'control' of each of the different arenas involved.[23] At least at first sight, it is only through such control that they are likely to ensure their own survival as organisations, and their dominant role in national political agenda setting. This is also an old phenomenon – indeed, the classic literature on party development in western Europe is replete with analyses of the ways in which parties attempted to nationalise electoral competition, and to translate particular dimensions of partisan conflict from the national to the local arena, or, less usually, from the local to the national arena.[24] Moreover, this has been a largely successful strategy, at least so far. The nature of contests between parties necessarily varies from place to place within the local arena, not least due to the emergence and survival of minor regionalist parties; contests also sometimes vary across localities even within the national arena. But it is striking in well structured party systems to see precisely how particular contests and alignments tend to be replicated at many different levels within the polity and to note the extent to which there is now a uniformity in the range of alternatives offered to voters.

Second, we might anticipate that the issues at play in each of these different arenas – leaving aside the direct democracy arena, which is inevitably issue-specific – will be largely attuned to the competences of the particular arena concerned. Notwithstanding the arguments concerning second-order elections, it seems reasonable to assume that neither the voters nor the parties will be inclined to fight elections in one arena on the basis of issues and policy questions that can only be settled in another arena. Although the same parties might be present in more or less all contests, we can, therefore, reasonably assume that contests in local arenas, for example, will focus primarily on issues at the local level, whereas contests in national arenas will revolve primarily around issues at the national level.

Both of these traditional assumptions can now also be easily applied to the distinction between the national arena and the more recently created European arena. First, it was always likely that the national parties in the EU member states – many of which were long-established and traditionally dominant within national politics long before the European electoral arena was inaugurated – would have attempted to control the new European arena. It was obviously in their interest to do so, since any new challengers that might emerge to contest the European arena could also possibly end up reaching across to contest the national arena.[25] Hence, to avoid contagion and to see off any potential challengers, national parties would have to enter the European electoral arena with as much force as they have traditionally done in the national context. Indeed, their incentive to do so in the European arena has probably been greater than is often the case in the local arena, since the former involves a national contest. Second, we might also assume that a crude division of issue responsibility would emerge, with national political issues continuing to be contested in the national arenas, and with the European arena becoming the domain for 'European' issues. In other words, questions of public policy in the more functional sense of the term are probably best contested within the national electoral arena, whereas the key questions regarding Europe, including the extent to which Europe may exert authority over national governments, are best contested in the European electoral arena. Put more simply, national elections should be about everyday questions of policy-making – social policy, economic policy, education policy, and so on – whereas European elections should be about European politics and the question of Europe itself. This seems an eminently reasonable assumption on which to operate.

In fact, however, the assumption is implausible, and not least because of the asymmetry of the two arenas involved. Although the two arenas are formally distinct, their remits are quite seriously confused. Moreover, this confusion operates to the advantage of the national arena. Thus, while national political decision-making, however circumscribed, can reasonably be portrayed as falling more or less exclusively within the remit of the national political arena, European political decision-making clearly falls within the remit of both arenas. For the voters, therefore, there are in fact two different channels through which access to Europe might usefully be directed (see Figure 1). On the one hand, and most obviously, access to European decision-making can be channelled through the European electoral arena itself (channel *B* in Figure 1). Preferences expressed in the direct European elections become translated into party strengths within the European Parliament, and hence, albeit not always authoritatively, into EU policy. On the other hand, and more indirectly, preferences expressed in national elections become translated into party strengths within national parliaments, and hence into the formation of particular governments. The latter, in turn, enjoy a major say in both the EU intergovernmental bodies (the various EU Councils) as well as in the nominations to the European Commission (channel *A* in Figure 1).

But there is also more to it than this. As far as the European Parliament is concerned, for example, the principal competences clearly lie in the area

FIGURE 1

ELECTORAL ACCESS TO EUROPEAN DECISION-MAKING

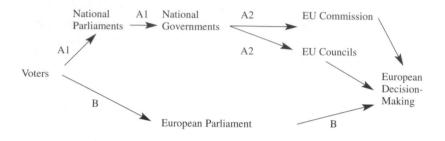

of day-to-day policy-making at the European level. It seems hardly necessary to go into this question here. Suffice it to recall that since the Maastricht Treaty in 1992, and most especially since the coming into operation of the Amsterdam Treaty in 1999, the European Parliament has come to enjoy an authoritative co-decision role in a wide variety of different policy areas, including environment, culture, technology and transport. The Parliament also enjoys the right to approve the overall budget of the EU, and to judge how that budget has been implemented. In some policy areas, to be sure, the European Parliament's powers remain quite limited. It still enjoys no formal say in foreign and security policy, for example, and its role in EMU policy-making as well as in the detailed working of the Common Agricultural Policy is non-authoritative. Nor can the Parliament formally initiate legislation. But given the increasing variety of policy areas in which its voice must be heard, at least in the sense that its views must be taken on board by both the Commission and the Council of Ministers, the European Parliament can be considered to have a major policy-making function within the EU system.

The competences that are associated with the national electoral arena, on the other hand, as channelled through national governments to the EU itself, not only include co-decision making in these selfsame policy areas, but also relate to the structure of the European polity itself. Hence any decisions on extending the powers of the EU, for example, including the adoption of new treaties such as those of Maastricht or Amsterdam, the establishment of EMU, or questions of enlargement, are the exclusive authority of the intergovernmental organs of the EU. Hence, they properly fall within the national electoral arena. Moreover, the key powers of appointment to the

European Commission, including the nomination of the President of the Commission, as well as of the other Commissioners, rests primarily with the national political leaderships. The European Parliament has an increasingly important voice here, too, especially since the Treaty of Amsterdam by which it acquired the formal right to approve the nomination of the President; it has also long enjoyed the formal right to dismiss the Commission as a whole.[26] Nevertheless, the key powers in this regard still remain with the national governments.

In sum, not only do two distinct channels exist whereby voters can affect issues that concern EU politics, but these channels may also be associated with alternative functions. Day-to-day policy-making across an increasing variety of fields within the EU constitutes the principal function of the European Parliament, and hence is especially suited to competition within the European electoral arena. Of course, this day-to-day policy-making also constitutes part of the functions of the intergovernmental organs of the EU, and, in certain fields (for example, foreign and security policy) actually remains within the exclusive authority of these inter-governmental organs. Yet the key European issues that are clearly most readily suited to competition within the national electoral arena are those concerning the question of Europe itself, including the distribution of powers to the various organs, as well as questions relating to enlargement and further integration. In other words, any questions concerning the *constitution* of Europe are likely to fall most firmly within the national electoral arena, whereas any questions concerning the day-to-day *functioning* of Europe are likely to be *at least as* appropriate within the European electoral arena. To put it yet another way, while questions regarding the day-to-day functioning of the EU might be usefully contested in both arenas, questions regarding the make-up of the European polity itself are best contested within the national arena alone, since it is there that the principal competence lies.

We might even take the argument a little further, particularly as the polities in Europe become even more integrated. Since so much of contemporary policy-making now has a European dimension, in that so many of the parameters within which policy manoeuvre is possible are set by the EU, the national electoral arena might be considered as suited to the contestation of policy issues only in an increasingly *indirect* sense. In other words, where major policy questions are at stake, these are perhaps best resolved through the national electoral arena only when that arena becomes translated onto the European level, that is, only when influence is directed – at one remove – along the A_2 channel as indicated in Figure 1. At the strictly national level, on the other hand, Europe increasingly restricts policy manoeuvre, and the scope for government discretion is quite severely constrained. In terms of any *direct* influence on policy-making, therefore, voters might better be advised to contest these policy issues within the European electoral arena rather than (exclusively) within the national political arena.

It is in this sense that the initial assumption about the 'division of labour' between the two arenas is implausible. Indeed, not only is it implausible, there are even grounds for its reversal. That is, there are grounds on which it could be argued that the national political arena is most suited to the contestation of European issues – principally European constitutional issues, but also certain European policy issues – whereas the European electoral arena is perhaps most suited to the contestation of everyday policy issues, including those issue areas that were normally seen to fall within the remit of independent national governments. We might then reasonably anticipate that national elections should be more and more 'about' Europe, whereas European elections should be more and more about questions of day-to-day policy-making. To divide the responsibilities otherwise would be to risk having more and more meaningless contests in each of the arenas.

In practice, however, this is not what happens – at least not throughout the EU. In fact, the opposite is often true: national elections continue to be dominated by conflicts over policy alternatives, the scope for the exercise of which is severely constrained by the European dimension. By contrast, European elections tend to be dominated by debates over Europe itself, despite the fact that the room for institutional manoeuvre concerning Europe is severely constrained by national governments. Thus, the issue of Europe scarcely figures in national elections – with the potential exception, as noted above, of the next general election in the United Kingdom – most of which are devoted to day-to-day policy issues. These selfsame policy issues are often neglected in European elections, many of which largely involve half-hearted debates about the future of Europe. In other words, contests in each arena appear to involve questions that can often be resolved only outside that arena itself.

Why should this seeming incongruity prevail? Two possible answers suggest themselves. The first is perhaps the more realistic and relates simply to popular traditions and expectations. Since national elections have always been about everyday issues of policy, it might seem absurd for the parties to attempt to contest these elections while at the same time admitting their abdication of responsibility for these policies. It is one thing for competing political leaderships to acknowledge that Europe imposes restrictions on the scope for national policy initiatives; it is quite another for them to enter an election while admitting that their hands are tied. National elections may now prove less decisive in policy terms, but it is important for the competing parties to maintain the sense that these contests matter. Moreover, it can also be argued that the diffuse support that these national elections provide is at least as important as any specific mandate for action that they produce. At the same time, both in the minds of voters and in the nature of media coverage, there also exists an inevitable tendency to associate European elections with the issue of Europe. Accordingly, it might seem even more absurd for a party to contest elections within the European arena without reference to its position on Europe itself. The stances adopted by the parties in this regard might have no implications in practice, but the terms of reference of the contest would appear to demand that they be enunciated – even if, as we have seen to be the case within the party mainstream at least – the positions which are advocated are scarcely likely to differ from one another. In addition, of course, the association between European issues and the European arena is such that parties may also be inclined to use the contests there simply to showcase their attitudes to Europe, particularly since these positions are largely excluded from the national arena.

The second answer is perhaps more sceptical, in that it might be argued that this incongruous division of debate across the two different arenas actually serves the interests of the parties – the contestants – themselves. That is, by debating Europe within an arena (the European arena) where competence in the area is negligible, and by debating policy questions in another arena (the national arena) where choices are increasingly circumscribed, voters are being offered a voice that is likely to have little or no effect on the practice of decision-making. In other words, voters are being offered a say over questions that do not really count at the particular level involved. What this also means is that the issue of Europe is taken out of the national arena, where it properly belongs, and is hence depoliticised. At the same time, many issues of public policy are taken out of the European arena, where they properly belong, and are, therefore, also depoliticised. The result is that the party leaderships which emerge victorious from the contests in each arena have the capacity to remain relatively insulated from electoral constraints and enjoy a relatively free hand to develop their appropriate policy alternatives as they themselves see fit. From a strictly rational perspective, this consideration then suggests another reason why party systems appear to remain relatively impervious to the direct impact of Europeanisation: the parties make it so.

DEPOLITICISATION AND EUROPEANISATION

Following from this last argument, we might conclude that Europe fails to impact on national party systems because it is held at one remove by the competing political leaderships, such that, in terms of domestic politics at least, it is often depoliticised. Nor does one even need to be sceptical about the intentions of the various political leaderships to entertain this argument. Indeed, given the mainstream consensus within most member states, it is likely that even if Europe were to be brought into these national arenas, the choice facing those voters who are concerned with governing alternatives would still remain largely non-existent.[27]

In either case, however, the result is self-evident: Europe becomes a matter for the governing politicians and their bureaucracies; it is not something that requires the active engagement of, or consultation with, the electorate at large. In this regard it is also striking to note the coincidence between the group of countries in which parties adopting an anti-European stance have succeeded in cornering a reasonable niche of the electoral market and that in which there have recently been important referendums on the issue of European integration – Austria, Denmark, France and Sweden (see Table 2).[28] This overlap might suggest that it is at least partly through the arena of direct democracy that the issue of European integration may gain access to national politics. Thus, while Europe may normally be taken out of political debate in partisan competition at the domestic level, it is sometimes forced back in by means of popular referendums.

More importantly, it is also here that we might see the strongest evidence of the *indirect* impact of European integration on national party systems. The depoliticisation of the European issue is far from being a unique phenomenon within contemporary political systems. Indeed, there are strong arguments to suggest that European democracy in general is becoming increasingly depoliticised,[29] and, in this sense, Europe serves as yet another, albeit major, component that may promote increased popular disengagement from, and indifference to, the wider political process. Partly through Europe, therefore, albeit indirectly, the democratic process risks becoming devalued. But that is another story, for to move from the direct to the indirect impact of Europeanisation on party systems is to open a Pandora's box in which it becomes increasingly difficult to specify the particular factors at play. As indicated above, however, two of these indirect influences may be of particular and lasting importance. In the first place, European integration increasingly operates to constrain the freedom of movement of national governments, and hence encourages a hollowing out of competition among those parties with a governing aspiration. As such, it promotes a degree of consensus across the mainstream and an inevitable reduction in the range of policy alternatives available to voters. Second, by taking Europe itself out of national competition, and by working within a supranational structure that clearly lacks democratic accountability, party and political leaderships do little to counteract the notion of the irrelevance of conventional politics. For both these reasons, it may be possible to trace a link, however indirect, between Europeanisation and the more widespread malaise that increasingly tends to characterise much of democratic life in modern Europe. In the end, therefore, it seems hardly coincidental that it is precisely during this period of deepening European integration that we begin to see the most obvious signs of electoral dealignment and disengagement. Party leaderships – and the party systems of which they are part – may well have proved capable of protecting themselves from the direct impact of Europeanisation. Nevertheless, by so doing, they may have risked undermining the legitimacy of their calling.

NOTES

An earlier version of this paper was presented to the workshop on *Europeanised Politics? The Impact of European Integration on Domestic Politics*, at Nuffield College, Oxford, 18–19 June 1999. I am grateful to the participants in that conference, and in particular to Paul Taggart, Klaus Goetz and Simon Hix, for their helpful comments on that earlier draft.

1. This is true for the nine member states then in the EC. Thereafter, Greece held its first direct European elections in 1981, Portugal and Spain in 1987, Sweden in 1995, and Austria and Finland in 1996. All 15 member states participated in the most recent round of direct elections in June 1999.
2. See G. Sartori, *Parties and Party Systems* (Cambridge: Cambridge University Press 1976).
3. Note that I am deliberately excluding any new parties that might have emerged to contest solely within the European electoral arena (see also below). Although the European electoral arena is clearly important, for the purposes of this present paper I am considering only effects which can be seen at the level of party system within the national electoral arena. For a more detailed analysis of the emergence of new parties in established party systems, see P. Mair, 'New Political Parties in Long-Established Party Systems: How Successful Are They?', in E. Beukel, K.K. Klausen and P.E. Mouritzen (eds.), *Elites, Parties and Democracy: Festschrift for Mogens N. Pedersen* (Odense: Odense University Press 1999), pp.207–24.
4. The three parties concerned are the Austrian 'No-Citizens Initiative' (average vote 1.0 per cent), the Finnish 'Alliance for a Free Finland' (average/only vote 1.0 per cent) and the British 'Referendum Party' (average/only vote 2.6 per cent). Details on new parties are derived from T.T. Mackie and R. Rose, *The International Almanac of Electoral History* (Basingstoke: Macmillan 3rd edn. 1991), and their *A Decade of Election Results: Updating the International Almanac* (Glasgow: CSSP 1997), as well as from the *Political Data Yearbook*, published as part of the *European Journal of Political Research*. The data cover elections held through to the end of 1998.
5. In passing, it should be emphasised that the opportunities available for the formation of new parties in the European electoral arena are probably far greater than those in the national

electoral arena are. The former offers a number of advantages in this regard, including financial subsidies from the European Parliament itself, relatively high levels of publicity, a fixed election date that allows for greater preparation and anticipation, a less decisive contest, which permits more expressive or protest voting, and, at least in some cases (e.g., France and the UK) lower electoral thresholds.

6. L. Ray, 'Measuring Party Orientations Towards European Integration: Results from an Expert Survey', *European Journal of Political Research* 36 (1999), pp.283–306.
7. P. Taggart, 'A Touchstone of Dissent: Euroscepticism in Contemporary Western European Party Systems', *European Journal of Political Research* 33 (1998), pp.363–88.
8. Ibid., p.384.
9. See, for example, J. Garry, 'The British Conservative Party: Divisions over European Policy', *West European Politics* 18 (1995), pp.170–89.
10. See G. Smith, 'Core Persistence, System Change and the "People's Party"', *West European Politics* 12 (1989), pp.157–68; see also S. Hix, 'Dimensions and Alignments in European Union Politics: Cognitive Constraints and Partisan Responses', *European Journal of Political Research* 35 (1999), pp.69–106.
11. See H.-M. ten Napel, *'Een Eigen Weg': De Totstandkoming van het CDA (1952–1980)* (Kampen: Kok 1992).
12. See, among others, L. Bardi, 'Transnational Trends in European Parties and the 1994 Elections of the European Parliament', *Party Politics* 2 (1996), pp.99–114; S. Hix and C. Lord, *Political Parties in the European Union* (Basingstoke: Macmillan 1997); G. Marks and C. Wilson, 'National Parties and the Contestation of Europe', in T. Banchoff and M.P. Smith (eds.), *Legitimacy and the European Union* (London: Routledge 1999), pp.113–33.
13. See R. Andeweg, 'The Reshaping of National Party Systems', *West European Politics* 18 (1995), pp.58–78; M.N. Pedersen, 'Euro-Parties and European Parties: New Arenas, New Challenges and New Strategies', in S.S. Andersen and K.A. Eliassen (eds.), *The European Union: How Democratic Is It?* (London: Sage 1996), pp.15–40.
14. See K. Reif and H. Schmitt, 'Nine Second-Order National Elections: A Conceptual Framework for the Analysis of European Election Results', *European Journal of Political Research* 8 (1980), pp.3–44.
15. See Hix and Lord, *Political Parties in the European Union*; L. Bardi, 'Transnational Party Federations. European Parliamentary Party Groups and the Building of Europarties', in R.S. Katz and P. Mair (eds.), *How Parties Organize: Change and Adaptation in Party Organizations in Western Democracies* (London: Sage 1994), pp.357–72.
16. See Sartori, *Parties and Party Systems*; see also P. Mair, *Party System Change* (Oxford: Clarendon Press 1997), pp.199–223, and L. Bardi and P. Mair, 'The Parameters of Party Systems' (unpublished paper).
17. See also H. Eckstein, 'Party Systems', *International Encyclopedia of the Social Sciences, Vol. 11* (New York: Crowell, Collier & Macmillan 1968), pp.436–53.
18. Pedersen, 'Euro-Parties and European Parties', p.16.
19. Hix and Lord, *Political Parties in the European Union*; Marks and Wilson, 'National Parties and the Contestation of Europe'; Bardi, 'Transnational Trends in European Parties and the 1994 Elections of the European Parliament'.
20. For an attempt to revise this more or less standard interpretation, see G.M. Pomper, 'The Alleged Decline of American Parties', in J.G. Geer (ed.), *Politicians and Party Politics* (Baltimore: The Johns Hopkins University Press 1998), pp.14–39.
21. See R.S. Katz and R. Kolodny, 'Party Organization as an Empty Vessel: Parties in American Politics', in Katz and Mair (eds.), *How Parties Organize*, pp.23–50.
22. G. Sartori, *Comparative Constitutional Engineering: An Enquiry into Structures, Incentives and Outcomes* (Basingstoke: Macmillan 1994), pp.100–112.
23. Pedersen, 'Euro-Parties and European Parties'; S. Bartolini, *Exit Options, Boundary Building, Political Structuring* (Florence: EUI Working Papers SPS 98/1 1998).
24. See the extensive discussion in D. Caramani, 'The Nationalisation of Electoral Politics: A Comparative and Historical Analysis of Territories, Elections and Parties in Western Europe' (Ph.D. thesis, EUI Florence, 1997), pp.14–47.
25. See Andeweg, 'The Reshaping of National Party Systems'.

26. See M. Westlake, 'The European Parliament's Emerging Powers of Appointment', *Journal of Common Market Studies* 36 (1998), pp.431–44.
27. See also Hix, 'Dimensions and Alignments in European Union Politics', pp.87–9.
28. See also Taggart, 'A Touchstone of Dissent', p.369. Although it might be tempting to add the UK to this list, thus linking the promise of a referendum on the EMU with the increasingly partisan divide over Europe in Britain, it is also worth noting that Ireland, which has had a number of referendums on Europe, has no recent record of electoral support for anti-European parties. By contrast, Italy, which has never voted in a referendum on Europe, currently records the highest level of support for parties regarded as strongly anti-European – see Table 2 above.
29. As, more than 30 years ago, it was predicted to become in the then very convincing arguments advanced by both Robert Dahl and Arend Lijphart. See R.A. Dahl, 'Epilogue', in idem (ed.), *Political Oppositions in Western Democracies* (New Haven: Yale University Press 1966), pp.387–401; and A. Lijphart, 'Typologies of Democratic Systems', *Comparative Political Studies* 1 (1968), pp.35–9. See also P. Mair, 'Representation and Participation in the Changing World of Party Politics', *European Review* 6 (1998), pp.161–74.

European Integration, Voters and National Politics

MATTHEW GABEL

By joining the European Union (EU), member states accept a particular set of policy choices regarding a broad range of economic and social issues (the *acquis communautaire*) and a supranational political authority to govern these policies. A large body of research has studied and documented how national politics in the member states has influenced the content and development of the *acquis* and the construction of EU political institutions. The usual story is that national representatives, concerned about the interests of key voters, have promoted particular policies and reforms, thereby shaping the process of European integration.[1] For example, President De Gaulle promoted the Common Agricultural Policy as a means to attract and maintain the farm vote in France. The general premise underlying such explanations is that the outcome of EU policies is sufficiently consequential to voters for the national representatives to promote EU policies that advance their electoral fortunes.

Given this premise, we might expect European integration to influence national politics through mass voting behaviour. This article investigates that assertion. Specifically, it considers whether and how EU membership, as a set of national policy and institutional commitments, shapes voting behaviour in national elections. Unfortunately, previous research provides little systematic evidence of this relationship. This is due, in large part, to the lack of scholarly attention. With one notable exception, researchers have only recently begun to address this question systematically across the EU member states. Since there is only limited relevant research to survey, a significant portion of the following discussion is devoted to describing and executing part of an agenda for further research on this question.

The analysis focuses on three particular areas where European integration intersects with national voting behaviour. First, we consider the impact of elections to the European Parliament on voting behaviour in national elections. Research on this topic is relatively well developed, offering several general theoretical propositions with supporting empirical evidence. Second, we address the question of whether issues of European integration influence electoral behaviour. Recent research suggests that, particularly for the United Kingdom, European integration has altered party competition and voting behaviour in national elections. Indeed, EU issues may now serve as a new electoral cleavage for the United Kingdom. We explore empirically how well these results generalise to all the EU member states. Third, the article examines the theoretical importance of European monetary unification for traditional models of economic voting. From this discussion, a research agenda is set out for future empirical research on economic voting in the EU member states.

VOTING BEHAVIOUR IN EUROPEAN ELECTIONS AND NATIONAL ELECTIONS

European integration has introduced an institutional dynamic to voting behaviour in EU domestic electoral arenas. That institution is the European election, in which EU citizens elect representatives to the European Parliament. One of the primary findings about these elections is that they are predominantly fought on national political issues, constituting a second-order national election.[2] This national focus means that European elections can convey meaningful information to national parties and voters regarding parties' electoral prospects.[3]

The study of European elections reveals several concrete examples of their effect on national politics generally, and voting behaviour specifically. For example, the electoral performance of the French National Front and German Green Party in European elections was crucial to their subsequent success in national elections.[4] The country chapters in *Choosing Europe*, by Cees van der Eijk and Mark Franklin provide more examples of this impact on national elections.[5] Central to these accounts is the claim that the results of European elections have altered voting behaviour in subsequent national elections. These accounts of specific events in particular nations are valuable, but they beg a more fundamental question. We want to know why European elections are influential on voting behaviour in some national contexts at particular times but not in others. Fortunately, research on European elections provides clear answers to this question. Studies by Michael Marsh and by Marsh and Franklin show that the outcomes of national elections are systematically related to the outcomes of European elections.[6] Specifically, these scholars have demonstrated that European elections vary in their effect on national elections according to their temporal relationship to these national elections. According to Marsh and Franklin, European elections serve as more than opinion polls on the governing parties, reflecting trends in the government's popularity cycle.[7] Instead, they claim that European elections can serve as 'marker' elections, providing useful information to parties and voters about the relative standing of political parties. According to van der Eijk, Franklin and Marsh:

> When European elections are held concurrently with, or very shortly after, national elections, they appear to be seen more or less as "throw-away" elections. The marker set by the concurrent or recent national election has not yet lost its plausibility and, whatever the difference between the European election outcome and the result that would have occurred in a national election, it will have no political consequences simply because no-one will pay any attention to it. Apparently, voters are aware of this, because these are the electoral situations in which sincere voting seems most frequent, with voters supporting their preferred party even if that party has little chance of playing a prominent part in government. Contrasting strongly with this situation is the one in which a European election is conducted at a considerable temporal distance from the previous national election, possibly with the next national election already in sight. In this situation the marker set by the previous national election has become obsolete, and politicians are tempted to regard the results of the European election as a new indicator of their own and other parties' electoral strength. Voters apparently sense this – presumably as a result of media coverage and the way in which politicians approach them during the campaign.[8]

When the European election serves as a marker, voters appear to register protest rather than express sincere preferences over parties. As a result, marker elections often change the dynamics of future national elections. Parties in government react to these protests, protest parties attempt to build on their electoral success, and voters re-appraise parties and their electoral potential.[9] In turn, voters behave differently in the subsequent national elections. Specifically, governing parties that attain higher (lower) vote shares than expected in European elections gain (lose) more votes in the ensuing national elections than would be expected in the absence of European elections.[10] Table 1 summarises the basic conclusions of this research.

TABLE 1
EFFECTS OF EUROPEAN ELECTIONS ON NATIONAL ELECTIONS

	Vote Share of Governing Parties in EP Election	
	Higher than expected	Lower than expected
EP election soon after national election	little effect on national election outcome	little effect on national election outcome
EP election long after national election	governing parties attract more votes than expected in subsequent national election	governing parties attract fewer votes than expected in subsequent national election

EUROPEAN INTEGRATION AND ISSUE-VOTING IN NATIONAL ELECTIONS

Membership in the European Union requires a national commitment to a specific set of social and economic policies. As integration has progressed, these policies have increasingly involved issues of high salience to EU citizens (for example, a single currency), and the current agenda for policy integration and reform includes areas of foreign affairs, defence and justice. Thus, EU membership and the direction of integration are relevant to citizens' welfare and political interests.

National elections provide an important channel through which citizens can express their interests regarding these policies and attempt to influence related political decisions. For one, the national government that emerges from national elections designates the national representatives that participate in the EU Council of Ministers, which must approve all EU laws. In addition, elected national heads of government directly represent their member states in the European Council, which sets the agenda for further European integration. Consequently, there is good reason to expect voters to express their preferences over EU membership and European integration in their voting behaviour in national elections.

If voters' preferences over EU issues influence voting behaviour in national elections, then European integration may have transformed national electoral politics. Several studies have noted that issues of European integration shaped voting behaviour in specific national elections. First, two studies by Geoffrey Evans demonstrated that voters' perceptions of the Conservative Party's position on European integration influenced its electoral support during the 1990s.[11] Evans also showed voters' perceptions of the Tories' mismanagement of the exchange rate mechanism (ERM) crisis hurt the Tories' electoral support. Second, Tapio Raunio found that Finnish political parties have engaged in strategic manoeuvring on issues of European integration in order to maintain electoral support in the 1990s.[12] Implicit in this study was the assertion that European integration is a sufficiently salient issue in these electorates to generate internal party conflict and party competition.

In addition, European integration may influence the saliency of non-EU issues in national elections. Voters may alter the issues they consider salient in national elections according to the level of governance responsible for the policy. For example, Clifford Carrubba and Richard Timpone demonstrated that environmental concerns were more important determinants of vote choice in European Parliament elections than in national elections.[13] They accounted for this finding by contending that voters prefer environmental policy-making at the EU rather than the national level. This argued that, since stringent national environmental regulations hamper the competitiveness of national firms *vis-à-vis* other EU member states with less stringent regulations, voters should prefer that regulations be imposed at the EU rather than the national level. Thus, voters pursue their environmental policy interests in European elections, but not in national elections.

This conclusion obviously points to the significance of European integration in determining which issues are important for national elections. EU authority over environmental issues changed the context of national voting behaviour. One could clearly extend this reasoning to other issues over which the EU governs. The general expectation would be that issues for which voters prefer EU-level governance are less salient in national elections once the EU acquires competence in that area.

More profoundly, EU issues may also introduce a new electoral cleavage to national politics in the member states. For this to be true, EU issues must determine, to some degree, voter choice and they must change the patterns of voting behaviour from their traditional configuration. Thus, it is important to note that the observation that voters' preferences over EU issues relate to their party choice is not, by itself, a signal that European integration has changed voting behaviour in national elections. Citizens may choose parties largely on non-EU issues, but their positions on EU issues may still correlate with their vote choice. For example, traditionally voters in the EU member states have chosen among parties based on their positions on the left–right dimension, which is commonly understood to represent a summary of policy preferences across a broad array of national political issues.[14] If a voter's position on an EU issue were highly correlated with that voter's left–right position, we would find a connection between EU issue preference and vote choice. However, unless EU issues largely define the left–right dimension, EU issues would not have transformed voting behaviour. Voting behaviour would remain driven by traditional left–right politics. Thus, for EU issues to transform voting behaviour in national elections, voters' preferences on these issues must be independent, to a significant degree, of the traditional sources of their vote choice.

Meeting this condition would be necessary but not sufficient to demonstrate that EU issues transform electoral politics. In the above example, voters' positions on EU issues may not correlate highly with their left–right positions, but the independent variation in voters' EU issue positions may be unrelated to their vote choice. In this case, voters' positions on EU issues would do more than simply reflect their left–right positions, but these positions would be inconsequential for understanding voting behaviour.

In sum, the general point is that for issues of European integration to generate a new electoral cleavage in national politics, voters' preferences on these issues cannot neatly map onto traditional sources of vote choice and they must be sufficiently salient to influence vote choice independent of these traditional sources. Several recent studies indicate that EU issues do in fact serve as a new electoral cleavage in the United Kingdom and France. Three studies by Evans provide different types of evidence that issues of European integration shaped recent British elections.[15] In particular, Evans showed that EU issues significantly affected voting behaviour in the 1997 British parliamentary elections.[16] First, Evans demonstrated that voters' preferences over EU membership were either unrelated or weakly related to policy issues defining the left–right dimension in the United Kingdom.[17] Since the left–right dimension is traditionally an important source of voting behaviour in the national elections in the UK, this means that voters' positions on EU membership had the potential to serve as a new electoral cleavage. Furthermore, voter positions on EU membership were not simply due to their partisanship. The level of support for EU membership of the core constituencies of the Labour and Conservative parties has remained fairly stable over time, while the parties have changed positions dramatically. Thus, British voters' positions on EU membership met the first condition for providing a new electoral cleavage: they were largely independent of traditional determinants of vote choice.

Evans then demonstrated that voters' support for EU membership influenced their vote choice in national elections, independent of their positions on left–right issues. The effect of support for EU membership on vote choice changed over this period. Up to 1992, support for European Community membership decreased the likelihood of voting for the Labour Party over the Conservative Party. In 1992, support for membership had no effect on vote choice. And, in 1997, support for EU membership increased the likelihood of voting for Labour over the Conservatives. Moreover, in that election support for EU membership had a significant impact on vote choice, clearly dividing Labour and Liberal Democrat voters from Conservative voters.

Kenneth Scheve has also investigated whether and how voters' positions on European integration influence their vote choice in national elections.[18] Specifically, he examined whether French and British voters chose among parties in recent national elections based on their preference for European monetary integration. He showed that vote choice depended on the proximity of a party's position on European monetary union to that of the voter. In both the 1997 British parliamentary election and the 1995 French presidential elections, this proximity influenced voting behaviour independent of traditional determinants of vote choice in these countries. Moreover, in the French case, this issue was responsible for several unexpected aspects of the elections, particularly the success of the far right and other small parties in the first round of the elections.

These studies, although nation- and time-specific, demonstrate that EU membership and issues of European integration can provide a new electoral cleavage in national electorates. Do these findings generalise to all EU member states? To generate a preliminary answer, this study uses the research design of Evans to explore this question across all EU member states.[19] Recall that Evans first examined whether citizens' support for EU membership was related to their position on left–right issues. He then examined whether, independent of their left–right positions, voters' support for EU membership influenced their vote choice. Applying this research design to all national elections in EU member states is beyond the scope of this article. However, it is possible to address these two empirical questions at one point in time across all the EU member states. Specifically, survey data from the January–March 1996 Eurobarometer mega-survey for the 15 EU member states is analysed.[20] This survey provides significantly larger national samples than regular Eurobarometer surveys and includes necessary questions to execute the Evans research design.

The first question is whether citizens' support for EU membership is related to their positions on left–right issues. To answer this question, Evans examined the relationship between citizens' position on particular policy issues that he expected to define the left–right ideological dimension and

TABLE 2
CORRELATION BETWEEN CITIZENS' EVALUATIONS OF EU MEMBERSHIP AND
THEIR LEFT-RIGHT SELF-PLACEMENTS

Member state	Correlation Coefficient
Austria	0.07*
Belgium	–0.03
Denmark	–0.30*
Finland	–0.15*
France	0.01
Germany	0.07*
Greece	–0.22*
Ireland	–0.08*
Italy	0.04*
Luxembourg	–0.05
Netherlands	0.05*
Portugal	–0.06*
Spain	0.06*
Sweden	–0.38*
United Kingdom	0.06*

Note: * 0.05 significance level

their support for EU membership.[21] While Evans may have chosen an appropriate set of left–right issues, there is no 'gold standard' that identifies exactly which issues are appropriate, particularly across countries. Thus, citizens' left–right self-placement is used rather than their positions on specific issues. An advantage of self-placements is that they do not impose an assumption about the issue-content of left–right ideology. In addition, previous studies show that (a) left–right self-placements are important predictors of vote choice and (b) that these self-placements reflect citizens' positions on a variety of salient policy questions, independent of their partisanship.[22] Thus, voters' left–right self-placements provide an indicator of an important traditional source of vote choice, but without imposing any particular assumptions about the issue-content of left–right ideology in a particular nation in 1996.

Table 2 presents the correlations between citizens' left–right self-placements and their support for EU membership.[23] Left–right self-placement ranges from 1 (left) to 10 (right). To measure citizens' support for EU membership, the following survey question was used: 'Generally speaking, do you think that [your country's] membership in the European Union is: (0) a good thing; (1) neither good nor bad; (2) a bad thing.'[24] The correlation coefficients differ in direction and significance across member states, indicating that there is no uniform relationship across EU national electorates.[25] For most EU member states, the relationship is either not statistically different from zero or is very close to zero. The correlation coefficient is relatively large for respondents in Denmark, Sweden and Greece. In these countries, respondents with a right ideology expressed stronger opposition to EU membership than respondents of the left. But, even for these member states, variation in respondents' evaluations of EU membership was largely independent of their left–right positions. Thus, for all the member states, support for EU membership fulfils the first condition for providing a new electoral cleavage in national elections.[26]

Do EU citizens choose among parties based on their support for EU membership? Following Evans, this question is examined by estimating the effect of voters' support for EU membership on their vote choice, while controlling for their left–right positions.[27] Specifically, separate statistical models of vote choice for respondents in each of the member states were estimated. The dependent variable in these models is the intended vote choice of the respondent in the next general election, which was asked in the Eurobarometer survey in all member states.[28] The independent variables are the two variables described above: left–right self-placement and support for EU membership.[29]

Modelling vote choice in a multiparty setting – such as elections in the EU member states – involves several methodological concerns. First, the vote choice is bounded, since the probability of voting for a party can only vary between zero and one. This rules out ordinary least-squares regression as an appropriate statistical method. In addition, with more than two parties, the electoral space may be multidimensional and, thus, it is not clear whether or how voters compare parties or order them on a single dimension. This rules out an ordered probit or logit model. An appropriate method in this setting is a multinomial logit (MNL) model of vote choice.[30] The MNL model does not impose restrictions on the electoral space and it estimates non-linear effects, which are appropriate given the bounded values on vote choice. In addition, MNL does not constrain the independent variables to have a common effect on vote choice between different parties. That is, a change in support for EU membership could increase a voter's likelihood of voting for several different parties (perhaps in varying amounts) and decrease the likelihood of the voter voting for yet another party.

Specifically, MNL extends the binomial logit model to a setting with more than two choices. But MNL provides more efficient estimates than a set of binomial logit models for each pair-wise comparison.[31] For each pair of parties, MNL estimates a model of the change in the probability of choosing one party over another due to a change in the independent variables.[32] For example, an MNL model of vote choice in a five-party

TABLE 3
LIKELIHOOD-RATIO (LR) TEST THAT SUPPORT FOR EU MEMBERSHIP
DOES NOT INFLUENCE VOTE CHOICE

Member State	LR Statistic (degrees of freedom on parentheses)	p-value
Austria	72.5 (4)	0.00
Belgium	33.7 (8)	0.00
Denmark	282.7 (8)	0.00
Finland	420.7 (14)	0.00
France	140.2 (13)	0.00
Germany	124.8 (5)	0.00
Greece	36.1 (4)	0.00
Ireland	20.3 (8)	0.01
Italy	43.4 (4)	0.00
Luxembourg	9.5 (4)	0.05
Netherlands	128.9 (11)	0.00
Portugal	41.9 (6)	0.00
Spain	125.3 (14)	0.00
Sweden	197.3 (7)	0.00
United Kingdom	3.6 (6)	0.73

system requires four model estimations. Consequently, due to the space required, the parameter estimates from the MNL models for all 15 EU member states are not presented.[33]

Moreover, the parameter estimates of these models are not the most relevant statistics for answering the empirical question at issue here. What we want to know is whether, for a given national electorate, voters' support for EU membership had a statistically significant impact on vote choice, independent of left–right self-placement. Since the effect of EU membership on vote choice may vary across parties, we need a summary statistic that indicates the total effect of EU membership on vote choice across all parties. A likelihood ratio (LR) test provides such an indicator.[34] This LR test compares the log-likelihood for a restricted model, which includes only the left–right self-placement variable, with the log likelihood for an unrestricted model, which includes both support for EU membership and left–right self-placement. The resulting difference is distributed as a chi-square and can be evaluated in terms of statistical significance. The null hypothesis is that only left–right self-placement is relevant for vote choice – that is, the restricted model is appropriate.

Table 3 presents the LR test for each of the 15 EU national electorates. The LR statistics indicate that the restricted model can be rejected for the vast majority of national electorates. That is, we can reject the hypothesis that support for EU membership has no effect on party choice for most EU member states. The only exceptions are Luxembourg and the United Kingdom.[35] For all other member states, respondents' support for EU membership had a statistically significant effect on vote choice, independent of left–right ideology.

What is the magnitude and direction of the effect of support for EU membership on vote choice in the EU member states? Space does not allow a presentation and assessment of the effects of voters' support for EU membership on their vote choice across all parties in all 15 member states. Thus, only the effect on the vote choice in Italy, Spain and Greece will be assessed. These three nations had elections soon after the Eurobarometer survey.[36] Consequently, survey responses to the question of vote choice in the next general election – the dependent variable in the MNL models – would be particularly relevant to respondents in these nations. Inferences about actual voting behaviour from these survey responses should therefore be more accurate than for the other electorates.

Figures 1–3 illustrate the impact of changes in voters' support for EU membership on their probability of voting for major parties in national elections in these three member states. The probability of supporting each party conditional on a moderate left–right self-placement (5, on the 1–10 scale) was calculated. Thus, the difference in the probability of vote choice across parties does not reflect the total electoral support of the parties in the electorate. In all three figures, support for EU membership has different effects on vote choice – both in magnitude and direction. In Figure 1, Italians' support for EU membership had basically no effect on their likelihood of voting for Forza Italia or the Democratic Party of the Left, but greater support for membership was negatively related to the probability of a vote for the Northern League. In Figure 2, Spaniards' support for EU membership was positively related to their probability of voting for the Socialist Party and negatively related to their probability of voting for the People's Party and the United Left. In Figure 3, Greeks' support for EU membership increased their probability of voting for New Democracy and had little effect on their probability of voting for the KKE or PASOK.

In sum, European integration has influenced mass voting behaviour in some national elections in the EU member states. Furthermore, issues of European integration may serve as a new electoral cleavage in many of the EU member states. EU citizens' support for EU membership appears both to be independent of their left–right positions and to have a statistically significant influence on vote choice in most EU member states. However, these findings are preliminary in that they concern only prospective vote choice at one point in time for all the member states. Further research is

FIGURE 1
THE EFFECT OF ITALIANS' EVALUATIONS OF EU MEMBERSHIP ON
THEIR VOTE CHOICE (1996)

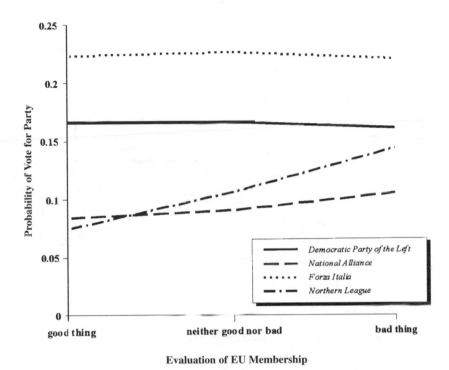

Evaluation of EU Membership

required in order to estimate the magnitude of EU issues on voting behaviour across national elections and to identify how and when these issues emerged on the national electoral agenda. Specifically, three important research questions remain. First, there may be country- or time-specific determinants of vote choice that confound the relationship between attitudes towards integration and vote choice. Including controls for such determinants of vote choice would thus improve the quality of our inferences about how attitudes towards the EU influence vote choice. Second, future research could compare the impact of EU issues on vote choice across elections in a particular nation. Temporal comparisons would inform us about the dynamics of the impact of EU issues on vote choice, generating inferences about how integration will shape future elections. A good template for such research would be the recent study by Evans, which provides a temporal comparison for the United Kingdom.[37]

FIGURE 2
THE EFFECT OF SPANIARDS' EVALUATIONS OF EU MEMBERSHIP ON THEIR
VOTE CHOICE (1996)

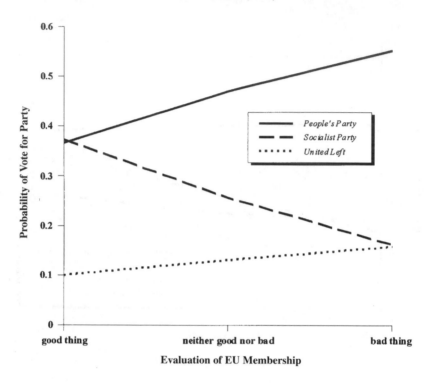

Finally, the present analysis focused only on one aspect of mass political attitudes related to European integration: citizens' support for EU membership. While citizens' support for EU membership is generally correlated with their support for specific integrative policies, specific issues of European integration may have distinct effects on vote choice for particular parties in certain national contexts.[38] For example, Scheve showed that support for European monetary unification has a significant effect on vote choice in France and the United Kingdom.[39] Thus, future research could explore the impact of particular issues of integration on voting behaviour in national elections.

FIGURE 3
THE EFFECT OF GREEKS' EVALUATIONS OF EU MEMBERSHIP ON THEIR
VOTE CHOICE (1996)

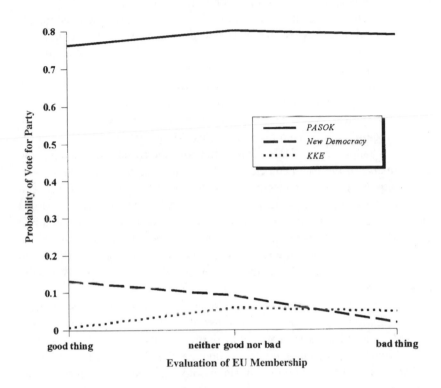

EUROPEAN INTEGRATION AND ECONOMIC VOTING

An important development in the economic voting literature is the theoretical concern for how the clarity of responsibility of incumbent parties for economic policy-making influences how voters punish and reward these parties for macroeconomic outcomes. Studies by G. Bingham Powell and Guy Whitten and by Christopher Anderson have shown that voters increasingly hold an incumbent party accountable for economic outcomes as the clarity of the party's responsibility for government policy grows.[40] Note, however, that these studies have focused on a party's responsibility for governing in general (for example, the number of cabinet portfolios held by a party), not responsibility for economic policy-making. Given the constraints that European integration has imposed on national economic policy-making, we may want to revise our conception of and measurement of 'clarity of responsibility' to incorporate this reality.

Specifically, one of the key results of open economy macroeconomics under capital mobility is that national governments forfeit control of monetary policy when exchange rates are fixed and they forfeit control of fiscal policy when exchange rates are flexible.[41] The EU member states have operated in such an open macroeconomic world for much of the last 30 years, but with varying degrees of exchange-rate flexibility. Membership in the Exchange Rate Mechanism (ERM) of the European Monetary System (EMS) required quasi-fixed exchange rates. Membership in EMU requires fixed exchange rates. Thus, depending on the time and nation, the governments of the EU member states have operated with varying degrees of autonomy in shaping macro-economic conditions. William Clark and Mark Hallerberg provide evidence that EU member state governing parties have responded to these constraints by selectively manipulating national economic conditions.[42] Based on evidence from the 1980s and early 1990s, they showed that opportunistic fiscal cycles occur particularly when exchange rates are fixed and that opportunistic monetary policy occurs under flexible exchange rates.

These findings indicate that EU national governments are constrained in their ability to manipulate economic outcomes. Therefore, they should only be held responsible for the conduct of particular economic policies – fiscal or monetary – depending on the exchange-rate regime. One important revision to economic voting models would thus be to incorporate this constraint in measuring the clarity of government responsibility in the EU. Regardless of whether an incumbent party governed in coalition or alone, its responsibility for particular macroeconomic outcomes varied due to whether it participated in the ERM or EMU. Thus, in estimating the relationship between a particular economic outcome (such as inflation) and incumbent party vote-share in the EU member states, we would want to take into account whether the incumbent party could manipulate that outcome, given the constraints of the exchange-rate regime.

The findings of Clark and Hallerberg are also relevant to a related strand of the economic voting literature. Previous studies have theorised that governing parties are held electorally sensitive for different macroeconomic outcomes depending on their ideology. Left-wing parties put a greater emphasis on unemployment while right-wing parties emphasise inflation. Thus, voters may judge parties' responsibility for economic outcomes differently depending on their emphasis.[43] Returning to the findings of Clark and Hallerberg, this partisan difference in responsibility may lead to electoral advantages and disadvantages for particular parties due to European integration. For example, if it is easier to manipulate the inflation rate via monetary policy than via fiscal policy, Conservative parties should be better able to attract votes when exchange rates are flexible, that is, when the country is not in the ERM or EMU.

Finally, a study by Harvey Palmer and Guy Whitten also identifies a channel through which European integration could influence economic voting.[44] Palmer and Whitten argue that economic performance matters most when it surprises voters. That is, the absolute level of inflation or growth is not as important to the electoral fortunes of governing parties as deviation from public expectations about these levels. Specifically, as inflation and growth rates diverge from trends in these indicators prior to an election, these indicators increasingly influence voters' likelihood of supporting the incumbent. Thus, to the extent European integration causes deviation from economic trends, it will influence economic voting.

Might European integration generate such economic deviations? Economic and Monetary Union may have such an effect on its member states. Many economists contend that one of the primary economic effects of the single market and the single currency is greater disparity in economic performance across the EU member states.[45] The basic claim is that, with a single currency, low labour mobility and little fiscal federalism at the EU level, regional and national variation in economic conditions (particularly unemployment) will increase across the EU member states.[46] In turn, this increase in the variability of economic outcomes would generate greater deviations from national economic trends. Thus, by joining EMU, EU member states are likely to experience greater unexpected changes in macroeconomic conditions, causing economic conditions to have a greater impact on national voting behaviour than they had before joining EMU.

CONCLUSION

This study has considered whether and how EU membership, as a set of national policy and institutional commitments, shapes voting behaviour in national elections. The first section discussed recent research showing how the introduction of direct elections to the European Parliament (EP) has transformed electoral politics in the EU member states. The key finding was that the later an EP election follows a national general election, the greater impact the results of the EP election have on governing parties' fortunes in the subsequent national election. The reason for this appears to be that, when the previous national election is distant, voters use EP election results as markers regarding the electoral prospects of national governing parties and they adjust voting behaviour accordingly. The second section explored whether and how issues of European integration have influenced voting behaviour in national elections. Several studies have identified the effect of a particular issue on a specific national election, particularly in France and the United Kingdom. Extending these previous studies, it was shown that for most of the EU member states, voters' support for EU membership appears to provide the basis for a new electoral cleavage. However, a variety of interesting questions remain to be addressed regarding the extent and character of this electoral cleavage. Finally, the third section speculated about how European economic integration has changed and will change the relationship between economic conditions and vote choice in the EU member states. In particular, this section developed several theoretical expectations about how EU monetary co-ordination and unification alter traditional hypotheses about the link between macroeconomic performance and support for governing parties.

In concluding, a research agenda is proposed, following from these theoretical and empirical results. These research questions can be placed in one of three categories: empirical questions that we can currently address with existing data; empirical questions about future events, which we need to consider in future data collection; and conceptual questions that require theoretical attention prior to empirical analysis. In the first category, we can clearly use existing national election surveys to identify and estimate the effects of voters' attitudes on issues of European integration on their party choice. Existing data allow for comparisons over time, across nations, and potentially across aspects of European integration. Also, existing economic and political data are sufficient to test the aforementioned hypotheses about how European monetary integration has influenced incumbent parties' electoral fortunes through its impact on their accountability for economic policy-making. Finally, scholars can extend the work of Carrubba and Timpone in investigating how citizens' preferences over the level of authority for particular issues influence the importance of these issues in determining vote choice.[47] Several Eurobarometer surveys ask respondents explicitly which policies they would prefer decided at the EU level, their position on these issues and their vote choice in national elections.

A research question in the second category is whether participation in the single currency – the Euro – changes the impact of macroeconomic conditions on voting behaviour. Based on the model of Palmer and Whitten, Euro membership is expected to increase the relevance of changes in macroeconomic conditions to the electoral fortunes of incumbent parties. This expectation is predicated on the assumption that a single currency will increase variability in national economic performance, causing greater deviations from historical trends in macroeconomic conditions. Thus, future research could address two questions (a) whether membership in the Euro increases the variability of economic performance of its members, and, if so, (b) whether these unexpected macroeconomic changes increase the impact of macroeconomic conditions on voting behaviour.

Finally, while issue voting may be the most obvious way that European integration can influence national elections, we could further develop a theoretical guide to how and when we would expect this effect to obtain. Obviously we need to be able to distinguish voters who are likely to vote based on issues – the 'apartisans' as defined by Russell Dalton – from voters likely to vote on partisan or sociological bases.[48] We then need to distinguish which of these voters are sensitive to EU issues, perhaps due to their position in the national economy – for example, nationalised industry or exporting sector. The study by Scheve provides a notable example of how to make such a distinction and connect it to voting behaviour.[49] Finally, we need to consider contextual factors that may enhance or decrease the saliency of EU issues in an election – such as media coverage or emphases by political parties.

NOTES

The author would like to thank the participants in the workshop on 'Europeanised Politics: The Impact of European Integration on Domestic Politics', at Nuffield College, Oxford, June 1999, for helpful comments. Particular gratitude goes to Geoffrey Evans, Simon Hix and Guy Whitten for criticism, advice and suggestions.

1. See, for example, A. Moravscik, *The Choice for Europe* (Ithaca, NY: Cornell University Press 1998).
2. See, for example, K. Reif and H. Schmitt, 'Nine Second-Order National Elections: A Conceptual Framework for the Analysis of European Election Results', *European Journal of Political Research* 8 (1980), pp.3–44.
3. C. van der Eijk, M. Franklin and M. Marsh, 'What Voters Teach Us About Europe-Wide Elections: What Europe-Wide Elections Teach Us About Voters', *Electoral Studies* 15 (1996), pp.149–66.
4. Ibid., p.159.
5. C. van der Eijk and M. Franklin (eds.), *Choosing Europe?* (Ann Arbor, MI: University of Michigan Press 1996).
6. M. Marsh, 'Testing the Second-Order Election Model After Four European Elections' (Paper presented at the ECPR Joint Sessions, Bordeaux, France, April 1995); M. Marsh and M. Franklin, 'Understanding European Elections, 1979–1994', in van der Eijk and Franklin (eds.), *Choosing Europe?*
7. Ibid.
8. Eijk, Franklin, and Marsh, 'What Voters Teach Us About Europe-Wide Elections', p.156.

9. Ibid.
10. Expected vote shares were based on the predictions due to an electoral cycle. See Marsh and Franklin, 'Understanding European Elections, 1979–1994'.
11. G. Evans, 'Economics and Politics Revisited: Explaining the Decline in Conservative Support 1992–1995', *Political Studies* 47 (1998), pp.139–51; G. Evans, 'Euroscepticism and Conservative Electoral Support: How an Asset Became a Liability', *British Journal of Political Science* 28 (1998), pp.573–90.
12. T. Raunio, 'Facing the European Challenge: Finnish Parties Adjust to the Integration Process', *West European Politics* 22 (1999), pp.138–59.
13. C. Carrubba and R. Timpone, 'Strategic Voting in Federal and Quasi-Federal Systems: Evidence from European Elections' (Paper presented at the annual meeting of the Midwest Political Science Association, Chicago, IL, April 1999).
14. On this definition of the left–right dimension, see M. Gabel and J. Huber, 'Putting Parties in Their Place: Inferring Party Left–Right Ideological Positions from Party Manifestos Data', *American Journal of Political Science* 44 (2000), pp.94–103.
15. G. Evans, 'Europe: A New Electoral Cleavage?', in G. Evans and P. Norris (eds.), *Critical Elections: British Parties and Voters in Long-Term Perspective* (Thousand Oaks, CA: Sage 1999); Evans, 'Euroscepticism and Conservative Electoral Support'; Evans, 'Economics and Politics Revisited'.
16. Evans, 'Europe: A New Electoral Cleavage'.
17. Evans, 'Eurosceptism and Conservative Electoral Support'.
18. K. Scheve, 'European Economic Integration and Electoral Politics in France and Great Britain' (Paper presented at the Annual Meeting of the American Political Science Association, Atlanta, August 1999).
19. Ibid.
20. K. Reif and E. Marlier, *Eurobarometer 44.2bis Mega-survey: Policies and Practices in Building Europe and the European Union, January–March 1996* (Ann Arbor, MI: Inter-university Consortium for Political and Social Research [distributors] 1998).
21. Evans, 'Europe: A New Electoral Cleavage'.
22. See J. Huber, 'Values and Partisanship in Left–Right Orientations: Measuring Ideology', *European Journal of Political Research* 17 (1999), pp.599–621; R. Inglehart, 'The Changing Structure of Political Cleavages in Western Society', in R. Dalton, S. Flanagan and P. Allen Beck (eds.), *Electoral Change in Advanced Industrial Democracies* (Princeton, NJ: Princeton University Press 1984), pp.38–40; R. Dalton, *Citizen Politics* (Chatham, NJ: Chatham House, 2nd edn. 1996).
23. Respondents who (a) did not place themselves on the left–right scale or (b) either did not respond or responded 'don't know' were omitted from the analysis.
24. Responses of 'don't know' (5 per cent of respondents) were omitted.
25. Note that the correlations between left–right self-placements and other standard Eurobarometer survey questions related to European integration reveal a very similar pattern to that presented in Table 2. Specifically, I estimated the correlations between left-right placement and (a) whether the respondent concluded that his/her nation had benefited or not from EU membership and (b) whether the respondent supported further efforts to unify western Europe.
26. These results are consistent with evidence presented in S. Hix, *The Political System of the European Union* (London: Macmillan 1999), ch. 5.
27. Evans, 'Europe: A New Electoral Cleavage'.
28. I omitted respondents who indicated that they 'don't know', would not vote, would spoil the ballot, would vote for a party not mentioned by the interviewer, or would not answer.
29. As in the previous analysis, respondents who (a) did not place themselves on the left–right scale or (b) either did not respond or responded 'don't know' when asked to nation's EU membership were omitted from the analysis.
30. Note that multinomial logit models differ significantly from multinomial probit models. On multinomial logit models of vote choice, see G. Whitten and H. Palmer, 'Heightening Comparativists' Concern for Model Choice: Voting Behavior in Great Britain and the Netherlands', *American Journal of Political Research* 40 (1996), pp.231–60; M. Alvarez and

J. Nagler Alvarez, 'When Politics and Models Collide: Estimating Models of Multiparty Elections', *American Journal of Political Science* 42 (1998), pp.55–96, advocate multinomial probit models in multiparty settings. However, these models are only appropriate where the vote choice model includes choice-specific variables – for example, the position of the party on the left–right dimension. Where the independent variables are all individual-specific (such as the voter's left–right position), MNL is appropriate. Since the analysis presented here involves only individual-specific variables, I use MNL.

31. Alvarez and Nagler Alvarez, 'When Politics and Models Collide', p.56.
32. See J.S. Long, *Regression Models for Categorical and Limited Dependent Variables* (London: Sage 1997), ch. 6.
33. The results are available from the author upon requests.
34. Ibid., p.161.
35. The results for the United Kingdom are surprising, since Evans, 'Europe: A New Electoral Cleavage', found that voters' attitudes toward the EU were an important determinant of vote choice in the 1997 British elections. Thus, it is worth noting that my analysis differs from that of Evans in some important ways. Evans did not use a MNL to estimate the effect of support for EU membership or voters' left-right self-placements. Also, he studied actual vote choice while my dependent variable is a survey respondent's expected vote choice in the next election. All of these differences in research design may account for the difference in results.
36. The Italian general election was held in April 1996. The Spanish general election was in held in March 1996. The Greek national election was held in September 1996.
37. Evans, 'Europe: A New Electoral Cleavage'.
38. On the relationship between citizens' attitudes toward specific aspects of integration and their general support for integration, see M. Gabel, *Interests and Integration: Market Liberalization, Public Opinion, and European Union* (Ann Arbor, MI: University of Michigan Press 1998).
39. Scheve, 'European Economic Integration and Electoral Politics in France and Great Britain'.
40. C. Anderson, *Blaming the Government* (New York: M.E. Sharpe 1995); G.B. Powell and G. Whitten, 'A Cross-National Analysis of Economic Voting: Taking Account of Political Context', *American Journal of Political Science* 37 (1993), pp.391–414.
41. W. Clark and M. Hallerberg, 'Mobile Capital, Domestic Institutions, and Electorally-Induced Monetary and Fiscal Policy', *American Political Science Review* 94 (2000), pp.323–46. See V. della Sala, 'Hollowing Out and Hardening the State: European Integration and the Italian Economy', *West European Politics* 20 (1997), pp.14–33, for a description of how EMU has constrained domestic economic policy-making institutions.
42. Clark and Hallerberg, 'Mobile Capital, Domestic Institutions, and Electorally-Induced Monetary and Fiscal Policy'.
43. See M. Weatheford, 'Economic Conditions and Electoral Outcomes: Class Differences in the Political Response to Recession', *American Journal of Political Science* 22 (1978), pp.917–38; and D. Hibbs, 'Economic Outcomes and Political Support for British Governments Among Occupational Classes: A Dynamic Analysis', *American Political Science Review* 76 (1982), pp.259–79.
44. H. Palmer and G. Whitten, 'The Electoral Impact of Unexpected Inflation and Economic Growth', *British Journal of Political Science* (forthcoming).
45. For examples, see P. Krugman, *Geography and Trade* (Cambridge, MA: MIT Press 1991); and B. Eichengreen, *European Monetary Unification* (Cambridge, MA: MIT Press 1998).
46. In the future, the EU may counter these asymmetric shocks by increasing the size of its fiscal transfers through such instruments as the structural funds. This would dampen the effects of EMU on economic voting, as described in this section. However, it would open up another potential avenue for European integration to influence voting behaviour in national elections: pork-barrel politics. In a recent paper, G. Whitten, H. Palmer and M. Gabel, 'Euro-pork: How EU Fiscal Policy Influences Public Support for European Integration' (Paper presented at the Annual Meeting of the American Political Science Association, Washington, DC, September 1998), showed that the distributional consequences of even the small level of EU spending in the early 1980s shaped voters' attitudes about European integration. Thus, if EU spending were dramatically increased, it seems reasonable to expect the increased distributional

consequences to shape voters' political attitudes toward the EU. In turn, since major distributional decisions about the EU budget are usually inter-governmental bargains, we might also expect voters to voice their demands regarding these resources to their national representatives in national elections.

47. Carrubba and Timpone, 'Strategic Voting in Federal and Quasi-Federal Systems'.
48. Dalton, *Citizen Politics*.
49. Scheve, 'European Economic Integration and Electoral Politics in France and Great Britain'.

Political Contention in a Europeanising Polity

DOUG IMIG and SIDNEY TARROW

EUROSTRIKE!

On 27 February 1997, the President of the ailing French Renault firm announced the imminent closure of the company's plant in Vilvoorde, Belgium. Louis Schweitzer, a former aide to Socialist Prime Minister Laurent Fabius, would soon announce massive financial losses and job cuts in France itself for Europe's sixth largest carmaker. Closing Vilvoorde was but a prelude to these politically more risky cuts, for Renault's largest shareholder is the French state.

Prelude it might be, but the mainly Flemish and heavily unionised Vilvoorde workforce would not go quietly, nor would the outraged Belgian government, whose Prime Minister, Jean-Luc Dehaene, had his political base in the Brussels industrial suburb.[1] As local, federal and regional policy-makers expressed their outrage (the city council of Vilvoorde briefly banned the use of French in the public market!), the Vilvoorde workers occupied the plant and began a series of public protests that would make Vilvoorde synonymous with a new term in the European political lexicon – 'the Eurostrike'.

European Union (EU) officials also expressed outrage at the plant closure and its unexpected announcement, for it soon emerged that Renault was hoping to use EU structural funds to expand its plant in Valladolid, Spain, just as it was closing Vilvoorde. European Competition Commissioner Karel Van Miert quickly announced that he would soon propose ways to stop companies from 'aid shopping' from the EU.[2] Responding to Brussels' anger, and its own embarrassment at what seemed like an attempt to steal jobs from a fellow EU member state, the Spanish government quickly shelved its plan to subsidise the Vallodolid expansion.

Renault had also ignored EU regulations that it must inform and consult its workers – presumably through its newly formed European Works

Council – of the decision to close the plant and negotiate measures of 'accompaniment and reconversion' for the laid-off workers. Not only the Commission, but also the European Parliament – peppered with e-mail petitions from constituents and unions – expressed shock and outrage at this 'Anglo-Saxon' restructuring. Echoing the concerns of unionists from Belgium, France and Spain, the assembly urged the EU to penalise Renault for its failure to consult and inform its workers, as EU regulations require, accusing the carmaker – and indirectly the French government – of 'arrogance and disdain for the most fundamental rules of social consultation'.[3] Even European Commission President Jacques Santer said the French government should have intervened to prevent Renault from laying off some 3,100 workers.[4]

The French government, in turn, was clearly embarrassed. Reeling from a series of work disputes that began in autumn 1995, the last thing that President Jacques Chirac and Prime Minister Alain Juppé needed was a 'brouille' with France's nearest neighbour and trading partner. While Chirac criticised Schweitzer's lack of tact, and Juppé called the Président-Directeur Généva (PDG) in for consultations, their apparent shock was belied by reports that the French government had known of Renault's decision months earlier. Indeed, French Industry Minister Franck Borotra backed the company. 'You talk about a strategy of job-cutting', he said. 'The strategy at stake here is the strategy of survival for the company.'[5]

But other French politicians were less than happy. On television, Confédération Française Démocratique Travail (CFDT) general secretary Nicole Notat chided the company for failing to consult the workers. In parliament, deputies of both the majority and the opposition were up in arms about Renault's decision,[6] and created an information mission to keep track of Renault and its workers.[7] Both Philippe Seguin and Charles Pasqua, Gaullist stalwarts who had clashed with Chirac before, used the Vilvoorde case to reinforce their scepticism about the EU.

However, if Belgian, French and EU officials were ruffled by Renault's move, their response was nothing compared to the reaction of the unions of both countries. Co-ordinated by the European Federation of Metalworkers – based in Brussels – their joint actions took two complementary forms – 'guerrilla actions' involving small number of participants intended for maximum media impact, and mass demonstrations designed to show the workers' power in numbers. Both types of action quickly took 'European' forms:

- On 2 March, a small contingent of Vilvoorde workers crossed the French border to Warin, near Lille, where they occupied a parking lot filled with new Renault vehicles ready for shipment.[8]

- On 7 March, strikes were called across the sprawling Renault empire, bringing out half its workforce in France and Spain.[9] In Seville, about two-thirds turned out,[10] and in France, some 48 per cent of workers in the Orleans facility participated in the strike.[11]
- In Brussels, the Vilvoorde workers hurled a Renault chassis across police barricades protecting the French embassy.[12]
- When it was announced that Schweitzer would meet with the European Works Council (EWC) on 11 March, a convoy of 80 buses left Vilvoorde before dawn to transport 3,000 workers in their red and green union jackets to demonstrate in front of his office in Paris.[13]
- At the EWC meeting, French unionists backed the Belgian unions' call to reverse the Vilvoorde closure and demanded a reduction of working hours throughout the company in lieu of further job losses.[14]
- When Schweitzer refused to budge on both counts, the Vilvoorde workers responded with a surprise 'commando action' across the border at the Renault plant in Douai. As they marched through the factory, about 600 French workers joined them, and production ground to a halt.[15]

These actions were small potatoes compared to what came on Sunday, 16 March. For several months, European trade unionists and left-wing groups had been planning a 'European march against unemployment' timed to coincide with the EU Amsterdam Summit.[16] Beginning with a planning conference in Brussels in February, the 'march' was to be mounted in stages in every EU country on different dates, culminating in Amsterdam on 14 June. The Vilvoorde crisis led the Belgian unions to move the date of their demonstration forward by two months, and to call for participation from across the EU.[17]

Given the politically charged atmosphere around the Renault case, and the growing tension over the Euro and its consequences for jobs and social benefits, the turnout on 16 March was extraordinary. The rapidity with which the event had been scheduled kept many European unions away;[18] even so, between 70,000 and 100,000 workers turned up in Brussels to march from the Gare du Nord to the Gare du Midi.[19] While only 60 Spanish unionists made the long trip, and the British and Dutch unions were lightly represented, the French left – with an election approaching – was massively and visibly present, from CFDT leader Nicole Notat to Confédération Générale du Travail (CGT) Secretary Louis Viannet, and from Communist leader Robert Hue to Socialist leader Lionel Jospin and SOS-Racisme founder Harlem Désir.[20] As Schweitzer was hung in effigy and a giant wicker figure carried by demonstrators made nazi salutes, the Vilvoorde workers dumped a yellow car body in front of the Brussels Bourse. 'This is a signal of anger and indignation', Belgium's Christian Democratic union leader, Willy Peirens, told the crowd, 'a signal of solidarity against brutality'.[21] Michel Nollet, head of Belgium's Fédération Générale des Travailleurs Belges (FGTB) union, called attention to the transnational character of the protest: 'Today's demonstration is not the end … Together united we will continue our struggle for a social Europe, for a Europe of solidarity.'[22]

The joint pressure from the union demonstrations, from the EU and from the Belgian government was too much for French Prime Minister Juppé. On 20 March he appeared on French television to announce that 800,000 francs per worker would be disbursed for 'reconversion and accompaniment'.[23] These figures turned out to combine both 'social measures' and the loss of value due to the abandonment of Renault's investment in the plant, but Juppé's tactic was enough to disarm the unionists. 'If a minority wants to struggle to the end', *Le Monde* observed, 'the silent majority of the workers – "illusioned" by the amount of money pronounced by Alain Juppé – are pushing for negotiations.'[24]

THE LESSONS OF VILVOORDE

The Renault crisis ended as it had to – with the plant's closure and the distribution of generous severance packages to the workers. But before it ended it had angered and embarrassed members of the EU, forced European Commission and European Parliament figures to take positions critical of a member state, united unionists of three nations against 'American'-style capitalism, and identified a possibly catalytic future role for an institution – the European Works Council – that had been created as a tame instrument for transnational communication.[25] Even the courts became involved, with tribunals in Paris and Brussels supporting the workers and judging that Renault had violated EWC obligations.

The Renault affair may represent a growing reality for contentious politics in Europe as challengers respond to the processes of integration. It shows that contention can become European in its *sources*, *processes* and *outcomes*:

- *The sources of contentious politics*: contentious politics can be Euro-centred when domestic actors are stimulated to take action as a result of decisions taken by the EU.
- *The processes of contentious politics*: contentious politics can take European form through the actions of social actors. Such processes may

include cross-border co-operation, actors crossing borders to strike against antagonists in another country, or even transnational social movement events that draw participants from across the continent.

- *The outcomes of contentious politics*: finally, contentious actions become Europeanised where they are resolved through the intervention of international bodies such as the European Commission, the European Parliament or the European Court of Justice.

In time, a fabric of trans-European social movement organisations which regularly interact with opponents and each other may emerge out of these processes, just as national social movements grew out of the process of state-building in the early nineteenth century.[26] We have found slim evidence that such a transnational development of social movements has yet occurred on a broad scale. However, a systematic look at European contention shows that European integration is producing a complementary process: the *domestication* of European contention, by which we mean *the mounting of claims triggered by EU decisions within national or subnational politics*. After summarising the obstacles to transnational movement formation and describing the data archive we have constructed to study that process, we shall present results that support our view that European integration is affecting the structure of internal politics of the EU's member states.

TRANSNATIONAL CONTENTION AND ITS OBSTACLES

The Vilvoorde episode was a spectacular example of how – in a Europeanising polity – domestic and supranational politics can intertwine to produce episodes of transnational contention. But note that this case brought together several factors that make it less than representative of the trends we hope to analyse:

- First, the source of the workers' claims was not the EU but a multinational firm.
- Second, the role of EU officials was to cheer from the sidelines and offer tools that the workers could use in their conflict – they were not the target of the protest. Indeed, the real target was the French government, which responded to transnational protest with pressure on the firm to settle with the laid-off Belgian workers on terms that would solve its domestic political problem.
- Third, if the Vilvoorde case became a 'eurostrike', it was at least in part due to the unusual factor that it occurred in a suburb of the capital of

Europe, where the European Metalworkers' Federation is based, in the presence of a press corps which framed it as a European event.

Such a concatenation of factors does not come together every day. We can illustrate this more sharply by placing the combination of factors that produced the Vilvoorde events schematically in a two-dimensional grid based on the intersection of two variables: first, whether the actors in contention are *national* or *transnational*; and, second, whether the targets of their action are *domestic* or *European*. Vilvoorde pitted a transnational coalition of actors against a domestic (French) political target – what we call in Figure 1 *co-ordinated domestic protest*.

Co-ordinated domestic protests are only one of the ways in which European integration can influence political contention. It may prove increasingly important as firms make decisions on product factors largely without reference to national boundaries within the EU – but protests against them would be *indirect* effects of European integration. We wish to focus on two more direct ones, those that appear in the two right hand cells of Figure 1: the *domestication* of conflict, in which national actors protest at home against policies of the EU; and *transnational contention*, in which transnational coalitions of actors target the EU or other supranational or transnational actors in response to EU policies.

Then, of course, there is the much more familiar pattern, *routine domestic protests*, in which national actors target domestic opponents. We predict that, even in an integrating Europe, routine domestic protests will continue to dominate political contention for decades to come – as they overwhelmingly do today. This is not only because the EU is a union of states; it is also because – for reasons spelled out below – transnational

FIGURE 1
A TYPOLOGY OF EUROPEAN PROTESTS

		Target of Protest	
		Domestic	*European*
Actors in Protest	*National*	Typical Domestic Protest	Domestication
	Transnational	Co-ordinated Domestic Protest	Collective European Protest

mobilisation must overcome important obstacles and will depend on favourable conjunctions of factors like those we listed for the Vilvoorde case. For similar reasons, we predict that the type of protest found in the upper right-hand cell of Figure 1 – what we call 'domestication' – will be the major contemporary effect of European integration on contentious politics for the foreseeable future. Not only does the EU continue to allocate to national courts and administrations the implementation of the policies decided in Brussels; domesticating European conflict enables claimants to continue to exploit the opportunities and resources that national social movements have created and offers the EU as the source of citizens' grievances, to the great relief of national governments.

French farm protests are the classic case of 'domesticated' European contention. Although 'European institutions have become the fulcrum of protest activity in the 1980s and 1990s', concludes Christilla Roederer from her detailed study of French farmers' protests, French 'farmers saw at the *domestic* level a more probable venue for pressure'.[27] This is not simply because farmers are 'locals'; it is also, and primarily, because they follow a strategy of targeting the agents against whom they can have maximum leverage, in the hope that this will translate into more robust governmental policies on their behalf in Brussels. French farmers are not alone. German miners protesting against pit closures; Italian milk producers objecting to EU fines for overproducing; British farmers opposed to EU policies on BSE disease: such groups routinely target their governments for evils ascribed to the EU. They frequently protest to demand that their governments defend their interests in Brussels.

Transnational protests – whether aimed against domestic actors like Renault or the French government or against European targets – are much harder to organise. Some scholars have seen transnational movement activity developing rapidly around globalisation, liberalisation and the growth of transnational media in a direct reflection of structural change on collective action. But social movement theorists think that it is not only when macrostructural or cultural conditions are conducive that mobilisation occurs, but also where indigenous social networks, collective identities, and political opportunities come together.[28] Let us summarise these elements from social movement theory before turning to our broader findings on European contention.

Social Networks

Movements are most likely to take root among pre-existing social networks in which relations of trust, reciprocity and cultural learning are stored. This is the thesis that Charles Tilly developed when he placed 'organization' in a triangular relationship with interest and collective action in his 'mobilisation model'.[29] The resulting idea of 'catnets' stressed a group's inclusiveness as 'the main aspect of group structure which affects the ability to mobilize'.[30] Social networks provide the interpersonal trust, the collective identities and the social communication of opportunities that galvanise individuals into collective action and co-ordinate their actions against significant others in a social movement.

The key role of interpersonal networks in movement mobilisation has obvious implications for the likelihood that social movements can form across transnational space. Even if 'objective conditions' (such as economic interdependence, cultural integration or hegemony, or institutional diffusion) produce the preconditions for the appearance of similar movements in a variety of countries, the transaction costs of linking them into integrated networks across national boundaries would be difficult for any social movement to accomplish. Cheap international transportation, electronic communication and lobbying, and international subcontracting provide resources for various kinds of social networks to form across national borders.[31] But the same mechanisms work in the opposite direction. For example, international subcontracting can as easily produce economic nationalism as transnational co-operation.

Collective Identities

In the social movement field, just as macro-structural causal arguments have given way to social network analysis, pure interest-borne models have been challenged by identity arguments.[32] Many of the political identities that emerge in contentious politics are based on familiar social networks and include family, friendship group, neighbourhood or work group. But others are detached from the structures of everyday life. Movements often strive to construct such detached identities. This makes it plausible to think of transnational identities developing around parallel claims in widely differing sites of conflict. But that identities can be 'imagined' does not make the imagining automatic. First, identities embedded in the relations of everyday life are often the basis of aggregation in social movements, and this is an obvious obstacle to building movements across national boundaries. Second, social movements require solidarity to act collectively and consistently; creating common identities around their claims is only the first step in mobilising. Third, building a movement around strong ties of collective identity cannot do the work of mobilisation – which must translate shared identities into collective action, alliance formation and conflictual interaction with opponents.

Political Opportunities

By the concept of political opportunity, we mean consistent – but not necessarily formal or permanent – dimensions of the political environment that provide incentives for collective action by affecting peoples' expectations for success or failure. These political opportunities are *external* to the resources held by the group, and they must be *perceived* by insurgents, for structural changes that are not experienced can hardly be expected to affect people's behaviour, except indirectly. Most political opportunity theorists specify the mechanisms of opportunity in local, regional or national terms.

In spite of these obstacles, transnational social movements do arise – as the Vilvoorde case and the current movement against genetically modified organisms demonstrate. And when they do they can cause tremendous clamour. But citizens are more likely to mount their protests where opportunities are most promising or most proximate: where physical targets offer themselves, where officials they have voted for are susceptible to their pressure, and where familiar routines of collective action are known and understood by both the actors and their antagonists. Moreover, the regulatory/implementation structure of the EU separates European citizens politically, as well as spatially, from the site of European decision-making, while leaving them closer to national and local officials with whom they have routine relations. But this is still speculation; let us turn to the data we have collected to examine the paths of European contention.

THE CHANGING WORLD OF EUROPEAN CONTENTION

If we were to limit our analysis to single cases like Vilvoorde, we would risk, first, selecting on dramatic cases that might turn out to be rare or idiosyncratic. Second, by looking at contention at one point in time, we would have little grasp of whether European contention of whatever kind is growing as the EU expands its competencies. To side-step these dangers, we needed a source of data that would allow us to track the evolving pattern of collective political action across the member states of the EU and over the recent history of European integration. To develop such a cross-national and longitudinal data set, we turned to the techniques of contentious events analysis, drawing from the record of political events reported in the international news media. But to do so we needed to find a data source that would both cover a significant period of the EU's development and provide comparable information for a number of different countries. National newspapers – the usual source of protest event analysis[33] – would be problematic because of their bias towards coverage of their own national news, and because they are written for different audiences. For these reasons, we drew our event reports from the *Reuters* news wire, which is available in electronic format for the past 15 years, has an explicitly international perspective, and is consistent in style and coverage. Below we briefly describe our reasoning and methodology, before presenting our major findings about domestic and transnational protest against the EU.[34]

Instrumentation and Sampling

There are good reasons to be cautious about the use of media data as a source for the study of political protest.[35] But by collecting and coding articles and press releases drawn from the *Reuters World News Service* and *Reuters Textline*, we found we could compile a data set containing a record of the shifting forms of contention in western Europe over the recent history of European integration. To maximise the reliability of our data, we first used an automatic coding system to 'read' and assign basic events-data codes to every political event reported in our *Reuters* sources. We used these tools to code the location, source, event type and target of political events reported in the media. Automated sentence parsing and coding programmes offer the promise of constructing and coding contentious events data sets from electronic media sources in a comparatively short period of time.[36] Within this collection of event reports, we isolated a subset of some 33,727 reports of political events that fit the following criteria: they occurred in one of the 12 member states that were members of the EU on 1 January 1984 to 28 February 1998 (when our *Reuters* archive ended); they were initiated by a private group or actor; and they were contentious in nature rather than routine political events.

We then drew a sample of some 9,872 discrete contentious political events of all kinds mounted by private groups in at least one of the member states between 1 January 1984 and 28 February 1998, using a keyword system that combined the social actors who are frequently active in protest plus a long list of typical collective action forms.[37] This set of nearly 10,000 contentious events contains a range of forms of protest action, from bombings in the Basque country, to border blockades by olive growers, marches against skinhead violence, peace camps, strikes by students, labour unions and professional groups, and relatively peaceful street demonstrations, rallies and processions.

As expected, by far the largest share of these events belongs in the upper left-hand cell of Figure 1: typical domestic protest, in which domestic actors protest against domestic grievances. This finding alone is a healthy corrective to the notion that the nation-state is withering as a focus of citizens' claims and that western Europe is becoming a transnational polity in short order. But what can we say about the share of contentious events motivated by the EU? In order to address this issue, we first needed to be able to isolate the share of our set of 9,872 events that were launched in response to the policies or institutions of the EU.

Identifying this subset was complicated by the composite relationship between national governments and European institutions. While some claimants who are directly affected by EU decisions are likely to frame their grievances in terms of European institutions and policies, others – at greater remove from the European source of their grievances – are more likely to continue to frame their grievances in national and domestic terms. This makes it difficult – short of generous and possibly subjective interpretation of the press data – to define protests as 'European'. The dislocations caused by the process of monetary union well illustrate this difficulty. In the spring of 1997, for example, coal miners shut down all 18 of Germany's coal pits and laid siege to the city of Bonn to protest against federal proposals for drastic cuts in subsidies to the coal industry. While government ministers and the news media blamed European integration – particularly the budgetary qualifications for monetary union – for the subsidy cuts, the miners and their union representatives instead framed their protest in terms of jobs and survival – and targeted the Kohl government rather than European institutions and policies.[38]

To respond to the problem of attributing European status to protests from brief media reports, we chose two strategies: first, a series of case studies based on more qualitative analysis that will be reported in detail elsewhere;[39] and, second, for this analysis, a conservative operationalisation of the concept of European contentious events. In the findings reported here, an institution or policy of the EU had to be mentioned in the first sentence of the media report of a protest action in order to be included in our subset of European contentious events. Keyword searches of the first sentence of each news account within the 9,872 contentious political events led us to identify 1,448 that were likely to be motivated by claims against the EU. Our trained coders reviewed these 1,448 events and, from them, gleaned 490 contentious events that fit our definition of European protest. This subset of 490 events is the basis for our discussion of European contentious politics. All 490 of these events fit in the co-ordinates of the two right-hand cells of Figure 1 and give us the opportunity to gauge the incidence of domesticated and transnational European protest up to 1998, and to measure the changes over time in these two categories of contention and the types of participants mounting each kind of protest.

Euro-Protest: A Small but Growing Phenomenon

Even allowing for the fact that our conservative coding criteria probably limited the number of European protest events we found, 490 protest events over a period of 14 years of European integration is not an impressive number: it constitutes a mere five per cent of the population of events that our search of the *Reuters* data unearthed. Most people, for most issues, continue to protest against national or sub-national targets about domestic issues. This suggests that Europe is still a continent of states where contentious politics is concerned.

But there is also evidence in the data that European conflict patterns are changing. Figure 2 plots the European protests over time as a percentage of total protest events in each year. It suggests that Europeans are increasingly targeting the EU, its agents or its policies when they go into the streets – though in much smaller numbers than when they protest against domestic actors. Reading across the figure, we see that the share of contention motivated by the EU is on the rise: accounting for less than five per cent of all contention in Europe through 1992, but rising thereafter to account for more than ten per cent of western European contention as we approach the end of the decade.

FIGURE 2
ANNUAL PERCENTAGE OF WESTERN EUROPEAN CONTENTIOUS EVENTS
GENERATED IN RESPONSE TO EU POLICIES AND INSTITUTIONS, 1984–97

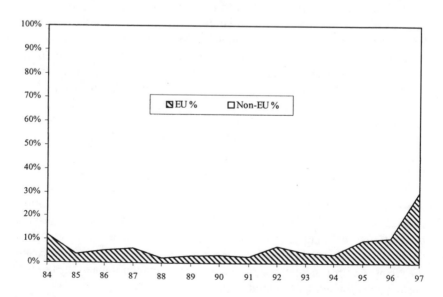

A second general finding relates to the relationship between peaks of protest activity and phases in the development of the EU. In a recent analysis, Doug McAdam and William Sewell Jr. stressed the importance of crucial junctures in the timing and frequency of contentious politics.[40] Do specific sets of events trigger peaks in European protest, or is there a more incremental and linear process of European contention? For European farmers, for example, we might project that periods of EU deliberation over Common Agricultural Policy accords would lead to protests against the EU.[41] Periods of national agricultural policy implementation, in contrast, should provoke higher levels of national and domestic claims. We have found general support for this thesis in other analyses,[42] as has Christilla Roederer in her study of French farmers.[43] At the same time, the upward slope of European protest in Figure 2 suggests that both processes may be at work simultaneously, with domestic actors learning to engage supranational policy makers incrementally, while specific policy disputes selectively heighten the incentives for particular sets of actors to attempt contentious claims across national borders. For example, the recent wave of protests against genetic modification not only came as the EU was implementing the Maastricht and Amsterdam treaties – a general source of Europeanisation – but also coincides with specific political junctures like the 'mad cow' crisis and debates about approval and labelling of GM products in both Europe and the United States.[44]

Domestication and Transnationalisation

What form does this growth in Euro-centred protest take? We have suggested that domestic actors are most likely to respond to policy initiatives of the EU by attacking domestic targets rather than engaging in collective European protest. But we were not prepared for the overwhelming predominance of 'domesticated' protests that our analysis would turn up. Table 1 confirms our suspicion that the preponderance of protest against the EU to date has occurred within domestic rather than transnational political spheres. Almost 83 per cent of the EU-directed protests in our sample are examples of 'domestication'; only 17 per cent were transnational.

A closer examination of these domestic protests launched in response to European grievances shows that they take the familiar forms pioneered by national social movements, including marches and demonstrations, blockades of roads and ports, and occupations of factories and public buildings mounted on national territory and against domestic actors.

Most of these domestic protests were aimed at national states or at their subnational agencies;[45] but a small percentage targeted domestic proxies to

TABLE 1

DISTRIBUTION OF PROTESTS AGAINST THE EU DIVIDED BETWEEN CASES OF
DOMESTICATION AND COLLECTIVE EUROPEAN PROTEST, 1984-97

	Domestication N=406	Collective European Protest N=84	Total N=490
1984-92	84.2%	15.7%	42.8% (210)
1993-97	81.7%	18.2%	57.1% (280)
Total	82.8%	17.1%	100 % (490)

stand in for distant European policies and institutions. For example, to protest against relaxed EU agricultural import restrictions, farmers overturned market carts stocked with east European produce. Angry at EU concessions to the United States, farmers ransacked McDonald's restaurants, and blockaded Euro-Disney. To put pressure on the European Commission to label GM foods, environmental protestors frequently aimed at American corporations present in European markets.

'Domesticated' protest was slightly more common in the first nine years than in the last half-decade, while transnational protest became slightly more common in the later period (though not at a statistically significant level). If collective European protests are growing in relation to globalisation, liberalisation and the Europeanisation of policy-making, they are doing so at a glacial pace. But students of European integration would do well to watch these protests – for they may become more and more common as national groups explore their commonalities with one another and experiment with collective forms of European protest. As they become more common, they would give a more robust indication of the growth of European citizenship than public opinion polls purporting to prove that citizens of the EU member states 'feel' European.

Types of Transnational Protest

When protests are organised transnationally, who is protesting and against whom? Within the subset of transnational events, we identified three principal forms of action, which may be characterised as international co-operation, collective European protest events and international conflict.

International co-operation finds actors from various countries joining together in linked and co-ordinated protest campaigns in each national setting against a shared antagonist. In April 1993, for example, workers from across the European Community launched strikes and took to the streets in protest of the failure of governments to halt and reverse the steep rise in unemployment. From 1996 on, anti GMO campaigners co-ordinated their efforts against the approval of genetically modified foods and in favour of their labelling. And in 1998, a major campaign of farmers' protests was mounted across the EU.

International conflict suggests a different dimension of transnationalisation, which we usually think of as transnational collective action. In these instances – extremely common among farmers – protesters have targeted, rather than joining with, their competitors from other nations. Examples include seizures of fishing vessels by fleets from other nations, provoked by arguments over EU fishing regulations. In July 1994, for example, French and Spanish fishermen clashed off the northern coast of Spain as part of their long-simmering dispute over the use of oversized drift-nets.[46] And in December 1997, Scottish farmers turned back 20 truckloads of cheap Irish beef destined for British markets. The Scotsmen were 'jubilant over this show of solidarity with their English and Welsh colleagues'.[47]

Collective European protest is the more familiar and anticipated form of transnational contentious politics. Here, major protest events draw the participation of citizens from across the EU. In April 1992, 30,000 European farmers gathered outside the European Parliament and US embassy in Strasbourg to demonstrate against proposed EC agricultural reforms. In November 1997, thousands of trade unionists from across Europe converged on Luxembourg to demonstrate for jobs as EU leaders gathered for a two-day summit on joblessness.

These different forms of European transnational protest follow different trajectories and involve different combinations of social actors, and need to be differentiated and separately traced. For example, the implications of 'international conflict' for the formation of European citizenship are very different from those of international co-operation or collective European protest. The first is entirely compatible with a Europe of States and contradicts the goals of those who see a unified European polity developing in short order.

Who Protests?

European integration may encourage certain social and political groups to mount protests against European institutions or policies while others continue to engage in routine national protests. Some scholars doubt that well-organised occupational groups – such as workers – will easily abandon their well-worn national opportunity structures to organise at the European level.[48] Others, like Turner,[49] think that such a change depends on the development of a cross-national mobilising capacity that European unions currently lack. On the other hand, *non*-occupational groups such as ecologists – drawing on a largely educated, middle-class constituency – may be more likely to be attracted to the European level. But once they reach Brussels, according to scholars like Gary Marks and Doug McAdam,[50] such groups are likely to take advantage of the lobbying opportunities that the EU makes available rather than take to the streets.

Our data do not allow for a direct comparison of general levels of lobbying and protest in European politics. But we do find evidence that *occupational* groups initiated a large majority of protests against the EU (82.1 per cent of the total). Over time, the amount of European-aimed protest is increasing for both occupational and non-occupational groups, but the proportion of protests coming from the latter groups increased at a much faster level – from 12 per cent of the total in 1984–92 to 22 per cent since 1993. These data are summarised in Table 2.

Who are the occupational groups who protest most against EU policies? Readers may quickly conjecture that the EU-oriented protests by occupational groups probably consists predominantly of farmers – whose long involvement with the Common Agricultural Policy makes them more attuned to European policy than other groups. Table 3 summarises the distribution of EU protests by farmers when compared with other

TABLE 2
DISTRIBUTION OF OCCUPATIONAL AND NON-OCCUPATIONAL PROTESTS
AGAINST THE EU, 1984–97

	Occupational N =402	Non-Occupational Groups N=88	Total N=490
1984-92	88.1%	11.9 %	42.9 % (210)
1993-97	77.8 %	21.2 %	57.1 % (280)
Total	82.1 %	17.9 %	100 % (490)

TABLE 3
DISTRIBUTION OF PROTESTS BY FARMERS AND OTHER OCCUPATIONAL
GROUPS AGAINST THE EU, 1984–97

	Farmers N=200	Other Occupational Groups N=202	Total N=402
1984–92	47.1 %	52.9 %	46.0 % (185)
1993–97	52.1 %	47.9 %	54.0 % (217)
Total	49.7 %	50.3 %	100 % (402)

occupational groups. It verifies that farmers are the most likely European economic groups to protest against EU policies and that the proportion of farm protests increased from 47 per cent of the total in 1984–92 to 52 per cent after 1992.

DOMESTICATION AND THE CHANGING ROLE OF STATES

As the Renault campaign showed, the emergence of a supranational realm of European government presents a series of new opportunities and constraints for domestic social actors. In this new transnational political realm, autoworkers not only can undertake traditional domestic forms of contentious action, but can also be linked in cross-border actions with others like themselves from across the continent. While workers and their intermediaries continue to press claims before both regional and national governments, their representatives in the European Trade Union Confederation (ETUC) and the Industry Federations press their claims directly before the EU.[51]

But set against the rapid development of policies and institutions at the transnational level, barriers remain to launching contentious action in the transnational realm. Most individuals continue to have difficulty ascribing the sources of their grievances directly to the EU. Transaction costs impede their efforts to co-ordinate collective action across national boundaries. National governments continue to play a primary role in policy-making before the EU, and tried-and-true routines of collective action and institutions attach citizens to their national political systems.

Which groups of actors have launched protests against EU policies? In addition to farmers, we found a vigorous range of contentious actions launched by fishermen, construction workers and miners, for example. Not coincidentally, it is these same groups who are confronting the painful realities of integration at first hand: through reductions in agricultural subsidies and production quotas, shifting trade restrictions, limitations on net sizes and fishing territories, and layoffs and closures in the name of fiscal austerity and monetary union. We are now entering a period of increased moves of west European plants to newly acceding countries of east-central Europe and to forms of subcontracting and contracting-out that will complicate the task of EU labour unions in defending the interests of their members. Against such moves, domestic protests against national states can have little impact.

The activism of these occupational groups highlights the much more fragile presence of other social actors in contention against European policies and institutions. Over and over, representatives of non-governmental organisations (NGOs) in the environmental, migrants' and women's sectors interviewed in Brussels bewailed the indifference of their members at the grassroots to the growing importance of European decision-making.[52] Without grassroots support, their lobbying efforts lack the clout of the better-financed business and professional groups they oppose. While there are dramatic cases of contentious action on the part of the environmental, student, anti-nuclear, animal rights and anti-racist movements in Europe – and these are growing as a proportion of total European protests – the largest proportion of contentious responses to the EU continue to involve farmers and other economic groups.

Our overview of contention in Europe also suggests that, rather than seeing an immediate and direct displacement of contentious politics from the national to the supranational levels, we are more likely to see a range of social movement approaches to the European level of governance: transnational co-operation against domestic actors, as in the Vilvoorde case, collective European protests, as in the recent campaign against GMOs, and the domestication of European issues within national politics. Across the recent period of European integration, we find the largest proportion of contentious political responses to the policies of the EU is located in national rather than transnational political space. In other words, domestic claimants exert pressures domestically to demand that their governments take action on behalf of aggrieved citizens' groups in the EU.

What are the likely consequences of this finding? For one thing, it allows Commission bureaucrats to live inside the ring that surrounds Brussels in a charmed world in which protests are held at a great distance. Secondly, it deprives movement activists who have chosen to make their careers in Brussels-based NGOs of the weapons they need to back up their claims.[53] Third – and here we go well beyond our data – in the long term this process may lead to a partial transformation of national states from autonomous centres of sovereign decision-making to pivots between domestic collective actors who cannot reach the European level, but use their traditional repertoire of contention to put pressure on their elected officials to act on their behalf in Brussels. In short, the empirical record we examine suggests that European integration, rather than provoking the transnationalisation of European politics, is leading instead to the Europeanisation of domestic politics and to the intermediasation of the national state.

NOTES

This research is supported in part by a grant from the National Science Foundation (#SBR-961819), and by a grant to the second author from the German Marshall Fund of the United States. We thank Doug Bond, Simon Hix, Gary Marks, David Mason and Doug McAdam for comments on earlier versions of this paper.

1. *Reuters*, 7 March 1997.
2. *Reuters*, 7 March 1997. Nearly $8 million would have come from the European Regional Development Fund, in effect, helping Renault to move jobs from one member state to another, according to a spokeswoman for Regional Policy Commissioner Monika Wulf-Mathies.
3. *Reuters*, 12 March 1997; *Le Monde*, 13 March 1997, p.14.
4. *Reuters*, 9 March 1997.
5. *Reuters*, 11 March 1997.
6. *Le Monde*, 9–10 March 1997, p.5.
7. *Le Monde*, 13 March 1997, p.14.
8. *Le Monde*, 2 March 1997.
9. As usual, the figures released by the unions and management varied widely. For the range of figures in the three countries, see *Le Monde*, 9–10 March 1997, p.24.
10. *Reuters*, 7 March 1997.
11. *Le Monde*, 9 March 1997, p.24.
12. *Reuters*, 9 March 1997.
13. *Reuters*, 11 March 1997; *Le Monde*, 13 March 1997, p.14.
14. *Reuters*, 11 March 1997; *Le Monde*, 12 March 1997, p. 21.
15. *Le Monde*, 15 March 1997, p.19.
16. *Le Monde*, Feb. 1997.
17. *Le Monde*, 16–17 March 1997, p.13.
18. *Le Monde*, 18 March 1997, p.18.
19. Ibid.
20. Ibid.
21. *Reuters*, 17 March 1997.
22. *Reuters*, 16 March 1997.
23. *Le Monde*, 26 March 1997, p.18.
24. Ibid.
25. A. Martin and G. Ross, 'In the Line of Fire: The Europeanization of Labor Representation', in A. Martin and G. Ross (eds.), *The Brave New World of European Labor: European Trade Unions at the Millenium* (New York and Oxford: Berghahn Books 1999), pp.312–67.
26. C. Tilly, *Popular Contention in Great Britain, 1758–1834* (Cambridge, MA: Harvard University Press 1995); S. Tarrow, *Power in Movement: Social Movements and Contentious Politics* (Cambridge and New York: Cambridge University Press 1998).
27. C. Roederer, 'CAP Reforms and the Transformation of Domestic Politics: The Paradox of Farm Protest in France (1983–1993)' (Paper presented at the Fourth European Conference of Sociology, Amsterdam, 18–21 August 1999).
28. B. Klandermans, H. Kriesi and S. Tarrow (eds.), *From Structure to Action: Comparing Social Movement Research across Cultures*, International Social Movement Research, vol.1 (Greenwich, CT: JAI 1988); D. McAdam, J. McCarthy and M.N. Zald (eds.), *Comparative Perspectives on Social Movements* (Cambridge and New York: Cambridge University Press 1996).
29. Tilly, *Popular Contention in Great Britain*, p.57
30. Ibid., p.64.
31. C. Bob, 'The Marketing of Rebellion in Global Civil Society: Political Insurgencies, International Media, and the Growth of Transnational Support' (Ph.D. dissertation, Massachusetts Institute of Technology, Boston, 1997); M. Keck and K. Sikkink, *Activists Beyond Borders: Transnational Activist Networks in International Politics* (Ithaca, NY and London: Cornell University Press 1998); B. Wellman and M. Giulia, 'Net Surfers Don't Ride

Alone: Virtual Communities as Communities', in P. Killock and M. Smith (eds.), *Communities in Cyberspace* (Berkeley and Los Angeles: University of California Press 1999).

32. A. Melucci, 'Getting Involved: Identity and Mobilization in Social Movements', in Klandermans *et al.* (eds.), *From Structure to Action*.

33. For representative studies, see H. Kriesi *et al.*, *The Politics of New Social Movements in Western Europe: A Comparative Analysis* (Minneapolis: University of Minnesota Press 1995); D. Rucht, 'Limits to Mobilization: Environmental Policy for the EU', in J. Smith, C. Chatfield and R. Pagnucco (eds.), *Transnational Social Movements and World Politics: Solidarity Beyond the Nation-State* (Syracuse: Syracuse University Press 1996); Tilly, *Popular Contention in Great Britain*; Charles Tilly, *The Contentious French* (Cambridge, MA: Harvard University Press 1986); Tarrow, *Power in Movement*; J.W. White, *Ikki: Social Conflict and Political Protest in Early Modern Japan* (Ithaca, NY and London: Cornell University Press 1995).

34. For earlier reports on the research, see D. Imig and S. Tarrow, 'Developing a European Repertoire of Contention' (prepared for the conference on 'Citizens, Parties and Elections in the EU', Center for European Studies, University of North Carolina, Chapel Hill, 30–31 August 1999); D. Imig and S Tarrow, 'The Europeanization of Movements? A New Approach to Transnational Contention', in D. della Porta, H. Kriesi and D. Rucht (eds.), *Social Movements in a Globalizing World* (New York: St. Martin's Press 1999); and S. Tarrow, 'The Europeanisation of Conflict: Reflections from a Social Movement Perspective', *West European Politics* 18 (1995), pp.223–51.

35. See, in particular, S. Hug and D. Wisler, 'Correcting for Selection Bias in Social Movement Research' (working paper 1998); J. McCarthy and C. McPhail, 'The Institutionalization of Protest in the USA', in D. Meyer and S. Tarrow (eds.), *The Social Movement Society: Contentious Politics for a New Century* (Boulder, CO: Rowman and Littlefield 1998). There are also reasons to be cautious about using any single media source for such analyses (see C. McClurg Mueller *et al.*, 'International Press Coverage of Protests in East Germany', *American Sociological Review* 62 (1997), pp.820–32), and still further reasons to be cautious about the coverage of contentious politics in the *Reuters* news service. *Reuters* focuses on business news, in particular, which is likely to mean that this service will devote higher levels of coverage to industrial conflict than to other sectors of contention. Likewise, *Reuters* devotes relatively greater coverage to larger western European countries and cities, which makes it difficult for us to engage in reliable comparisons between the EU member states. Against these limitations, *Reuters* offers a number of advantages for a cross-national, longitudinal study of contention. First, this service provides an extensive, continuous daily record of western European political events available from January 1984 to the present. *Reuters* also avoids the partisan and national biases of many other European news sources, and its news reports are widely available to researchers. Moreover, *Reuters* news reports are written in a consistent format, allowing the preliminary steps in data collection and analysis to be automated. Finally, while print news sources contain large seasonal variations in the percentage of space they allocate to advertisements versus news coverage, *Reuters* does not. See J. Bond and D. Bond, 'The Protocol for the Assessment of Nonviolent Direct Action (PANDA): Codebook for the P24 Data Set', *Program on Nonviolent Sanctions and Cultural Survival* (Weatherhead Center for International Affairs, Harvard University 1998).

36. Specifically, we employed the PANDA (Protocol for the Assessment of Nonviolent Direct Action) data system to establish a set of decision-rules that, in turn, guided a sentence parsing and coding program (named KEDS, for the Kansas Events Data System). Intercoder reliability statistics on KEDS/PANDA indicate a human to machine convergence of between 70 and 80 per cent. See D. Bond *et al.*, 'Contours of Political Contention: Issues and Prospects for the Automated Development of Events Data', *Journal of Conflict Resolution* 41 (1997), pp.553–79. Still, automated coding is a developing technology, and we are cautious about its limitations. For other uses of similar sources and methods, see ibid.; Bond and Bond, 'The Protocol for the Assessment of Nonviolent Direct Action'; U. Reising, 'Taking European Integration to the Streets: Results from France and Belgium, 1980–1989' (Paper presented to the Annual Meeting of the Midwest Political Science Association 1997);

and U. Reising, 'Domestic and Supranational Political Opportunities: European Protest in Selected Countries, 1980–1995' (Paper presented to the Annual Meeting of the Midwest Political Science Association, 1998).

37. Our keywords identified over 100 groups of European social actors engaged in contention in Europe that have been identified either in the case study literature or through our own earlier empirical analysis of the record of contentious politics found in media data. These included not only groups likely to launch contentious political action in response to EU policies and institutions, such as farmers, fishermen, and, more recently, trade unionists and other labour and professional groupings, but also actors reported to be slower to engage supranational institutions, including national extremist groups, racist and anti-immigrant organisations, ethnic and religious representatives, migrant and undocumented workers, and representatives of the women's, student and jobless movements. Additionally, we included keywords to identify actors that historically have had both national and transnational presences, but that may or may not engage the EU through contentious political action, including the environmental and peace movements. To augment this list, we also drew 65 keywords from the PANDA event dictionary that identified a wide range of contentious political action. See Bond and Bond, 'The Protocol for the Assessment of Nonviolent Direct Action'. These included forms of protests and demonstrations, strikes and boycotts, blockades and property occupations, and riots, violent clashes, and property destruction.

38. The coal miners strike was covered in numerous media sources the week of 7–14 March 1997. English accounts were found in the *Reuters Western European News Service, The Independent, The Daily Telegraph, The Glasgow Herald, The Irish Times* and *The Guardian.*

39. D. Imig and S. Tarrow (eds.), *Contentious Europeans: Protest and Politics in an Integrating Europe* (Boulder, CO: Rowman and Littlefield, in press).

40. D. McAdam and W. Sewell, 'Temporality in the Study of Social Movements and Revolutions', in R. Aminzade *et al.* (cds.), *Silence and Voice in the Study of Contentious Politics* (New York and Cambridge: Cambridge University Press, in press).

41. See E. Bush and P. Simi, 'Harvesting Contention: European Integration, Supranational Institutions, and Farmers' Protests, 1992 97', in Imig and Tarrow (eds.), *Contentious Europeans.*

42. Imig and Tarrow (eds.), *Contentious Europeans.*

43. Roederer, 'CAP Reforms and the Transformation of Domestic Politics'.

44. Bush and Simi, 'Harvesting Contention'; V. Kettnaker, 'The European Conflict over Genetically-engineered Crops, 1995–97', in Imig and Tarrow (eds.), *Contentious Europeans.*

45. Roederer, 'CAP Reforms and the Transformation of Domestic Politics'.

46. S. Tarrow, 'Fishnets, Internets and Catnets: Globalization and Transnational Collective Action', in M. Hanagan, L. Page Moch and W. te Brake (eds.), *Challenging Authority: The Historical Study of Collective Action* (Minneapolis: University of Minnesota Press 1998).

47. *Reuters,* Dec. 1997.

48. W. Streek, 'Public Power Beyond the Nation-State', in R. Boyer and D. Brachem (eds.), *States Against Markets* (New York: Routledge 1996).

49. L. Turner, 'The Europeanization of Labour: Structure Before Action', *European Journal of Industrial Relations* 2 (1996), pp.325–44.

50. G. Marks and D. McAdam, 'Social Movements and the Changing Structure of Political Opportunity in the EU', *West European Politics* 20 (1996), pp.111–33; G. Marks and D. McAdam, 'On the Relationship of Political Opportunities to the Form of Collective Action: The Case of the EU', in della Porta *et al.* (eds.), *Social Movements in a Globalizing World.*

51. Martin and Ross, 'In the Line of Fire'.

52. See Imig and Tarrow (eds.), *Contentious Europeans.*

53. Turner, 'The Europeanization of Labour'.

Policy Networks in a Multi-Level System: Convergence Towards Moderate Diversity?

GERDA FALKNER

Does the European Union (EU) represent a case of transnational pluralism which will trickle down through the European multi-level system? Or is it a 'statist pluralist' model, which impinges on both statist and corporatist national polities? Or does the EU herald a completely new form of governance, a problem-solving style of co-operation between public and private actors, which will supersede hierarchy between public and private actors and competition amongst interest groups in both the supranational and the national spheres?

There are good arguments to support each of these hypotheses. If this is the case, there must be an analytical key to open the doors between these seemingly contradictory scenarios. The argument advanced here is that the *inclusion of the meso level* in the analysis – that is, the systematic examination of policy-specific and sector-specific characteristics in European governance – will do the trick. In addition, it is necessary to recognise *different types of impact potentials* of Euro-level patterns on the national systems. Based on this analytical differentiation, a long-term effect of European integration is expected to be 'moderate diversity'. The latter is characterised by the co-existence of different types of policy networks within the same political system. While *intra-system diversity* of public–private interaction may even increase, this development is likely to be accompanied by a *trend towards inter-system convergence* in specific policy areas, as a consequence of Europeanisation. Since the effect of Euro-politics is, in most cases, indirect, 'soft' and mediated by national institutions (in the wider sense), no uniform (sub-)systems of interest intermediation are likely to emerge, not even in the same policy field and in the longer term.

The following discussion starts by reviewing the relevant literature and identifies several analytical shortcomings. Against this background, a new approach is set out. This new approach stresses, first, meso-level policy networks as the typical settings of public–private interaction in policy-making and outlines four simple ideal-types to characterise them at both the EU and the national levels. Second, the approach distinguishes three different mechanisms of a potential EU impact on national interest intermediation. The conclusion then formulates some preliminary hypotheses on future developments.

EUROPEAN INTEGRATION AND NATIONAL PUBLIC–PRIVATE RELATIONS: DEFINITIONS, CLASSIFICATIONS AND EXPECTATIONS VARY

In the EU, one finds quite diverse models of public–private interaction in the making of public policies. At least at first glance, they may be distinguished with reference to three classic political science paradigms. *Statism* refers to a model in which private interests have no significant role in public decision-making. In *pluralist* polities, there are many interest groups that lobby individually, that is, they express their views in an effort to influence the politicians who actually take the decisions. In *corporatist* systems, a few privileged interest groups – usually the peak associations of labour and industry – are incorporated in public decision-making as decisive co-actors. But a closer look reveals that the precise definitions of these concepts employed in the literature vary a great deal, especially as far as corporatism and, albeit to a lesser extent, pluralism, are concerned.

Differing Definitions of 'Corporatism' and 'Pluralism'

At least in the academic mainstream, a specific type of interest group system,[1] combined with a particular form of co-operative policy-making,[2] has been regarded as the hallmark of corporatism.[3] This two-dimensional definition of corporatism also informs the ideal-types presented below. But corporatism has also variously been 'defined as an ideology, a variant of political culture, a type of state, a form of economy, or even as a kind of society'.[4] Even in the most recent writing, for example in accounts of public–private patterns and European integration, authors do not necessarily refer to the same animal when they talk about 'corporatism'. Vivien Schmidt, for instance, defines corporatism as a situation in which private interests have privileged access to both decision-making and implementation, whilst pluralism is characterised by a large set of interests that are involved in decision-making, but have no influence in implementation, since in this regard a regulatory approach prevails. Statism, according to Schmidt, is marked by the exclusion of societal interests from decision-making, which are, however, accommodated during the policy implementation phase.[5] Beate Kohler-Koch, by contrast, develops another definition of corporatism for the macro-level of political systems. Her typology of 'modes of governance' is based on two categories: 'the organising principle of political relations' (majority rule versus consociation); and 'the constitutive logic of a polity' (politics as investment in a common identity versus reconciliation of competing self-interests). In her view, corporatist governance captures, first, the pursuit of a common interest and, second, the search for consensus instead of majority voting.[6] For their part, Svein Andersen and Kjell Eliassen have implicitly defined 'a corporatist structure' as one in which bodies consisting of both interest organisations and Community institutions are decisive.[7]

Such a definitional 'mess' is not a novel problem in political science; after all, the older concept of pluralism, too, has presented its critics with a moving target.[8] In contrast to the previously dominant élite model, 'pluralists' originally assumed widespread, effective, political resources; multiple centres of power; and optimum policy development through competing interests. What seems unclear is whether these interests can merely all make themselves heard at some consultative stage during the decision-making process or whether all of them possess equal influence on the decision-makers. Pluralism is typically associated with a clear separation of state and society, with the state being an arbiter of the competition amongst interest groups;[9] this would seem a strong argument against the presumption of equal influence for all groups. Nevertheless, the latter is frequently assumed in contemporary writing that touches pluralist thought, including scholars writing on European integration. For example, Elizabeth Bomberg speaks of 'similar access and influence'.[10] But when it comes to detailed empirical studies, the assumption of equal influence for all lobbies is shown to be highly unrealistic. Hence, the definition of the pluralist form of policy network, that is, the issue network, discussed below, does not assume such a characteristic.[11]

Differing definitions are not only problematic for scholarly discourse; they also make classifications of political systems partly inconsistent with one another. This problem is aggravated by the lack of a single authoritative classification of the EU member states as concerns their patterns of interest politics. Moreover, even where the same classifications are employed, comparative studies do not always draw the same conclusions.[12] Thus, recent contributions by Europeanists have regarded France, Italy and Spain as statist polities, while Austria, Germany and the Netherlands are usually considered corporatist – notwithstanding partly differing definitions.[13] No agreement exists for the case of the UK. Maria Green Cowles speaks of pluralist government–business relations, while Schmidt takes the UK as a statist example.[14] It is interesting to note that pluralist systems in Europe are scarcely explicitly discussed, but rather exist as a residual category; instead, the US is chosen as the textbook example of pluralism, even when a comparison of political systems with the EU is at stake.[15]

Differing Models and Expectations Concerning the EU

Most of the commentators on Euro-politics and interest intermediation tend to deduce effects on the national systems from one assumed cross-sectoral ideal-typical style of EU governance; but their ideal-types and the expected effects differ. In other words: the few available contributions[16] that go beyond individual case studies usually concentrate, as a first step, on describing the EU as one particular type of state–society relations. In a second step, they deduce from this general model of Euro-politics the likely effects on the member states. The best known of such accounts by Wolfgang Streeck and Philippe Schmitter – with the telling title 'From National Corporatism to Transnational Pluralism' – analyses why the EU falls short of centralised labour–industry–state relations. According to these authors, the most likely scenario for the EU is 'an American-style pattern of "disjointed pluralism" or "competitive federalism", organised over no less than three levels – regions, nation-states, and "Brussels"'.[17]

Not all scholars, however, agree on these specific characteristics attributed to 'European Community (EC) governance'.[18] While Streeck and Schmitter describe a pluralist style similar to American patterns, Vivien Schmidt detects important differences to the US model. She considers the EC to be 'less "pluralistic" in interest group access, given that business is the interest mainly represented in a majority of policy areas, and it contains statist elements in its control of the process of interest representation and its greater insulation from undue influence'.[19] She even speaks of 'statist pluralism' in policy formulation.[20] Like Streeck and Schmitter, Schmidt also infers impacts on national interest politics from her general ideal-type of EU-level governance.[21] Her conclusion is that 'statist polities have had a harder time adjusting to EU-level policy formulation, a more difficult task in implementing the policy changes engendered by the EU, and a greater challenge in adapting their national governance patterns to the new realities'. Conversely, 'the EU's quasi-pluralist process is in most ways more charitable to systems characterized by corporatist processes ... because the "fit" is greater in such areas as societal actors' interest organisation and access and governing bodies' decision-making culture and adaptability'.[22]

Schmidt argues that European integration enhances the autonomy of political leaders in pluralist or even corporatist states, but not in statist France, where it has 'diminished the overall autonomy of the executive at the formulation stage, while it has undermined its flexibility at the implementation stage'.[23]

To give a further example, Beate Kohler-Koch's ideal-typical EC-style, 'network governance', refers to a quite different animal, characterised by co-operation among all interested actors, instead of competition, and by joint learning processes.[24] In her account, hierarchy and subordination give way to an interchange on a more equal footing aimed at joint problem-solving[25] that will spread in the multi-level system. This suggests a much more co-operative process than self-interested lobbying of many individual private groups according to the pluralist ideal-type. There are, thus, divergent accounts of the basic characteristics of EC public–private relations and, based on them, diverse predictions regarding the effects of European integration on national interest intermediation.

Existing accounts need not, however, necessarily be contradictory. Rather, they can be read as useful pieces in a larger jigsaw. Breaking down the level of analysis to include the meso level – for both the EC/EU and its member states – might allow one to integrate these analyses, with each referring to different co-existing types of governance at the EU level and to specific forms of impact on the national systems.[26] The apparent current confusion stems mainly from two sources. First, the lack of systematic linkage of research on interest intermediation that points to considerable meso-level differences in the member states, on the one hand, and in the field of Euro-politics, on the other. And, second, the insufficient attention given to the need for an analytical distinction of the different kinds of potential effects that EU-level patterns may provoke in the member states. The remainder of this article seeks to fill this gap.

A NEW APPROACH TO STUDYING THE IMPACT OF EUROPEAN INTEGRATION ON NATIONAL INTEREST INTERMEDIATION

Varying Networks rather than '...isms' throughout the Multi-Level System

The approach developed here acknowledges differentiated governance sub-systems at both the national and the EU levels. Instead of 'plural*ism*', 'corporat*ism*' or 'stat*ism*', it seems useful to speak about specific policy networks with particular characteristics. Insights from the governance literature can, thus, be imported into cross-nationally comparative political science. The following discussion first summarises existing knowledge on the importance of the meso level in interest politics at the national and European levels. It then presents a scheme of ideal-types for both national and European politics. On that basis, the pressures exerted by European integration on particular policy networks at the national level can be established more precisely than hitherto.

The National Level

From the beginning of the corporatism debate in the 1970s, it was evident that corporatist patterns were much more frequent in some policy areas, notably in social policy, than in others.[27] A multitude of case studies on patterns of interest intermediation in EU member states quickly uncovered that even in non-corporatist political systems, corporatist 'arenas' did, indeed, emerge at the level of industrial sectors, sub-national political units and/or single policy arenas.[28] Since then, changes at the economic and the political levels have made it even more improbable that within otherwise increasingly fragmented political systems, corporatism should still cover all crucial issues of policy-making, as Lehmbruch's ideal-type assumed.[29]

Even for the corporatist 'role model' of Austria, a strong trend towards sectoralisation of interest politics has recently been acknowledged. In fact, 'social partnership' is much less uniformly characterised by interest group co-decision in public policy-making than has often been assumed. In areas such as judicial policy, education, research policy, consumer protection, defence policy and telecommunications, the influence of the Austrian social partners is, at best, marginal.[30] Corporatist patterns are only prominent in a few core areas, notably social, economic and agricultural policies, and even there not in all relevant issue areas and, importantly, not in all specific decision processes.

The Austrian case is by no means exceptional, since sectoralisation of politics and a shift of industrial relations towards the sectoral level seem to represent a broader trend.[31] Compared to the 'classic' 1970s corporatism, which was indeed often macro-corporatism with demand-side steering of the economy, contemporary corporatist arrangements appear significantly restricted in functional scope, as the policy-making process is broken down and varies across policy subsystems.[32] Nevertheless, meso-level diversity has so far hardly been reflected in comparisons of the political systems of the EU member states. Political scientists still tend to label whole countries as pluralist, corporatist or statist, without referring to the important intra-state differences identified in the state-specific literature, although single-country studies now frequently prefer a refined heuristic approach based on the policy networks typology proposed by British scholars.

The policy networks approach was developed with the explicit intention to capture the sectoral constellations emerging as a response to the growing dispersion of resources and capacities for political action among public and private actors.[33] In parallel with the scope of state intervention targets, decentralisation and fragmentation of the state also increased over time and were complemented by increased intervention and participation in decision-making by a growing range of social and political actors. Policy networks were, thus, characterised as 'integrated hybrid structures of political governance' with the distinctive capacity for mixing different combinations of bureaucracy, market, community or corporatist association as integrative logics.[34]

While continental authors were more concerned with the characteristics of 'network governance' in general,[35] British political scientists tended to concentrate on the development of policy *network ideal-types*. On the basis of earlier work by authors such as Grant Jordan and Jeremy Richardson, David Marsh and Rod Rhodes elaborated the dominant typology. They distinguished closed and stable policy communities from loose and open issue networks as the two polar ends of a multi-dimensional continuum ('policy network' is thus a generic term encompassing all types).[36] The characteristics of both groups focus on the dimensions of membership,[37] integration,[38] resources[39] and power.[40] Marsh and Rhodes stress that the characteristics form an ideal-type to be compared with actual relationships between governments and interests, since no policy area is likely to conform exactly to either list of characteristics.[41] These ideal-types cannot explain politics within networks,[42] but they may be heuristically useful, notably for comparisons of national and EU-level networks that seek to determine the potential impact of the latter on the former (see below).[43]

The EU Level

That the emergence of a supranational form of macro-corporatism comparable to national patterns in the 1970s is unlikely has been underlined by a number of studies on EC interest politics.[44] At the same time, scholars have increasingly pointed to fragmentation as a typical feature of the EU's political system. Enormous cross-sectoral differences find a basis in the European treaties, since the participation of the European Parliament and the EC's Economic and Social Committee varies, as do voting procedures in the Council and its subgroups. Such constitutionally fixed differences are, however, merely the tip of the iceberg, as they have been further refined by long-standing political practice. For example, different directorates-general have very distinct styles of interaction with private interests, a fact that has been highlighted by a new generation of meso-level studies that addresses the question of EC governance at the area-specific and sector-specific levels.[45] This area-specific character of European integration is unlikely to change. Treaty reforms continue to deepen constitutional cleavages, and the large number of different actors from multiple levels could, in practice, hardly co-operate outside clear functional boundaries, even if any new central EU authority should ever try to harmonise the patterns of sectoral governance. The diverse styles of public-private interaction found in various EC policy networks include statist, pluralist and corporatist patterns.[46] To give just a few examples, private interest governments[47] and quasi-corporatist regimes have been detected in the regulation of pharmaceuticals,[48] consumer electronics,[49] steel production,[50] health and safety at work,[51] technical standardisation[52] and social policy.[53] These findings indicate that there is a plurality of sector-specific constellations rather than a pluralist macro-system of Euro-politics.[54]

This insight has important consequences for the effects of European integration on national public–private interaction styles. If Europeanisation does not necessarily imply that a policy is decided according to one particular pattern (for example, a pluralist one), assumptions about feedback into national systems must also be adapted. It seems that the impact of Euro-politics could be much more diverse, that is, differentiated between policy areas, than has hitherto been expected.

A Typology Connecting Two Strands of Literature

What is needed, therefore, are models of public–private interaction in the making of public policies that allow for the differentiation between varying situations in distinct policy areas or economic sectors (for the sake of stringency,[55] the stage of implementation shall be excluded here). At the same time, however, the well-established distinction between statist, pluralist and corporatist patterns, which is still frequently used by scholars working on Euro-politics, should not be discarded.[56] Thus, it is suggested that two strands of literature be combined by incorporating the corporatist and statist ideal-types with the issue network/policy community dichotomy.[57] Since the catalogue of characteristics elaborated by Marsh and Rhodes is, in fact, quite complex and may easily result in blurred empirical types, only two decisive dimensions have been chosen and all other characteristics mentioned by these authors are treated as empirical matters to be established on the basis of case studies.[58]

FIGURE 1
FOUR SIMPLE IDEAL-TYPES FOR THE ANALYSIS OF MESO-LEVEL INTEREST
INTERMEDIATION

	Statist cluster	Issue network	Traditional policy community	Corporatist policy community
Membership of interest groups in the network	–	*Unstable:* network is open for diverse interests	*Rather stable:* network tends to be closed	*Extremely stable:* exclusive group of members
Involvement of interest groups	*Insignificant:* lobbies do not exist or are not heard	*Consultative:* lobbying is common	*Participatory:* joint process of decision-shaping	*Decisive:* formal co-actors in the making of public policies

The two suggested core dimensions are membership and involvement of interest groups in the network. These two dimensions must not necessarily correlate empirically in all cases. However, if a network is stable over time – in the sense that it usually includes the same actors – the latter will more easily develop the kind of mutual acquaintance and trust relationships that favour giving a (co-)decisive role to participants other than state institutions. Clearly, many issues of interest in the study of public–private relationships in policy-making are outside the two basic dimensions of this typology. To give some examples, the number and type of public actors in the policy network, the number and type of interest groups involved, the balance of power within these two actor groups, as well as potential state influence on intra-group politics are not included in the typology itself, but should be considered in empirical enquiries.

The typology proposed here thus includes four basic ideal-types of policy networks, grouped along the continua of stability of interest group membership and of the degree of these groups' involvement in decision-making (see Figure 1). Accordingly, a *statist cluster* is a form of policy network where interest groups either do not exist at all[59] or are not paid any attention, since there is no significant public–private interaction. Empirically, this might be the rarest form, particularly at the EU level.[60] In an *issue network*, there is interaction between the state and, typically, a plurality of societal actors, who may easily join or leave such networks; but the interest groups' involvement is merely consultative, as the public actors decide quite independently. Obviously, this form is close to the pluralist paradigm. The *traditional policy community*, by contrast, is characterised by a much more stable network membership. It is not easy, but still possible, for a new interest group to be admitted. Private groups are incorporated into the process of decision-shaping, although without actual veto powers and without being formal co-actors. The qualifier 'traditional' is used to indicate that this type basically corresponds to how the label policy community has so far been used in the literature. Only in a *corporatist policy community* do interest groups actually come to share state authority. In this extremely exclusive form of policy network, a typically small number of privileged groups make public policies with state actors in a co-decisive capacity. As regards functionally oriented writing on policy networks and European integration,[61] it is important to mention that, in the understanding proposed here, 'network governance' would apply to traditional policy communities as well as to corporatist policy communities.[62] In both, the participating public and private actors co-operate in the search for consensual approaches.[63]

This typology allows us to distinguish between four basic types of policy networks at all levels of the European multi-layered system and promises to lead to new insights into the effects of European integration on the member states. Such a differentiated approach allows, for example, for distinctive effects of a specific European policy network on the functionally corresponding but diverging networks in different member states. Furthermore, this approach could show that a specific actor category, for example labour, might be disadvantaged by Europeanisation in one policy field, say transport, but not in another area, such as labour law.

The following section outlines in more detail what such a differentiated approach suggests for the analysis of the potential impact of specific European networks on their counterparts (see in particular Figure 2). When networks of the same kind operate at the member state and EU levels, no great pressures for change are to be expected. By contrast, an encounter of adverse types heralds the highest degree of potential[64] destabilisation, for example, when a statist cluster at EU level co-exists with a corporatist policy community in a member state, or vice versa.

TYPES OF POTENTIAL IMPACT ON NATIONAL INTEREST INTERMEDIATION

This section, first, further specifies the variegated influence of different EU decision patterns, as already briefly outlined above. It then considers two further mechanisms by which European integration may influence national public–private co-operation.

EU Decision Patterns

As noted above, commentators on the influence of Europeanisation on national interest intermediation until recently used to describe one typical form of interest politics for the EC and deduced from that an impact on the national systems, each of which was, again, assumed to conform to a single ideal-type. Accordingly, sectoral differences at both the EU and the national levels tended to be overlooked. The mechanism by which the pattern of public–private co-operation practised at the EU level affected the member states did not usually attract much attention; instead, there was an implicit assumption that the EC style would somehow trickle down into the national systems over time.

There are at least three different ways in which EU policy networks can make a difference domestically. First, since some or even many actors – both public and private –within the national policy network will also participate in European networks, their experiences 'in Europe' may lead to cognitive, normative and strategic changes. New ideas about 'best practice', for example on ways in which to engender consensus amongst actors in policy networks, can be imported into the domestic environment. Second, different norms regarding (non-)co-operative governance may be transferred by policy network members who are active in various arenas. What has been practised and accepted at the national level may look different if one knows various cultures and their norms. Finally, strategic alliances between specific actors or actor categories formed at the European level may have feedback effects in the national environment. In all three cases, the time dimension is important, since very short-term effects seem rather improbable.

In any case, if one acknowledges that EU-level public–private interaction may be variegated, the repercussions of EC decision patterns in the domestic context must be highly area-specific. An issue network at the EU level will tend to trigger different reactions at the national level than, for example, a corporatist policy community. Participation in an EC network of the former type might encourage some interest groups to show lobbyist behaviour also 'at home', at the expense of interest aggregation with other actors. If at the EU level a corporatist policy community exists, national social partnerships in the same field should have comparatively less to fear. In Figure 2, a 'tendency towards lobbying' combines pressures to open the network up for more diverse interests and to pay some attention to their lobbying efforts. The 'tendency towards stability and involvement' stands for the pressure to have more stable membership of interest groups in the network and to give them a more decisive say in policy-making.

FIGURE 2
DIRECTION OF DOMESTIC IMPACT OF EC DECISION PATTERNS

Specific EC Decision Patterns

	Statist cluster	Issue network	Traditional policy community	Corporatist policy community
Statist cluster	confirmation and potentially reinforcement	tendency towards lobbying	tendency towards stability and involvement	tendency towards stability and involvement
Issue network	tendency towards less lobbying	confirmation and potentially reinforcement	tendency towards stability and involvement	tendency towards stability and involvements
Traditional policy community	tendency towards less stability and involvement	tendency towards less stability and involvement (example 2)	confirmation and potentially reinforcement	tendency towards stability and involvement
Corporatist policy community	tendency towards less stability and involvement	tendency towards less stability and involvement	tendency towards less stability and involvement	confirmation and potentially reinforcement (example 1)

Specific National Policy Networks (left vertical label)

Based on the assumption that various 'cultures' of EU-level decision-making can trickle down, Figure 2 suggests that corporatist patterns will provoke effects that are quite different from those of a statist or pluralist field of EU activity (if changes take place at all).[65] To start with the left column, a *statist cluster*[66] will tend to confirm or even reinforce another statist cluster at the national level. For example, in countries where independent central banks have existed for a long time already, the role of private interests in this field will not be hampered by a similar style at the European level.[67] If a statist cluster meets an issue network, a traditional policy community or a corporatist policy community in a member state, the potential effect should be to the detriment of the network stability and relevance of involvement of private interests. A pluralist[68] EC *issue network*, in turn,[69] will tend to promote more lobbying by interest groups in a national statist cluster and will tend to reinforce another issue network. When a member state features a traditional policy community in the field, a possible impact will be in the direction of rather less stable and decisive involvement of private interests. National corporatist policy communities, too, will be pushed towards less stable public–private co-decision by an EC issue network. If we pursue this logic, a traditional EC *policy community* (as seems to exist in the automobile sector)[70] will tend to influence both national statist constellations and issue networks in the direction of increased participation of societal actors. Only the groups in national corporatist policy communities are likely to experience an impact that is detrimental to their stable membership and co-decisive role. Finally, a *corporatist policy community* (such as in EC social policy)[71] can be expected to increase the chances for stability in the network and for co-decision of interest groups in national statist clusters, issue networks and policy communities.

Empirical research on Austrian EU-adaptation supports such an approach. A recent study has revealed that corporatist patterns in the core area of Austrian social partnership, that is, social policy and particularly labour law,[72] have not been significantly altered by EU membership.[73] This fits the above hypothesis neatly, since in the aftermath of the Maastricht Treaty a corporatist policy community was established in the realm of EU social policy, too.[74] By contrast, environmental policy in Austria is not regulated in a 'social partnership' pattern, but managed in a traditional policy community without a crucial role for labour and industry.[75] At the EU level, an issue network exists in the environmental field, as described in detail by Bomberg.[76] Insofar as a shift in the Austrian network can already be discerned,[77] it is in the direction of more influence for the involved ministries, but rather less for the interest groups, notably for the environmentalists. These social and environmental policy cases in Austria appear as examples numbered 1 and 2 in Figure 2.

These brief remarks suggest that breaking down European policy-making patterns in meso-level constellations results in more realistic assumptions about their possible effects on equally variegated national public–private networks. Such expectations need to be tested through comparative empirical studies with research designs that explicitly include policy-specific and sector-specific patterns.[78]

While potential effects on the member states stemming from EU decision patterns have already been discussed by various authors, very little attention has so far been paid to the fact that the EU may also influence national styles in a more direct manner.

Positive Integration Measures

During the past decades, the EU member states have been confronted with an increasingly high incidence of European legislation, which affects, to varying degrees, almost all issue areas. It is not only policies that may be transmitted in this way, but also public–private interaction patterns. Partly as a side-effect of some policy goal, but sometimes intentionally, the EU fairly frequently impinges on national interest intermediation through acts of secondary law. Some examples from social policy reveal efforts to encourage corporatist patterns at the national level. In some cases, derogations from common EC standards need to be negotiated or at least discussed with the social partners in the member state concerned. Thus, the Working Time Directive allows for derogations 'by way of collective agreements or agreements concluded between the two sides of industry at the appropriate collective level' (OJ 93/L 307/18, Art. 17.3). The Directive on the posting of workers in the framework of the free provision of services (OJ 97/L 18/1, Art. 3.3) states that 'Member States may, after consulting employers and labour, in accordance with the traditions and practices of each Member State, decide' not to grant equal minimum pay to posted workers during the first month of their stay abroad. This means that even a national government that has no interest at all in co-operating with labour and industry on labour law matters must now consult these societal actors if it wants to derogate from specific EC norms.

Contacts between public and private national actors in all member states are also prompted by several recent EC social Directives, which prescribe that in the national reports to the Commission on the practical implementation of the respective Directive, the viewpoints 'of the two sides of industry' must be indicated (see, for example, Art. 17.4 Directive on the protection of young people at work, OJ 94/L 216/12). This is also common practice in the field of health and safety at work (see, for example, rules concerning chemical agents at work). In other cases, consultation or co-decision of interest groups is not directly prescribed as a condition for certain national actions or required to complete a national report on implementation, but may still be encouraged and facilitated. For example, the recent parental leave (OJ 98/L 14/9) and part-time work Directives (OJ 96/L 145/4) allow for one additional year of implementation delay if the EC provisions are implemented by a collective agreement instead of legislation. The recent part-time rules, which stem from a Euro-agreement between the major interest groups of labour and employers that was incorporated in the relevant Council Directive, also provide that 'Member States, *following consultations with the social partners* in accordance with national law or practice, should ... review obstacles ... which may limit the opportunities for part-time work and ... eliminate them' (clause 5, emphasis added).[79] The EC standards, furthermore, do 'not prejudice the right of the social partners to conclude, at the appropriate level ... agreements adapting and/or complementing the provisions of this Agreement in a manner which will take account of the specific needs of the social partners concerned' (clause 6.3). Finally, the provisions on implementation provide that 'Member States and/or social partners may maintain or introduce more favourable provisions' (clause 6.1 of part-time Agreement). Very similar passages are to be found in the parental leave Directive and Agreement.

In environmental policy, too, several recent Directives could impact on national public–private interaction, since they encourage more open structures *vis-à-vis* private groups. 'The plurality of actors associated with the different instruments will result in new complexity in territorial and public–private terms, counter-acting old hierarchical chains of command'.[80] However, such patterns are encouraged only in some Directives, while others might have the opposite effect, so that it is 'doubtful whether EC governance in the field of environmental policy is sufficiently comprehensive, coherent and stable to trigger a decisive and uniform response'.[81] This points to the fact that potential 'positive integration effects' as outlined here may well be contradictory. Only if the aggregate impetus from the various EC Directives in a specific policy area exceeds 'zero' can such influence be expected to produce significant adaptational pressure in a national policy network. But systematic and comparative empirical studies on the influences on public–private co-operation in the member states exerted by positive integration measures are still missing.

Competence Transfers

The third influence on the member states' public–private relations arising from European integration results from shifts of various competences to the EU level. The overall realm of national action capacity decreases parallel to each issue area that is covered by EU policy. This 'size' effect on the national interest intermediation systems exists regardless of any specific actor constellation in the member state. However, it is possible that not all public–private interaction patterns are affected by this development to the same extent. More co-operative policy network types, which rely on log-rolling and package-dealing, will be hampered, while types that know only individual lobbying by diverse groups according to each new issue at stake may not be affected. In particular, it seems reasonable to expect that cross-sectoral corporatist systems, that is, macro-corporatism, would be affected most adversely, since the number of issue areas available for corporatist exchange between the state and national interest groups decreases. This line of argument suggests that the impact of competence transfers would by now impede old-style national macro-corporatism in the member states anyway, even if sectoral differentiation had not already changed national patterns. At the macro level, Streeck and Schmitter were thus certainly right in pointing out that 'corporatism as a national-level accord between encompassingly organized socio-economic classes and the state, by which an entire economy is comprehensively governed, would seem to be a matter of the past', not least due to European integration.[82] However, this diagnosis is only part of the story about effects of Europeanisation on national interest intermediation – since at least at the meso level, EC decision patterns and positive integration measures might also provoke countervailing impulses. Even where 'only' negative integration[83] prevails in Euro-policies – for example, where positive integration measures are blocked in the Council – there may be an effect on national interest politics, as the neo-liberal options chosen at the EU level may pose restraints. In such cases, national networks in the relevant area are restricted in their policy choices. *De facto*, this affects the opportunity structure for national actors,[84] often at the expense of trade unions or consumer groups with an interest in state interventions that are no longer legal under EC law. As Streeck and Schmitter pointed out, mutual recognition in the internal market and the resulting inter-regime competition tended to devalue the power resources and political strength of organised labour.[85] This indicates that there are also effects of European integration on national policy networks that originate less in the lost competences at the national level than in the specific kind of policies decided at the supranational level. Once again, however, a meso-level approach may produce new insights, because a more integrated and co-operative public–private network at the national level may counterbalance such influences to some extent, while issue networks will hardly be able to do so.

The Role of Mediating Factors

As has already been mentioned, the present discussion centres on influences that European integration *might* exert on national interest intermediation. This is to say that the Euro-level side of the coin is the primary topic here, notwithstanding the fact that the national processes of adaptation (or non-adaptation) are another fascinating issue, which is not necessarily less significant in terms of the final result of the overall process.[86] To demonstrate the potentially crucial role of national mediation of impacts, Economic and Monetary Union (EMU) may serve as a case in point. The effects of the Maastricht convergence criteria for EMU membership on public–private relations in various member states could scarcely have been more divergent. They allowed (or forced) several governments to reform their national budgets by cutting public spending at a speed and in a form that would otherwise not have been acceptable to either employer or labour associations, most notably in Austria.[87] Euro-policies may thus increase the opportunities for governments to 'cut slack' and to gain leverage *vis-à-vis* the major national private players. At the same time, however, this EC policy reinforced public–private co-operation in other member states, where issue-specific[88] and fixed-term tripartite pacts – usually labelled 'social pacts' – were concluded with a view to reaching the convergence criteria.[89] Although EMU certainly constitutes a very special case of supranational steering of the national economies and polities, and EU influences on national interest intermediation in traditional policy areas can be expected to be somewhat less contingent, this example nevertheless indicates that mitigation of EU impulses in the national networks does play a major role in the field of interest intermediation.

Here, only a few hypotheses can be put forward concerning the potential transmission mechanisms and the forms of policy networks as outlined above. They suggest asking the following questions in future empirical research:

- Do more *direct* types of EC influence favour effects on the national level? It seems that a transfer of competences will often matter, regardless of national action or reaction. For example, a positive integration measure that allows a member state a derogation from EC law only under the condition of approval by labour and industry will involve national action, but still appears more likely to show effects than a mere divergence between EU and national decision patterns would. The latter has been much discussed in the existing literature, although it seems, in fact, the least direct of the mechanisms described here.
- Is the impact of European integration weaker and slower if the specific national policy network is more ingrained, as institutionalist assumptions suggest?
- Do concurring competences within the same policy field promote learning and adaptation processes? The impact of EU decision patterns, when they are diverging from the relevant national ones, could in such cases matter comparatively more, since there is more contact and, hence, potential exchange between the two levels. As long as there is no full Europeanisation, a higher EU share of activity in a policy field could make the supranational network style comparatively more influential.
- Finally, are the more demanding forms of public–private co-operation patterns in greater danger of being called into question by challenges from outside? The fact that corporatist patterns seem more difficult to

establish than pluralist competition of societal actors suggests that they might, in principle, be rather more vulnerable in the multi-level system.[90] Statist clusters, too, might be less stable than issue networks or traditional policy communities, since excluding all private interests from the policy arena can easily lead to de-legitimisation of the output. It might also prompt protest – in particular if more co-operative styles of governance are well known from other venues in the multi-level system. Moreover, the EU seems, in principle, rather open to lobbying,[91] so adaptive pressure from EC-level statist clusters might be less frequent than from the more co-operative forms of governance.

CONCLUSION: CONVERGING TOWARDS 'MODERATE DIVERSITY'?

This study has advocated the *inclusion of the meso level* of policy networks into the analysis of interest intermediation at both the European and the national levels, and, in particular, with a view to determining possible influences of the former on the latter. If the governance literature is right in highlighting the differentiation of policy subsystems, comparative political science could profit from adopting such a differentiated approach, which promises more realistic assumptions concerning the impact of EC patterns of public–private interaction on national policy networks. Some preliminary results of empirical research presented above seem to bear out this point (see Figure 2). While only empirical enquiries can authoritatively confirm how much policy-specific patterns do matter in terms of domestic Europeanisation, research designs that exclude the meso level cannot address this question at all.

The second main argument advanced here is that there is more than one type of EU impact on national interest intermediation. Thus far, the most frequently discussed effect has been the 'trickling down' of EC decision patterns. By contrast, the more direct impact of interest intermediation patterns imposed – in one way or another – on the member states through EC law have scarcely been studied as a relevant influence. Finally, the effects of the transfer of various competences to the EU level must also be taken into account. All three mechanisms have to be considered when it comes to assessing the effect of Europeanisation on national interest intermediation. At times, they may counteract each other.

One point that could not be discussed in detail in the present context is that European integration influences national public–private interaction patterns mostly in an indirect manner.[92] This points to the crucial role of mediating factors at the national or sectoral levels. These factors need to be established through empirical studies, but it is possible to generate some general assumptions from the conceptual approach suggested here, in the form of preliminary hypotheses on future trends in European interest intermediation.

First, a meso-level approach suggests that *inter-sectoral diversity* in private–public interaction during the policy process will persist or even increase. As outlined above, both the national and the European layers of the multi-level system are characterised by highly diverse styles of interest intermediation at the meso level. Since the EC is a particularly strongly sectoralised system, inter-sectoral differences in patterns of public–private interaction could be expected to increase even in unitary states.[93] As policy networks have recently been described as relevant meso-level constellations in the European states anyway, the EU will probably reinforce an already existing trend towards sectoral differentiation in the member states.

Second, the *inter-systemic diversity* – both amongst member states and between the EU and the member states – of policy networks might in the future be rather more moderate. As the EC patterns will influence all national systems in the same direction, the effect over time should be some convergence towards the EC model, since the latter is the point of reference for all national networks. In the words of Adrienne Héritier *et al.*, one may think of path-dependent corridors of adaptation that are open to each of the national policy networks.[94] Since all national networks are, however, influenced by the same Euro-level pattern existing in the relevant field, the result should be adaptation towards more similarity. Some divergence will persist, but probably in a more moderated form than before the EU gained influence on national policy networks.

In other words, one may expect systematic empirical studies to reveal a trend towards *cross-sectorally divergent* styles of public–private interaction with nevertheless rather more convergence than before between the geographic layers of the European Union and amongst the member states. We could thus be heading towards more *'uniform pluriformism'* in the European multi-level system.

NOTES

Previous versions of this paper were presented at two *West European Politics* Special Issue Conferences, Oxford, Nuffield College, 1998 and 1999; at the 6th Biennial International Conference of the European Community Studies Association, USA, Pittsburgh, 2–5 June 1999; at the Annual Meeting of the American Political Science Association, 2–5 Sept. 1999; and at the European Forum of the European University Institute, Florence. Thanks to the commentators (Hussein Kassim, Christopher Allen, J. Nicholas Ziegler) and participants for their feedback.

1. 'Corporatism can be defined as a system of interest representation in which the constituent units are organized into a limited number of singular, compulsory, non-competitive, hierarchically ordered and functionally differentiated categories, recognized or licensed (if not created) by the state and granted a deliberate representational monopoly within their respective categories in exchange for observing certain controls on their selection of leaders and articulation of demands and supports'. See P.C. Schmitter, 'Still the Century of Corporatism?', *Review of Politics* 35 (1974), p.13.

2. Lehmbruch contrasted 'corporatist' co-operation of organisations and public authorities, and 'pluralist' pressure politics. See G. Lehmbruch, 'Introduction: Neo-Corporatism in Comparative Perspective', in G. Lehmbruch and P.C. Schmitter (eds.), *Patterns of Corporatist Policy-Making* (London and Beverly Hills, CA: Sage 1982), p.8 with further references. Along these lines, a corporatist policy-making process was also described as 'a mode of policy formation in which formally designated interest associations are incorporated within the process of authoritative decision-making and implementation. As such they are officially recognised by the state not merely as interest intermediaries but as co-responsible "partners" in governance and social guidance', See P.C. Schmitter, 'Interest Intermediation and Regime Governability in Contemporary Western Europe and North America', in S. Berger (ed.), *Organising Interests in Western Europe: Pluralism, Corporatism, and the Transformation of Politics* (Cambridge: Cambridge University Press 1981), p.295.

3. For example, A. Cawson, 'Introduction: Varieties of Corporatism: The Importance of the Meso-level Interest Intermediation', in A. Cawson (ed.), *Organized Interests and the State. Studies in Meso-Corporatism* (London: Sage 1985), p.8.

4. P.C. Schmitter, 'Neo-corporatism and the Consolidation of Neo-democracy' (Paper presented at the 8th International Conference on Socio-Economics, Geneva, 12–14 July 1996), p.3. Until today, the comparative industrial relations literature tends to speak about 'corporatism' (without further specification) if in a state, labour markets and industrial relations are managed by co-operative governance of industry, unions and (partly) the state, even if other policy areas in the same political system may follow completely different patterns. In political science, Scandinavian scholars take the same approach because in their countries, centralised wage bargaining is empirically the major incident of corporatist patterns. See F. Traxler, 'Farewell to Labour Market Associations? Organized versus Disorganized Decentralization as a Map for Industrial Relations', in C. Crouch and F. Traxler (eds.), *Organized Industrial Relations: What Future?* (Aldershot: Avebury 1995), p.5, and F. Karlhofer and E. Tálos, *Sozialpartnerschaft und EU. Integrationsdynamik und Handlungsrahmen der österreichischen Sozialpartnerschaft* (Vienna: Signum 1996), p.245. Economists tend to speak about corporatism as a particular style of economic policy and the conceptual incongruencies become even more obvious if we look at the extreme diversity of specific indicators for, and detailed measurements of, corporatism. See H. Keman and P. Pennings, 'Managing Political and Societal Conflict in Democracies: Do Consensus and Corporatism Matter?', *British Journal of Political Science* 25 (1995), pp.271–81.

5. V.A. Schmidt, 'Loosening the Ties that Bind: The Impact of European Integration on French Government and its Relationship to Business', *Journal of Common Market Studies* 34 (1996), pp.224–54; and V.A. Schmidt, 'European Integration and Democracy: The Differences among Member States', *Journal for European Public Policy* 4 (1997), pp.128–44.

6. B. Kohler-Koch, 'The Evolution and Transformation of European Governance', in B. Kohler-Koch and R. Eising (eds.), *The Transformation of Governance in the European Union* (London: Routledge 1999), pp.26ff.

7. S.S. Andersen and K.A. Eliassen, 'European Community Lobbying', *European Journal of Political Research* 20 (1991), pp.173ff.

8. W. Grant, 'Introduction', in W. Grant (ed.), *The Political Economy of Corporatism* (London: Macmillan 1985), p.19. 'Since pluralism is so vague a set of ideas it is difficult to understand how opponents can have rejected it with such confidence', see G. Jordan, 'The Pluralism of Pluralism: An Anti-theory?', *Political Studies* 39 (1990), p.286. German authors may use a very different concept; 'pluralism' has a less specific meaning in German, since it was used to distinguish liberal societies from monist ones before the international debate on

corporatism started in 1974 – see G. Lehmbruch, 'Der Beitrag der Korporatismusforschung zur Entwicklung der Steuerungstheorie', *Politische Vierteljahresschrift* 37 (1996), p.736.

9. A. Cawson, 'Pluralism, Corporatism and the Role of the State', *Government and Opposition* 13 (1978), pp.182ff. The 'vectors of influence' were perceived to run only in one direction, i.e. from private lobbies to state agencies. See G. Lehmbruch, 'Wandlungen der Interessenpolitik im liberalen Korporatismus', in U. von Alemann and R.G. Heinze (eds.), *Verbände und Staat. Vom Pluralismus zum Korporatismus. Analysen, Positionen, Dokumente* (Opladen: Westdeutscher Verlag 1979), pp.51ff. No co-operation in the narrow sense was assumed, i.e. no multi-directional relations. However, it is very difficult to draw the boundary between 'negative co-ordination' (i.e. an implicit mutual adaptation of the competing actors which is included in the pluralist pattern) on the one hand, and the active mobilisation of consensus (i.e. direct negotiations which are a typical feature of corporatism), on the other. See R. Czada, 'Konjunkturen des Korporatismus: Zur Geschichte eines Paradigmenwechsels in der Verbändeforschung', in W. Streeck (ed.), *Staat und Verbände* (Westdeutscher Verlag 1994), p.53, and F. van Waarden, 'Dimensions and Types of Policy Networks', *European Journal of Political Research* 21 (1992), p.34.

10. E. Bomberg, 'Issue Networks and the Environment: Explaining European Union Environmental Policy', in D. Marsh (ed.), *Comparing Policy Networks* (Buckingham and Philadelphia: Open University Press 1998), p.183. Also see D. Marsh, 'The Utility and Future of Policy Network Aalysis', in ibid., p.189, and, implicitly, Schmidt, 'European Integration and Democracy', p.134.

11. Equal or unequal influence are here considered a matter of empirical fact, not of definition.

12. For various rankings of countries in terms of 'corporatism' see, for example, Schmitter, 'Interest Intermediation and Regime Governability'; G. Lehmbruch, 'Sozialpartnerschaft in der vergleichenden Politikforschung', in P. Gerlich, E. Grande and W.C. Müller (eds.), *Sozialpartnerschaft in der Krise* (Vienna: Böhlau 1985); and M.M. Crepaz and A. Lijphart, 'Linking and Integrating Corporatism and Consensus Democracy: Theory, Concepts and Evidence', *British Journal of Political Science* 25 (1995), pp.281–8; and the country studies in Lehmbruch and Schmitter (eds.), *Patterns of Corporatist Policy-Making*; P.C. Schmitter and G. Lehmbruch (eds.), *Trends Towards Corporatist Intermediation* (Beverly Hills and London: Sage 1979); and R. Kleinfeld and W. Luthardt (eds.), *Westliche Demokratien und Interessenvermittlung* (Marburg: Schüren 1993).

13. V.A. Schmidt, 'National Patterns of Governance under Siege: The Impact of European Integration', in Kohler-Koch and Eising (eds.), *The Transformation of Governance in the European Union*, pp.155–71; W. Streeck and P.C. Schmitter, 'From National Corporatism to Transnational Pluralism: Organized Interests in the Single European Market', in V. Eichener and H. Voelzkow (eds.), *Europäische Integration und verbandliche Interessenvermittlung* (Marburg: Metropolis 1994), pp.171–215; and A. Lenschow, 'Transformation in European Environmental Governance', in Kohler-Koch and Eising (eds.), *The Transformation of Governance in the European Union*, pp.39–59.

14. See M. Green Cowles, 'The TABD and Domestic Business–Government Relations: Challenge and Opportunity' (Paper presented at the conference on Europeanization and Domestic Change, Florence, 19–20 June 1998); and Schmidt, 'National Patterns of Governance under Siege', p.156.

15. For example, Schmidt, 'European Integration and Democracy', p.135.

16. The impact of European integration on interest intermediation in the member states has so far hardly been discussed in detail and broad-based comparative empirical studies on the practical effects in the member states are missing. There are at least a few recent exceptions offering interesting insights on the sectoral and case study level. For example, Maria Green Cowles looks at the 'Transatlantic Business Dialogue' and its impact on national government–business relations in France, Germany and the UK. See Green Cowles, 'The TABD and Domestic Business–Government Relations'. Andrea Lenschow discusses the implementation of EC environmental policy acts and their impact on state–society relations in Germany, the Netherlands, Spain and the UK. See Lenschow, 'Transformation in European Environmental Governance'. A study of the implementation of four EC-environmental Directives in Britain and Germany also allows some insights into

private–public relations, see C. Knill and A. Lenschow, 'Adjusting to EU Regulatory Policy: Change and Persistence of Domestic Administrations' (Paper presented at the conference on Europeanization and Domestic Change, Florence, 19–20 June 1998).

17. Streeck and Schmitter, 'From National Corporatism to Transnational Pluralism, p.215.

18. I choose the term EC – and not EU – in this section, since EU governance is often used to describe the entire multi-level system, not only the EU as a specific supra-national political system. As the debate on patterns of governance focuses on EC policy fields and usually neglects the second and third EU pillars with their very special style, using EC here is also correct in legal terms. The typology presented below can nevertheless be applied to the second and third pillars, too.

19 Schmidt, 'European Integration and Democracy', p.134.

20. Ibid., p.138.

21. Schmidt, 'National Patterns of Governance under Siege'; and Schmidt, 'Loosening the Ties that Bind'.

22. Schmid, 'National Patterns of Governance under Siege', p.157.

23. Schmidt, 'Loosening the Ties that Bind', p.249.

24. B. Kohler-Koch, 'Catching up with Change: The Transformation of Governance in the European Union', Journal of European Public Policy 3 (1996), pp.359–80.

25. Kohler-Koch, 'The Evolution and Transformation of European Governance', p.32.

26. In terms of our discussion of the impact of Europeanisation on national interest politics, it is important to note that much of the literature does not systematically distinguish changes in the national policy process due to a trickling down of impacts from the EU level, on the one hand, and the participation of national actors in the European decision process, on the other.

27. '(I)n point of fact, all the interest intermediation systems of Western Europe are "mixed". They may be predominantly of one type, but different sectors and subsectors, classes and class factions, regions and subregions are likely to be operating simultaneously according to different principles and procedures'. See P.C. Schmitter, 'Modes of Interest Intermediation and Models of Societal Change in Western Europe', in Schmitter and Lehmbruch (eds.), Trends Towards Corporatist Intermediation, p.70. Also see Lehmbruch, 'Introduction: Neo-Corporatism in Comparative Perspective', p.27.

28. For example, see the contributions in Berger (ed.), Organising Interests in Western Europe; Cawson, 'Introduction: Varieties of Corporatism'; Grant, 'Introduction'; W. Streeck and P.C. Schmitter (eds.), Private Interest Government. Beyond Market and State (London: Sage 1985).

29. Lehmbruch, 'Sozialpartnerschaft in der vergleichenden Politikforschung', p.94.

30. B. Kittel and E. Tálos, 'Interessenvermittlung und politischer Entscheidungsprozeß: Sozialpartnerschaft in den 1990er Jahren', in F. Karlhofer and E. Tálos (eds.), Zukunft der Sozialpartnerschaft: Veränderungsdynamik und Reformbedarf (Wien: Signum 1999), pp.118ff. Also see W.C. Müller, 'Die Rolle der Parteien bei der Entstehung und Entwicklung der Sozialpartnerschaft', in P. Gerlich, E. Grande and W.C. Müller (eds.), Sozialpartnerschaft in der Krise (Vienna: Böhlau 1985), p.220; E. Tálos, 'Entwicklung, Kontinuität und Wandel der Sozialpartnerschaft', in E. Tálos (ed.), Sozialpartnerschaft: Kontinuität und Wandel eines Modells (Vienna: Verlag für Gesellschaftskritik 1993), p.27; E. Tálos, K. Leichsenring and E. Zeiner, 'Verbände und politischer Entscheidungsgrozeß – am Beispiel der Sozial- und Umweltpolitik', in Tálos (ed.), Sozialpartnerschaft; and F. Traxler, 'Sozialpartnerschaft am Scheideweg: Zwischen korporatistischer Kontinuität und neoliberalem Umbruch', Wirtschaft und Gesellschaft 22 (1996), p.19.

31. F. Karlhofer and H. Sickinger, 'Korporatismus und Sozialpakte im europäischen Vergleich', in Karlhofer and Tálos (eds.), Zukunft der Sozialpartnerschaft, p.242.

32. For example, M.M. Atkinson and W.D. Coleman, 'Strong States and Weak States: Sectoral Policy Networks in Advanced Capitalist Economies', British Journal of Political Science 19 (1989), p.157. The fact that the sectoral economics, in turn, are increasingly internationalised represents one of several challenges to cross-sectoral corporatist regimes. See J.R. Hollingsworth and W. Streeck, 'Countries and Sectors: Concluding Remarks of Performance, Convergence, and Competitiveness', in J.R. Hollingsworth, P.C. Schmitter and W. Streeck (eds.), Governing Capitalist Economies – Performance and Control of Economic Sectors (Oxford: Oxford University Press 1994), p.289.

33. P. Kenis and V. Schneider, 'Policy Networks and Policy Analysis: Scrutinizing a New Analytical Toolbox', in B. Marin and R. Mayntz (eds.), *Policy Networks. Empirical Evidence and Theoretical Considerations* (Frankfurt am Main: Campus Verlag & Westview Press 1991), p.28.

34. Ibid., p.42; and R. Mayntz, 'Policy-Netzwerke und die Logik von Verhandlungssystemen', in A. Héritier (ed.), *Policy-Analyse. Kritik und Neuorientierung* (Opladen: Westdeutscher Verlag 1993), pp.44ff.

35. For example, see Marin and Mayntz (eds.), *Policy Networks*; J. Kooiman, 'Findings, Speculations and Recommendations', in J. Kooiman (ed.), *Modern Governance. New Government–Society Interactions* (London: Sage 1993), pp.249–62; F.W. Scharpf (ed.), *Games in Hierarchies and Networks* (Frankfurt am Main: Campus Verlag & Westview Press 1993); more recently see T. König, 'Modeling Policy Networks', *Journal of Theoretical Politics (Special Issue)* 10/4 (1998), pp.387–8. However, a common conceptual approach to 'policy networks' was not developed: 'By definition of what makes a theoretical "fashion", this term is attributed great analytical promise by its proponents, whereas critical commentators argue that its meaning is still vague and that the perspective it implies has not yet matured into anything like a coherent (middle range) theory. What they agree on is their subject of concern, discourse and dispute, and that is sufficient to establish "policy networks" on the theoretical agenda of contemporary social science, without necessarily guaranteeing the declared value. On the contrary, a speculative oversupply of networking terminology may inflate its explanatory power so that some form of intellectual control over the conceptual currency in circulation, both its precise designations and its amount of diffusion, becomes inevitably a clearance process within the profession.' See B. Marin and R. Mayntz, 'Introduction: Studying Policy Networks', in Marin and Mayntz (eds.), *Policy Networks*, p.11.

36. A.G. Jordan and J.J. Richardson, 'Policy Communities: The British and European Policy Style', *Policy Studies Journal* 11 (1983), p.603. Also see D. Marsh and R.A.W. Rhodes (eds.), *Policy Networks in British Government* (Oxford: Clarendon Press 1992); and R.A.W. Rhodes and D. Marsh, 'New Directions in the Study of Policy Networks', *European Journal of Political Research* 21 (1992), p.181.

37. A policy community has a very limited number of participants and some groups are consciously excluded, while issue networks comprise large numbers of participants; concerning the type of interest, in a policy community 'economic and/or professional interests dominate', while an issue network encompasses a 'range of affected interests'.

38. There are three sub-dimensions: *frequency of interaction* (in policy communities, there is 'frequent, high-quality, interaction of all groups on all matters related to policy issue', whereas in issue networks contacts fluctuate in frequency and intensity); *continuity* (changes from 'membership, values and outcomes persistent over time' to 'access fluctuates significantly'); and the *consensus* variable that reaches from 'all participants share basic values and accept the legitimacy of the outcome' to 'a measure of agreement exists but conflict is ever present'.

39. Two sub-dimensions, i.e. distribution within network and distribution within participating organisations: a policy community is characterised by all participants having resources and the basic relationship being an exchange relationship in which leaders can deliver members; in an issue network, by contrast, some participants may have resources, but they are limited and the basic relationship is consultative, plus there is varied and variable distribution and capacity to regulate members.

40. Rhodes' and Marsh's policy community is characterised by the somewhat contradictory statement 'There is a balance of power between the members. Although one group may dominate, it must be a positive sum game if community is to persist'. By contrast, an issue network comprises 'unequal powers, reflects unequal resources and unequal access. It is a zero-sum game'. See Rhodes and Marsh, 'New Directions in the Study of Policy Networks', p.187.

41. Ibid., p.187.

42. Ideal-types never 'explain' anything. One may certainly add on to the original Marsh/Rhodes approach hypotheses from theoretical concepts in political science (for example

structuralism) and thus change it; see suggestions in D. Marsh, 'The Utility and Future of Policy Network Analysis', in Marsh (ed.), *Comparing Policy Networks*, p.185. When adding different potential explanatory variables, however, there is a danger one will end up with only an over-complex inventory for empirical research.

43. Without doubt, there is also some impact of the national on the European level but this is beyond the scope of this article.

44. The mainstream of scholarly writing on interest politics at the European level describes specific groups and their development without asking explicitly whether the pattern of interest politics is corporatist or pluralist. The focus tends to be on the number of groups in a given field and the date of their foundation as well as on specifics of group membership and reasons for joining Euro-groups.

45. J. Greenwood, J.R. Grote and K. Ronit (eds.), *Organized Interests and the European Community* (London: Sage 1992); S. Mazey and J. Richardson (eds.), *Lobbying in the European Community* (Oxford: Oxford University Press 1993); R.H. Pedler and M.P.C.M. Van Schendelen (eds.), *Lobbying the European Union* (Aldershot: Dartmouth 1994); Eichener and Voelzkow (eds.), *Europäische Integration und verbandliche Interessenvermittlung*; in J. Greenwood (ed.), *European Casebook on Business Alliances* (London: Prentice Hall 1995); and H. Wallace and A. Young (eds.), *Participation and Policymaking in the European Union* (London: Oxford University Press 1997).

46. Most recently see Kohler-Koch and Eising (eds.), *The Transformation of Governance in the European Union*.

47. Streeck and Schmitter (eds.), *Private Interest Government. Beyond Market and State*.

48. J. Greenwood and K. Ronit, 'Established and Emergent Sectors: Organized Interests at the European Level in the Pharmaceutical Industry and the New Biotechnologies', in Greenwood *et al.* (eds.), *Organized Interests and the European Community*, p.69.

49. A. Cawson, 'Interests, Groups and Public Policy-Making: The Case of the European Consumer Electronics Industry', in Greenwood *et al.* (eds.), *Organized Interests and the European Community*, p.99.

50. T. Grunert, 'Decision-Making Processes in the Steel Crisis Policy of the EEC: Neocorporatist or Integrationist?', in V. Wright and Y. Mény (eds.), *The Politics of Steel: Western Europe and the Steel Industry in the Crisis Years (1974–1984)* (Berlin and New York 1987), p.222.

51. V. Eichener and H. Voelzkow, 'Europäische Regulierung im Arbeitsschutz: Überraschungen aus Brüssel und ein erster Versuch ihrer Erklärung', in Eichener and Voelzkow (eds.), *Europäische Integration und verbandliche Interessenvermittlung*; and V. Eichener and H. Voelzkow, 'Ko-Evolution politisch-administrativer und verbandlicher Strukturen: Am Beispiel der technischen Harmonisierung des europäischen Arbeits-, Verbraucher- und Umweltschutzes', in Streeck (ed.), *Staat und Verbände*.

52. V. Eichener, 'Entscheidungsprozesse bei der Harmonisierung der Technik in der Europäischen Gemeinschaft. Soziales Dumping oder innovativer Arbeitsschutz?', in W. Süß and G. Becher (eds.), *Politik und Technikentwicklung in Europa. Analysen ökonomisch-technischer und politischer Vermittlungen im Prozeß der Europäischen Integration* (Berlin: Duncker & Humblot 1993).

53. G. Falkner, *EU Social Policy in the 1990s: Towards a Corporatist Policy Community* (London and New York: Routledge 1998).

54. See Cawson, 'Interests, Groups and Public Policy-Making', p.99.

55. As outlined above, many definitions of corporatism, pluralism and even policy network ideal-types have actually included the implementation dimension. It was never quite clear, however, how an empirical network should be classified that fits the definition in only one dimension, policy-making or implementation. Since Euro-politics leave the implementation of policies to the national level, it seems useful not include an implementation dimension here. Whether private interests are included in the implementation of EU policies and whether the national policy networks analysed are involved in, the implementation of European or national policies should, where relevant, be studied empirically.

56. Streeck and Schmitter, 'From National Corporatism to Transnational Pluralism'; Schmidt,

'European Integration and Democracy'; Schmidt, 'National Patterns of Governance under Siege'.

57. See Falkner, *EU Social Policy in the 1990s*.

58. In practice, this necessarily happens anyway since authors are often confronted with contrary findings on different dimensions of the complex typology but nevertheless have to choose one ideal-typical label for the specific policy network in the end. This is easier with a more economic typology.

59. This would then be a network of exclusively public actors (for example a para-state agency, a parliamentary committee and one or two ministries).

60. However, monetary policy seems to qualify, or at least it did before the establishment in 1999 of a so-called macro-economic dialogue of the European Central Bank with different political and economic actors (the practical significance of which, however, still remains to be established).

61. Kohler-Koch, 'Catching up with Change'.

62. In fact, one could also perceive a 'corporatist policy community' as a specific subtype of a generic-type 'policy community'. However, since both the exclusivity of non-state group membership and the degree of involvement are typically stronger than in a traditional type of policy community, it seems plausible to make it a distinctive ideal-type in a two-dimensional typology as the one presented here.

63. This fits in very well with the style where 'political goals are not just determined by (legislation, regulations and public administration) alone, but by way of the multi-stratified informal decision-making process between groups', where 'the state' is more an arena than an actor and where the upgrading of common interests is as common as the pursuit of particular interests. See Kohler-Koch, 'Catching up with Change', p.370. Accordingly, the EU is seen to perform process management instead of steering from above, while the boundaries between the private and the public become blurred. It is perceived to bring together interested actors and promote social learning based on discourse and political entrepreneurship. Ibid., p.372, and Kohler-Koch, 'The Evolution and Transformation of European Governance', p.32.

64. Whether or not changes actually take place depends on mediating factors such as institutions and agency at the national level. They need to be studied in much more detail than hitherto. For example, so far, we know hardly anything about whether and how specific party systems or state forms favour stability or adaptation of particular policy networks.

65. As already mentioned above, the definitions of various public–private constellations in EU policy-making differ. The following examples are necessarily taken from case studies with differing conceptual backgrounds and even thematic focuses. Nevertheless, the presented evidence allows the characterisation of the cases with reference to the policy network ideal-types developed here, even though the author of the particular study may not necessarily have referred to a network ideal-type or even a label such as pluralist, statist or corporatist.

66. For example, for the case of European monetary policy see Dyson in Kohler-Koch and Eising (eds.), *The Transformation of Governance in the European Union*; in tourism, see J. Greenwood, 'Tourism: How Well Served, and Organized, is "The World's Largest Industry" in Europe?', in Greenwood (ed.), *European Casebook on Business Alliances*, p.139.

67. Note, however, that this field has meanwhile been 'Europeanised'. Empirical studies might reveal statist clusters at the EU level, but they seem, in fact, less frequent than other policy networks.

68. In the sense of the definition used here, i.e. not assuming equal influence for all groups.

69. For example, as described for environmental policy by Bomberg, 'Issue Networks and the Environment'; for biotechnology by J. Greenwood, 'European Bioindustry', in Greenwood (ed.), *European Casebook on Business Alliances*; for water supply by W.A. Maloney, 'Euro Awakenings: Water Supply Representation in Europe', in Greenwood (ed.), *European Casebook on Business Alliances*, p.155.

70. A. McLaughlin, 'Automobiles: Dynamic Organization in Turbulent Times?', in Greenwood (ed.), *European Casebook on Business Alliances*, p.175.

71. See Falkner, *EU Social Policy in the 1990s*. The Maastricht Treaty established patterns where collective agreements between labour and industry (in practice, by the three players UNICE,

ETUC, and CEEP) formulate the EC labour law standards to be applied in the member states. It is always the same major interest groups who co-decide public policies with the EC 'state actors', i.e. the Commission, the Council and the EP.

72. Kittel and Tálos, 'Interessenvermittlung und politischer Entscheidungsprozeß'.

73. Karlhofer and Tálos, 'Sozialpartnerschaft und EU'; G. Falkner et al., 'The Impact of EU Membership on Policy Networks in Austria: Creeping Change Beneath the Surface', Journal of European Public Policy 6 (1999), p.496.

74. As in Austria, labour law issues are predominant also in EC-level tripartite social policy-making under the Maastricht Social Agreement (incorporated in the EC-Treaty at Amsterdam). For details see Falkner, EU Social Policy in the 1990s.

75. Falkner et al., 'The Impact of EU Membership on Policy Networks in Austria'.

76. Bomberg, 'Issue Networks and the Environment'.

77. The basic type of network was changed neither in social nor in environmental policy since EU accession.

78. This is crucial in order not to simply confirm our limited knowledge on presumably 'national' styles. Clearly, the meso level is not necessarily always the ideal level of analysis. In fact, the most appropriate level of (dis)aggregation (national/policy-specific/single decision) for a given research question has to be established in empirical research and may differ from country to country. With a view to interest intermediation, however, it seems that the meso level is the most adequate for comparative purposes. On the one hand, there is a rich literature pointing towards increased sectoralisation of erstwhile national systems; on the other, it is scarcely possible to disaggregate further and study, say, all single decision-processes in the field of environmental affairs for all (or even several) member states.

79. In the following sub-paragraph, the national social partners are directly addressed and asked to review such obstacles 'within their sphere of competence and through the procedures set out in collective agreements'.

80. Lenschow, 'Transformation in European Environmental Governance', p.9.

81. Ibid., p.17.

82. Streeck and Schmitter, 'From National Corporatism to Transnational Pluralism', pp.203ff.

83. F.W. Scharpf, 'Negative and Positive Integration in the Political Economy of European Welfare States', in G. Marks et al. (eds.), Governance in the European Union (London: Sage 1996).

84. Also see M. Green Cowles and T. Risse, 'Conclusion', in T. Risse, M. Green Cowles and J. Caporaso (eds.), Europeanization and Domestic Change (Ithaca, NY: Cornell University Press forthcoming), p.5.

85. Streeck and Schmitter, 'From National Corporatism to Transnational Pluralism', p.203.

86. Lenschow, 'Transformation in European Environmental Governance'; T. Risse et al. (eds.), Europeanization and Domestic Change; Knill and Lenschow, 'Adjusting to EU Regulatory Policy'.

87. B. Unger, 'Österreichs Wirtschaftspolitik; Vom Austro-Keynesianismus zum Austro-Liberalismus?', in Karlhofer and Tálos (eds.), Zukunft der Sozialpartnerschaft; E. Tálos and G. Falkner, 'Österreich in der EU: Erwartungen – Gegenwart – Perspektiven', in E. Tálos and G. Falkner (eds.), EU-Mitglied Österreich. Gegenwart und Perspektiven (Vienna: Manz 1996).

88. This is another indicator that corporatist patterns nowadays tend to be located at a lower structural level and fulfil narrower functions than previously. In particular, they often facilitate labour law and pay adaptations to EMU rather than being a macro-level governance pattern as was the case during the 1970s. See G. Falkner, 'Corporatist Governance and Europeanisation: No Future in the Multi-level Game?', Current Politics and Economics of Europe 8 (1999), pp.387–412.

89. For example, G. Fajertag and P. Pochet (eds.), Social Pacts in Europe (Brussels: Observatoire Social Européen 1997); and A. Hassel, 'Soziale Pakte in Europa', Gewerkschaftliche Monatshefte 10 (1998), pp.626–38.

90. Notwithstanding the possibility that, at the same time, European integration or the EU as an institution might promote corporatist patterns in particular areas by other means.

91. See Mazey and Richardson (eds.), Lobbying in the European Community.

92. Research designs based on ideal-types always leave a number of other potentially relevant dimensions aside. This article is no different. A further issue that would have led too far here are the potential influences of the substantive policy output of the EU on national interest groups and their relations. It seemed both useful and necessary to focus on the *forms* of co-operation here, not on the *contents or styles of policies*. It will, however, certainly be of interest to study empirically if, for example, re-distributive policy areas are characterised by different feedback into the national systems than regulative or distributive fields. Moreover, European integration might also have some effects on national interest group *structure*. They could not be discussed here in any detail, in favour of analysing *procedural patterns* and effects (which are at the core of interest intermediation, as opposed of simple interest representation). In the frame of studies following the design presented here, these topics must be tackled as empirical matters – as must be issues such as the balance of power between groups and group categories (see explanation of Figure 1).

93. It seems likely, but remains to be established empirically, that the EU features the most differentiated policy subsystems of all European political systems.

94. A. Héritier *et al.*, *Die Veränderung von Staatlichkeit in Europa. Ein regulativer Wettbewerb: Deutschland, Großbritannien, Frankreich* (Opladen: Leske & Budrich 1994).

Europeanised Politics – Europeanised Media? European Integration and Political Communication

HOLLI A. SEMETKO, CLAES H. DE VREESE and JOCHEN PETER

THE IMPACT OF EUROPEAN INTEGRATION ON POLITICAL COMMUNICATION

While the processes of European integration have advanced in terms of a common currency, a common parliament, and policy and legislative harmonisation and convergence, there has been little research on integration in terms of news and information sources. There have been only a few studies on how European affairs are reported in various media in Europe.[1] These involved content analyses of newspaper articles based on simple measures of visibility of European news and the valence of the stories with respect to European Union (EU) institutions.[2] We know of no studies to date that have looked specifically at the role and impact of European integration on domestic political news coverage. This, however, seems an important question as most of what Europeans know about contemporary political issues and developments in the European integration process comes from their own national news media. More than 60 per cent of the citizens across the EU member states name television news and 40 per cent name daily newspapers as the most important sources for acquiring information about European affairs.[3] We know little about political communication and news organisations from a comparative perspective and even less about how news differs cross-nationally in terms of the reporting of domestic and European political affairs. In addition, we have very limited knowledge about how citizens in different European countries react to news about European affairs and processes of integration. Nevertheless, there is considerable concern among publics and elected officials about the potential power of (un-elected) editorial gatekeepers and journalists to exert an influence on public opinion about political institutions and issues, via the daily processes of news selection and presentation.[4]

A comprehensive framework for analysis of the impact of European integration in the realm of political communication needs to take account of developments in four areas: media and political systems, media and political organisations, media content and potential effects, and media audiences and audience characteristics. In this article, we focus, first, on changes in media systems, and, second, on media organisations and journalists' role orientations. Third, we summarise what is known about news concerning 'Europe' and discuss the impact of 'Europeanisation' on news content. We identify the conceptual, theoretical and empirical challenges facing students and scholars of political communication in understanding the impact of European integration in member states. We argue that it is important to consider the historical, institutional and media system contexts, and patterns in news content, and conclude by proposing new avenues for research on the link between media coverage of politics and potential effects on audiences.

Research in the field of political communication includes political actors (politicians, parties), intermediary actors (PR agencies, media strategists, spin-doctors), media actors (news organisations, journalists) and the public/electorate. The dynamics of the interaction between these actors can be studied from a variety of angles, including, for example, the role of news in the political process and influence on changes in public opinion. Taking a cross-national perspective offers an escape from the ethnocentrism common to most research in the field of political communication.[5] Such a perspective 'provides an opportunity to examine how those involved in the political communication process – publics, political parties, and media – behave when operating under different institutional constraints and to consider the consequences of this for democracy'.[6]

Cross-national research has demonstrated the importance of considering the characteristics of the media and political systems in which political communication occurs.[7] An understanding of the historical, institutional and political and media system contexts of political communication shape such a perspective. In this study we focus on Britain and Germany as two countries that represent two interesting cases in terms of European integration. Both countries are large and strong European political and economic players. Germany, on the one hand, is considered to be one of the driving forces behind European integration. Britain, on the other hand, is known for reluctance towards Europe and internal divisions in public opinion about the euro and the European Monetary Union. We discuss the British and German cases drawing on a cross-national study of news about the introduction of the euro.[8]

MEDIA SYSTEMS

At the dawn of the new century, the European broadcasting systems look remarkably different from only two decades ago. There has been a structural shift from national public service broadcasting monopolies towards international and national broadcasting markets with competing public and private outlets.[9] Only 20 years ago, all European countries (with the exception of Britain, Italy and Luxembourg) had only public service broadcasting channels. By 2000, all public broadcasting monopolies had come to an end. This change is important because of the consequences it may have on the provision of public affairs news and information. Research comparing various national broadcasting systems around the world in the early 1980s showed that the more 'commercial' the form of financing the system, the less room there was in prime-time schedules for information about political and current affairs.[10] Recent changes in British prime-time broadcasting seem to support these observations. The most notable change occurred in March 1999 with ITV's decision to reschedule the *News at Ten* – its flagship main evening news broadcast comparable with the BBC's *Nine o'Clock News* – and instead offer a shortened early evening news programme at 6.30 p.m., with a daily 11 p.m. late night news headlines bulletin. This provision of news outside the prime-time viewing hours is structurally similar to what the US networks offer. In the US, with its free market in broadcasting and abundance of channels catering to all sorts of specialised tastes and information, there is not only less visibility of public affairs news in the mainstream media and in prime-time, but also less interest for such information among the public in general. Robert Entman has described the US – with its array of media outlets but few programmes rich in political information – as a 'democracy without citizens'.[11]

While the shift from public monopolies to competitive broadcasting markets coincided historically with the increased pace of European integration processes in the 1980s and 1990s, it is not an easy task to determine the relative influence of European integration on the changes in broadcasting systems. Neo-liberal trends in governance (irrespective of whether left or right was in power) in different European countries and in EC policies in the 1980s undoubtedly contributed to the changes. The changes in party systems, governments and parliaments, which all define the field of political communication, are dealt with at length elsewhere in this volume (see contributions by Mair, Goetz, and Raunio and Hix). Whereas the impact of European integration is perhaps only *indirectly* related to some of the general changes in the structures of western European broadcasting systems, it is possible to identify a range of *direct* and specific impacts of European integration on broadcasting legislation, ownership, and quota restrictions on cultural products. This impact of increased European integration, in turn, shaped the European broadcasting landscape in which political communication takes place.

Broadcasting

Legislation in the field of broadcasting and media was essentially a national policy issue until the early 1980s. International broadcasting legislation was non-existent, with the notable exception of the telecommunications sector addressed in 1987 and 1990 Green Papers on telecommunications and satellite communication and the 1997 Status Report on European telecommunications policy. Media policy and telecommunications policy have a long tradition as distinct areas of policy-making.[12] With new media technologies entering the market and blurring the distinction between distribution and content, the separation in policy-making was insufficient and a new generation of integrated communication policies was required.[13] The rapid growth in the use of the Internet has posed new policy challenges and has raised new issues of copyright and ownership.

The European Community most notably addressed broadcasting in the 1984 Green Paper on 'Television without Frontiers'. As Peter Humphreys notes, the 'initial impulse for a European-level media policy was the optimistic expectation ... that transfrontier broadcasting might give a welcome fillip to the process of European cultural and political integration'.[14] Anthony Weymouth and Bernard Lamizet add to this that much policy-making in this field stemmed from sheer necessity and challenges posed by transnational satellite broadcasting.[15] The 'Television Without Frontiers' Green Paper, eventually adopted in the Directive of 1989 on television broadcasting, was aimed at opening national borders for a flow of television programmes creating a single market for broadcasting, unhindered by national legislation.[16] The core of this Directive was generally in line with the notions of deregulation and liberalism as embedded in the 1992 creation of the Single European Market.

The 1997 update of 'Television without Frontiers' was implemented to address the challenges of primarily digital-related televised services, tele-shopping and regulations on advertising and sponsorship. The directive now addresses such diverse issues as the necessity for major events (particularly sport) to be carried on an unencrypted network, protection of minors, and restrictions on broadcasting violence and pornography.[17] The 'notorious' quota system promoting European programme production, as defined in the 1989 directive, was confirmed (see regulation on content below).

Ownership

The liberal European legislation has fostered a new environment for media ownership, with several cases of large-scale cross-media ownership. Especially strong European publishers have entered the broadcasting market, notable examples being Germany's Springer and Bertelsmann, and Australia's Rupert Murdoch. Non-press media companies as well as large businesses have entered the broadcasting scene with Italy's Berlusconi (Fininvest) and Germany's Kirch as well-known examples. The emergence of international media conglomerates goes hand in hand with national restrictions on cross-media ownership and European competition legislation. Britain, Spain and the Netherlands, on the one hand, have very restrictive regulations on cross-ownership of press and broadcasting, whereas the Scandinavian countries, Germany and France, on the other, have no or only limited restrictions on cross-media ownership. The situation today seems to be one in which both national and European policy makers are dealing with cross-media ownership by adjusting current policies to national situations.

Cultural Products

The initial policies of the European Commission concerned with creating a unified European culture were later adjusted towards a more realistic attempt to preserve existing European cultural diversity.[18] With the introduction of the Single Market in 1992, fears that dominant market leaders with a high production of low-cost programmes would gain in strength entered the debate.[19] The fear of North-American market dominance and small countries' vulnerability to large, competitive, neighbouring countries led to cultural policy intervention. A first step was made by the creation of the 'MEDIA' programme aimed at supporting European audio-visual production and distribution by initiating cross-frontier co-operation, prioritising small and medium-sized operators as well as respecting national differences and cultural identities.[20] A second programme, 'Audio-visual Eureka', merged cultural and industrial European policies by stimulating production of programmes to feed and create a market for the scheduled introduction of HDTV, while a third programme, 'Euroimages', was aimed at stimulating European film and television production.[21]

The issue of protectionist European programme quotas was controversial in the 1980s. The French government, for instance, demanded a 60 per cent European-produced programme quota in broadcasting, so as to limit import of programmes, mainly from the US. Wolfgang Hoffmann-Riem pointed to the contradiction in the policies creating a liberal, deregulated market, on the one hand, while calling for national, protectionist quota interventions and subsidisation on the other.[22] Both public broadcasters within Europe, who considered the French proposal as a limitation in their programming policies, and US media companies opposed the quota system. The US companies used the argument that quotas would infringe the principles of the international General Agreement of Tariffs and Trade (GATT). However, the 1997 'Television without Frontiers' Directive confirmed the quota system until 2002, when it is to be reappraised and, unless modified, to be continued. Individual member states are given some discretion and flexibility in interpreting and implementing the requirements for European programming, as the article reads that 'member states shall ensure where practicable and by appropriate means that broadcasters reserve for European works ... a majority proportion of their broadcasting time'.[23]

Several observers have noted that the attempts by the European Community to contribute to increased European cultural and political integration have failed.[24] One direction of initiatives was the support of pan-European media channels to increase co-operation in production and exchange of programmes for viewing. The European Commission supported the European Broadcasting Union (EBU) in developing two pan-European channels. Both the 1982 Eurikon experiment and the 1985 'Europa TV', a satellite carrying a pan-European consortium of European public broadcasters, collapsed within a year of their launch as 'neither viewers nor advertisers were attracted by the channel'.[25] These failures gave support to studies documenting that European audiences by far prefer to watch nationally produced programmes in their own language.[26] Two later attempts, Eurosport (a joint venture between Sky and EBU members, launched in 1989) and Euronews (launched in 1993), have proven more successful, but both channels play only peripheral roles in terms of audience ratings and are only accessible via satellite and/or cable television.

While media systems in most European countries have been affected by the initiatives, policies and regulations as outlined above, the impact in individual countries differs somewhat. Britain, for example, seems to have been less affected than its neighbours on the Continent by the trends towards commercialisation and deregulation in the broadcasting market, because Britain has had a competitive market since ITV was introduced in 1954. In terms of production, European policies have fuelled an already innovative production infrastructure by co-funding, for example, Britain's

Channel 4 productions. Germany, on the other hand, experienced the emergence of several new private networks during the 1980s and 1990s. Though German companies have been active participants in pan-European projects, it is still an open question whether the processes of European integration have led to major changes in terms of programming, because the preference for German language programming remains very strong.

In contrast to Britain, which has had competition since the mid-1950s, Germany has had a competitive TV market only since the mid-1980s. The BBC and ITV (now Channel 3) continue to attract the widest audience, while audiences in Germany are more evenly distributed across four channels: the two public broadcasting channels – ARD and ZDF (with about 30 per cent market share) – and the two private networks – RTL and SAT1 (with in total about 25 per cent market share).[27] The German public broadcasting channels clearly provide more news than their private counterparts.[28]

JOURNALISM AND MEDIA ORGANISATIONS

Just as the media systems have changed, so too have media organisations. New technology, new media, new generations of journalists, and the more competitive marketplace all contributed to changes within news organisations. Studies of journalism as a profession and journalists' norms and values, for example, have revealed interesting cross-national differences. While journalists' own perceptions of the roles of news media have remained broadly similar in the US over the past decade, differences in the role perceptions have been observed in several European countries.[29] This has important implications for the way in which both domestic and European politics are covered in the news.

Cross-national differences in traditions surrounding the coverage of political parties during elections in broadcast news may also be changing (potentially diminishing) due to changes within news organisations.[30] Broadcasters today pay far more attention to what the audience wants, whereas the public service ethos in the past meant a greater emphasis on 'educating' and 'informing' the electorate with special attention to what politicians had to offer. Take, for example, the recent comments of a political editor in the Danish public service broadcasting organisation on the low turnout in the 1999 European Parliamentary Elections: 'It is not our responsibility if the turnout is so low. There have been no issues to cover and we know from our survey that our audience wants to know about fraud and scandals, so that is what we cover.'[31] In Holland, the second Editor-in-

Chief of Dutch public service broadcasting echoed these sentiments: 'The low voter turnout at recent elections is not our responsibility. An increase in the number of people choosing not to vote is a statement that we must respond to. If the lack of interest is evident, we will also make a deliberate choice not to give the elections too much attention.'[32]

European integration, in particular, has had implications for the European news organisations in terms of their allocation of resources, strategic placement of correspondents and editorial staff, and choices for constructing news stories. The organisation of news desks in media organisations has been largely national, but advances in European integration have led news organisations to respond to the shift towards supranational levels of governance. As the Editor-in-Chief of the BBC *Nine o'Clock News* put it: 'Earlier we compared ourselves to America, today we are much more likely to compare ourselves to another European country such as Germany or France ... We now have bureaux in Brussels, Frankfurt, Paris, Berlin and Rome and we can tap onto BBC World's correspondents in places such as Warsaw and Vienna.'[33] The implications of European political integration for news organisations is echoed by the Editor-in-Chief of Britain's Channel 5 news programme who said: 'When setting up the programme, we had to decide whether to have a bureau in Washington DC or in Brussels. We opted for Brussels as almost anything that comes out of there has importance, directly, for Britain, much more so than what comes out of Washington.'[34]

The range and scope of implications of European integration for news organisations and journalists are likely to increase in the coming years. More news will come out of Brussels and the European institutions. One interesting aspect will be whether the changes in volume and importance of European news will generate a further redistribution of staff resources away from the national European political capitals such as London, The Hague and Berlin towards Brussels and Strasbourg. Some of the availability and demand for European news may also be addressed by increased use of advanced information technologies such as 'desk-top journalism' which implies access to a wide variety of international information from local journalism headquarters. Information-gathering and distribution technologies will definitely play an important role in defining the future coverage of Europe. The post-graduate European Journalism Centre, for example, has launched a series of courses for journalists on 'Covering Europe from your laptop' in which advantages and pitfalls for dealing with news about Europe from distant locations are addressed.

National news organisations are operating in increasingly international markets and one apparent dimension seems to be the closer links to

'Europe'. The shift in importance of European and Brussels-based news will continue to pose challenges for the organisation of political coverage in news organisations as well as raise new questions for journalistic practices.

MEDIA CONTENT

While the changes in domestic media systems and news organisations can be linked both directly and indirectly to the processes of European integration, little can be said about the changes over time in media content, particularly news, as a result of 'Europeanisation'. Previous research offers little in the way of systematic cross-national comparisons of media content about Europe or European affairs. The most comprehensive cross-national study focused on the first European parliamentary elections in 1979.[35] Looking at the television coverage in both the run-up and the actual campaign period, a cross-national team of researchers found that 'European issues' did not really enter the media agenda before the actual campaign started. With some cross-national variation, it was found that economic topics, comments about the elections and the 'problems, strategies, and mechanics of waging the campaign predominated the television programming in nearly every country'.[36] Although there has been some continuation of this research on news coverage of European elections in individual countries, the 1999 European parliamentary elections presented the first opportunity for cross-national comparative research on the range and quality of political reporting. This research, now under way at the University of Amsterdam, will compare media content across EU countries in the 1999 elections to study the effects of media system differences on media content, as well as the effects of news coverage on public opinion and voting behaviour.[37]

European integration and the EU are not only present in news coverage of genuinely European issues, but also are increasingly an integral part of national political and economic coverage. In a Swedish context, researchers concluded that 'reports concentrating on the national economic consequences of the EU for monetary union' was an important theme in national television news coverage of the economy.[38] In Britain, a similar observation was made, and it was concluded that press releases by economic players, including major European finance houses, were a central element in economic news in Britain.[39] But these studies, valuable as they are, had neither a longitudinal nor a genuinely cross-national comparative perspective.

The EU itself has monitored press coverage of European news in different EU countries for a number of years.[40] The publicly available annual reports provide one of few cross-national attempts at gauging media attention devoted to 'Europe'. The reports document the volume and priority of information about the EU and provide an overview of the attention focus of the press coverage. The results of the 1995 and 1996 studies, for instance, both suggest that coverage of EU affairs was focused on economic and financial affairs. Specific issues such as the 'mad cow disease' as well as the debate about the enlargement of the EU, along with social matters, also surfaced in the news. These studies, however, were limited in their sampling by including only two, often elitist, newspapers from each European country. This tells us very little about the total news environment's coverage of Europe, not least because television news was excluded.

Another data source for the analysis of how European affairs have been covered in newspaper and television news in the EU countries are the monthly *Monitoring Euromedia* reports. Drawing on these data, Pippa Norris concluded with respect to the period from January 1995 to autumn 1997 that most European issues received minimal coverage in the news media.[41] If there was coverage, then it cyclically peaked around the EU summits. Throughout routine periods, however, coverage of European affairs remained ephemeral. The predominant topics in the 33-month period discussed by Norris were monetary union and EU development; in other words, issues that journalists could use for further analysis. Norris also noted that the coverage during this period was sometimes neutral, but had usually a modest, yet consistent, negative-leaning slant.[42]

As the number and depth of studies focusing on the coverage of European news are limited, it is useful to look at studies of coverage of national elections in various European countries to gain some idea of the influence of European integration on domestic political communication. While comparative survey data have been collected over several decades, comparable time-series of media content are rare. On the basis of what exists from various national election studies, one may conclude that 'Europe' as a subject in the news did not feature until fairly recently. Coverage of Germany's 1990 national election, British elections from the early 1980s and early 1990s, and Dutch elections in the early 1990s shows that Europe was on the periphery of the campaigns.[43] In the most recent elections, however, such as Britain in 1997, and Denmark, Germany and the Netherlands in 1998, 'Europe' moved centre stage or at least provided the backdrop against which much of the political debate occurred.

A comparative analysis of the main subject of both press and television news coverage of the 1992 and 1997 British elections revealed that the category 'foreign affairs' (defined as 'Europe and the EU, relation with foreign countries') increased its share of the campaign topics from one to six per cent on television and from 0 to 12 per cent in the press.[44] In the 1998 German national elections, campaign conduct and the economy rated as the by far most extensively covered issues with foreign policy/Europe as number three.[45] Foreign policy/Europe accounted for an average of seven per cent of the television news stories about the election, compared to six per cent in British television news.[46] The Dutch national elections of 1998 also had a strong focus on Europe, in particular via the French–Dutch power-play surrounding the nomination of Dutchman Wim Duisenberg as the first President of the European Central Bank, which received extensive coverage.[47] Europe also surfaced in national political discussion in relation to recent elections in Scandinavia, though in a more indirect manner. During the national Danish election of 1998, for instance, eight per cent of the electorate mentioned European integration as one of the most important problems facing the nation. Immigration and refugees were more prominent issues in the media coverage, but as political observers have noted, these issues were inherently 'Europe-related' as much of the debate on immigration was centred on the impact of the EU-based Schengen agreement.[48]

One fundamental problem when examining the visibility of European issues in relation to national elections over time is the lack of comparable data. Thus, it is often difficult to extract in a reliable and systematic fashion data that would show the role Europe played at earlier national elections. Europe-related matters are often found in discussions of immigration, the environment, and the economy, for example. What were once domestic issues is now some combination of *domestic and European* issues. Studies of media content and effects in national election campaigns have to date not been designed to capture this shift, neither in terms of media content nor in terms of voters' perceptions of issues. A related difficulty is that the definition of Europe and the EU has continuously been changing. Not only has the number of member states expanded, but the whole concept of Europe has changed in the aftermath of the political changes in 1989. Moreover, European policy-making is not a process that is easily distinguished from national policy-making.

Another shortcoming of studies on the visibility of European issues in the media has been a lack of integrating theoretical frameworks. In an attempt to address this weakness, a more recent study of national news media coverage of European affairs during the period surrounding the 1997 Amsterdam 'Eurotop' Summit drew upon the concept of framing.[49] The analysis of news content identified five predominant frames in the news and subsequent experimental studies assessed the effects of these frames on readers' thoughts about the introduction of the euro.[50] One part of the content analysis involved analysing the frames used to report political news and European news in Holland. Reliable scales provided evidence of the key frames used in news stories in the major national news outlets. The most common frame in the news was the responsibility frame, and it was more evident in the 'serious' news outlets in the press and television, which presented more political and economic news, than the 'sensationalist' (or less serious) outlets. Responsibility for causing or solving social problems can be attributed to the individual or to the government. Results showed that in Holland responsibility was often attributed to the government. The predominance of the responsibility frame in Dutch national media outlets suggested the importance and potential influence of political culture and context on the framing of problems and topics in the news. In Holland, where there continues to be a strong and relatively undisputed social welfare state, the government is expected to provide almost all the answers to social problems.[51]

News stories about Europe were also framed in terms of conflict and economic consequences. The conflict frame was the second most common frame in Dutch news. The emphasis on conflict in the news reflected the political tension surrounding the 'Eurotop' summit and a general emphasis on the disagreements among the various political parties and within the Dutch coalition government. The economic consequences frame reported an event, problem or issue in terms of the consequences it would have economically on an individual, group, institution, region or country. The analysis of Dutch news surrounding the Amsterdam 1997 Summit showed that news about European integration was more often framed in terms of economic consequences than domestic political news.[52]

NEWS AND THE EURO: A CASE STUDY OF BRITAIN AND GERMANY

We conducted a cross-national comparative study of the television news coverage of the introduction of the euro in a number of European countries. The 1 January 1999 launch of the common European currency provided an opportunity for an interesting case study of the news coverage of a key European event, with potentially wide-ranging implications for domestic economies and politics.

Only 11 of the current 15 EU member states participated in the EMU from January 1999. Two of Europe's most important political and economic players, Britain and Germany, took opposite stands on the introduction of the euro. The British government chose to stay outside EMU and the euro, whereas Germany was not only in from the beginning, but played a key active role in bringing about the 1 January 1999 launch. An analysis of the television news coverage in Britain and Germany around the introduction of the euro revealed some important national differences in the way this common European key event was covered.

The majority of news stories about the euro were concentrated between 31 December 1998 and 4 January 1999. The following qualitative analysis is based on 35 English and German TV stories about the introduction of the euro; 11 on the BBC and ITN and 24 on ARD, ZDF and RTL. Despite the fact that these stories were connected to a common event, news organisations put considerable national spin on the topic. The national spin in the news media reflected the positions of the countries with respect to their support for the euro. News in both countries followed the chronology of the introduction of the euro, in other words, the appearance of the euro first on the Asian stock markets, then in Europe and then in the US. All provided pictures of the champagne corks popping among EU finance ministers and the pie as it was being smashed in the face of the entirely unsuspecting Dutch Minister of Finance by an 'anti-authoritarian protester'. All provided fleeting coverage of the public euro event in Frankfurt, which was a major public relations effort, and according to German news involved '10,000 people [who] were eager to form the euro symbol, with moderate success'. All mentioned the enormous costs borne by companies and governments for the conversion, and described how companies were working through the night to be ready for the launch. Finally, all noted that the launch meant there was now a currency to compete against the dollar, which had been world-dominant for so long. Only Britain couched this in terms of the negative repercussions it could have for the pound's place in the world.

British news reported the launch of the euro with some anxiety and trepidation, judging from the reports in the main evening news. News reports presented the launch in terms of the potentially severe economic repercussions for the domestic macro-economy and for individual businesses. There was a strong focus on the 'bottom line' and the economic consequences for Britain. It was noted how the common currency would be more powerful than their own and it was viewed as having the potential to diminish the importance of the pound on the world market, with the future battles being waged between the dollar and the euro. In that way, British news reporters noted, it represented a much bigger step toward integration than Britain wanted to take, and it was a fundamentally important step over which Britain had no control. British news sought to educate viewers about the economic facts of the euro, not only what it meant for the 11 countries that were in, but more specifically what it meant for them, the countries that were out.

The British television reporters went so far as to explain why people should not run out to refinance their mortgages in euros, despite the much lower interest rates, and advised keeping UK mortgages in pounds sterling because of the 'uncertainty' of foreign exchange rates. British reporters also went shopping in Euroland to show how the price of groceries and various household goods compared with British prices, and found the prices lower in euros. It appeared that the educative role of the British news was especially tailored towards reinforcing (or at least not challenging) the government's and the country's official position on the euro, and people were advised to take a wait and see approach before opening bank accounts in euros or buying a home with a euro mortgage.

British news claimed that London was the financial centre for Europe even though the country remained outside the euro. It failed to note that German news claimed Frankfurt/Main to be Europe's new financial capital. British news did, however, pay special attention to Germany's role in, and reaction to, the launch of the euro, emphasising the stability it would bring to the German economy. One story had full screen headshot coverage of an undubbed and unsubtitled impressive German soundbite from Chancellor Gerhard Schröder's televised New Year's address. Viewers were then told that the German Chancellor described the euro as 'the key to the twenty-first century' and that Germany was at the forefront of this development.

In comparison with the British tabloid press, British television's comparatively objective coverage of Germany's reaction to this event should be understood in the context of the general public's concerns about Britain possibly taking a backseat to Germany in the Europe of the future. It also followed a period of excessively negative and actually insulting coverage of Germany in Britain's screamingly opinionated tabloids, especially since the time of the British beef crisis a few years ago. The *Sun's* notorious front-page headline on the resignation of German Finance Minister Oskar Lafontaine – 'VEE HAF VAYS OF MAKING YOU KVIT' – is but one more recent example of this anti-German attitude in the British tabloids.

In contrast to the British reports, German television news looked for conflict and problems but had difficulty finding them. In fact, news in Germany viewed the introduction of the euro as a positive development with positive consequences for the national economy, but also as a non-event in terms of public interest. ZDF noted 'The Euro conquered the international finance market with a dream start. The German share index reacted with fireworks'. Showing politicians having difficulty opening the champagne in celebration of the launch of the new currency, Germany's RTL reporter said 'little troubles sweeten the pleasure'. They then briefly showed Danish people demonstrating against the euro and then, as a contrast, how children from 11 'Euroland' countries sent balloons into the sky. ZDF news said 'price stability was the most important goal' and that the 'typically German fear of inflation' was 'not justified'. German Minister of the Economy Müller described it as 'a stable currency valid throughout Europe'. German journalists concluded it was an event that mattered largely only to politicians and bankers. Politicians were seen celebrating, bankers were seen working, and the general public were seen as not thinking very much about it. One reporter noted that 'There was only limited interest in the euro', and a person on the street said: 'It is simply a different sense of, well, community.' The ZDF reporter then concluded: 'At the moment, however, the sense of community is confined to cashless payment.'

The qualitative analysis of the coverage in Britain and Germany surrounding the launch of the euro suggested that this European event played an important role in defining the national news agenda. Similarities in the choice of topics of the news stories, however, did not mean that the event was reported similarly. The national news media played an active role in providing a national spin on this major event. Nevertheless, our qualitative analysis of the news in Britain and Germany suggests that a conflict frame and, in particular, an economic consequences frame were most common across all television news programmes. These two frames were also found to be quite visible in an earlier study of Dutch coverage of European and EU events.[53] These frames also were shown to have direct framing effects on the thoughts Dutch readers had about the euro.[54]

THE MEDIA, PUBLIC OPINION AND EUROPEAN INTEGRATION – AVENUES FOR FUTURE RESEARCH

Future research on the links between public opinion, news and European integration will benefit from media effects theories. This may also enrich our understanding of European integration in that it encourages a perspective which not only focuses on what Europe does with the citizens, but also on what the citizens do with Europe.[55] Theories concerning media agenda-setting/building, priming and framing provide a basis for theory-building research on news and European integration. We conclude with a brief discussion of these theories and avenues for research.

The basic idea of agenda-setting was formulated in 1963 by Bernard Cohen, who investigated the power of the press to influence public opinion about foreign affairs: 'The press may not be successful much of the time in telling people what to think, but it is stunningly successful in telling its readers what to think *about*.'[56] After Max McCombs and Donald Shaw first advanced the agenda-setting hypothesis in 1972,[57] more than 200 investigations have provided empirical evidence that the visibility of an issue in the news influences the perceived importance of that issue by the public.[58] Agenda-setting refers specifically to the visibility and perceived importance of a problem or issue due to its visibility or salience in the news. Agenda-setting is limited to visibility, and does not include the valence or evaluation of that issue in the news or by the public.

With respect to public opinion and European integration, one interesting aspect to investigate is to what extent the mere frequency of the coverage of European affairs influences how important European citizens consider those affairs to be. One would expect that the higher the frequency of European affairs is on the media agenda, the higher the perceived importance of those issues will be on the public agenda. Equally important is the question of how media, public and European policy agendas are related to one another: Do politicians react to the media and public agenda? Or do politicians shape the media and public agenda and, if so, how do they try to get their issues and messages across? A focus on the interrelatedness of policy, media and public agenda aims at a process usually referred to as agenda-*building*[59] in which journalists and news executives play an essential role.[60] Agenda-building and agenda-setting might prove useful for tackling questions such as whether Europeanised politics can produce Europeanised media contents (or, possibly, vice versa) and if that translates into a Europeanised public agenda. Another question may centre upon whether Europeanised politics are mediated or mediatised politics and to what extent the European policy agenda and public agendas differ.

Whereas agenda-setting is merely concerned with the perceived importance of an issue, media priming goes further by positing that frequently covered issues also become the basis for citizens' evaluations of political parties, leaders and institutions. Media priming emphasises that what is available in the media and most readily accessible in people's minds is given greater weight in the formation of evaluations. Support for the priming effect has been found in different methodological and topical settings.[61] With respect to public opinion and European integration, one interesting question is whether and to what extent the predominance of a certain issue (such as, for example, common foreign policy in the wake of the Kosovo war) has influenced the overall evaluation of European politicians and institutions. Another avenue to pursue might focus on the idea of the 'Europeanisation' of politicians, such as the increased visibility of politicians in the context of Europe, for example during the EU presidency of a country. Yet another aspect worth investigating is whether the success or failure of EU policies, initiated by a politician, affect his or her evaluation in the domestic arena. One might also ask whether those policies have an impact on the public's evaluation of a politician concerning his or her general ability to push European integration further. It could be expected that negative news about European integration, echoing topics such as bureaucracy, fraud and agriculture, may fuel a negative and cynical perspective of politics and current politicians in other areas, and one might ask whether news contents and effects differ cross-nationally.

Framing analysis shares with agenda-setting research a focus on the relationship between public policy issues in the news and the public perceptions of these issues. However, framing analysis 'expands beyond agenda-setting research into *what* people talk or think about by examining *how* they think and talk about issues in the news'.[62] Although there is no single definition of news frame or framing, the ones that have been employed centre on three aspects: selection, organisation and emphasis. A frame then selects particular aspects of reality (thereby excluding others), organises those aspects around a central idea and, thus, puts emphasises on how to look at and interpret those aspects.[63] Framing *effects* refer to changes in evaluations, judgements and interpretations as the result of aspects made salient through selection, organisation and emphasis. Linking the framing concept to public opinion and European integration requires an identification of the predominant frames in the coverage of European affairs. Consequently, it can be asked whether the frames the media apply to European affairs translate into patterns the public uses to interpret those affairs. Do the media employ a European perspective or do they emphasise us vs. them aspects? Is news about European integration overly concerned with the 'bottom line' of EU policies, for example, focused primarily on the economic consequences for citizens and countries? A next step would be to investigate the extent to which those frames are mirrored in public support for further European integration or the opinions concerning the reduction of national sovereignty in decision-making. A recent study suggested that news frames did provide the audience with direction on how to conceive of European issues, such as the introduction of the euro.[64]

These brief suggestions for future research on the relation between media content and public opinion may help us to understand European integration not only as a top-down process but also as a bottom-up process. By focusing on the effects of the coverage of Europe, the process of European integration is ultimately reconceptualised from a too simplistic unidirectional flow with European integration as independent variable to a more reciprocal model with European integration as both an independent and dependent variable.

NOTES

1. J.G. Blumler (ed.), *Communicating to Voters. Television in the First European Parliamentary Elections* (London: Sage 1983).
2. Fundesco/AEJ Annual Report, *The European Union in the Media 1995* (Madrid: Fundesco 1996).
3. European Commission, *Eurobarometer 46–50* (Brussels: Directorate-General X 1996–99).
4. For a historical discussion of news coverage of politics in the US see, for example, T. Patterson, *Out of Order* (New York: Alfred A. Knopf 1993).
5. M. Gurevitch and J.G. Blumler, *The Crisis in Public Communication* (London: Routledge 1995); A. Przeworski and H. Teune, *The Logic of Comparative Social Inquiry* (New York: John Wiley & Sons 1970); D. Swanson and P. Mancini, *Politics, Media and Modern Democracy* (London: Praeger 1996).
6. H.A. Semetko and A. Mandelli, 'Bringing Culture into the Concept: Cross-National Comparative Research on Agenda-Setting', in M. McCombs, D. Shaw and D.H. Weaver (eds.), *Communication and Democracy* (Hillsdale, NJ: Lawrence Erlbaum 1997).
7. Cross-national comparative studies on the formation of news agenda during national elections in Britain and the US and the political roles of journalists in Western democracies found important differences that have been linked to the media and political systems. See H.A. Semetko *et al.*, *The Formation of Campaign Agendas: A Comparative Analysis of Party and Media Roles in Recent American and British Elections* (Hillsdale, NJ: Lawrence Erlbaum 1991); and T.E. Patterson, 'Political Roles of the Journalist', in D. Graber, D. McQuail and P. Norris (eds.), *The Politics of News. The News of Politics* (Washington, DC: CQ Press 1998). Looking at the interaction between politicians and journalists, two of the core actors in the field of political communication, distinct cross-national differences were revealed. US journalists, for example, were found to exert considerably more influence than their British counterparts over the formation of the election news agenda. Moreover, with respect to journalists' perceptions of their roles, a comparison of German and British reporters found that in comparison with the former, the British more often saw it as their role to provide analysis and be a watchdog of the government. See D.H. Weaver and Wei Wu (eds.), *The Global Journalist: News People around the World* (Cresskill, NJ: Hampton Press), pp.466–7.
8. The content analysis of the introduction of the euro was funded by The Amsterdam School of Communications Research *ASCoR* and The Danish Research Academy. It is integral to a larger study of news and European integration which includes two Ph.D. projects, one by Jochen Peter and one by Claes H. de Vreese.
9. For a discussion of the initial rationale for a public service system see P.J. Humphreys, *Mass Media and Media Policy in Western Europe* (Manchester: Manchester University Press 1996).
10. J.G. Blumler and T.J. Nossiter (eds.), *Broadcasting Finance in Transition* (Oxford: Oxford University Press 1991); J.G. Blumler, M. Brynin and T.J. Nossiter, 'Broadcasting Finance and Programme Quality: An International Review', *European Journal of Communication* 1 (1986), pp.343–72.

11. R.M. Entman, *Democracy without Citizens: Media and the Decay of American Politics* (Oxford: Oxford University Press 1989).

12. D. McQuail and the Euromedia Research Group, 'Caging the Beast: Constructing a Framework for Analysis of Media Change in Western Europe', *European Journal of Communication* 5 (1990), pp.313–32.

13. J. van Cuilenburg and P.Slaa, 'From Media Policy Towards a National Communications Policy', *Journal of Communication* 8 (1993), pp.149–76; J. Melody, 'Communication Policy in the Global Information Economy: Whither the Public Interest', in M. Fergurson (ed.), *New Communication Technologies and the Public Interest* (London: Sage 1993).

14. Humphreys, *Mass Media and Media Policy in Western Europe*, p.258.

15. A. Weymouth and B. Lamizet, *Markets and Myths. Forces for Change in the European Media* (London: Longman 1996).

16. R. Collins, *Broadcasting and Audio-visual Policy in the European Single Market* (London: John Libbey 1994).

17. European Parliament and Council Directive, 97/36/EC, 30 June 1997.

18. Collins, *Broadcasting and Audio-visual Policy.*

19. P. Sepstrup, *Transnationalization of Television in Western Europe* (London: John Libbey 1990).

20. Humphreys, *Mass Media and Media Policy in Western Europe*, p.280.

21. Ibid., pp.282–4.

22. W. Hoffmann-Riem, 'National Identity and Cultural Values: Broadcasting Standards', *Journal of Broadcasting and Electronic Media* 31 (1987), pp.55–72.

23. European Parliament, 97/36/EC, article 4.

24. Collins, *Broadcasting and Audio-visual Policy*; Humphreys, *Mass Media and Media Policy in Western Europe*; Weymouth and Lamizet, *Markets and Myths.*

25. Humphreys, *Mass Media and Media Policy in Western Europe*, p.258.

26. Sepstrup, *Transnationalization of Television in Western Europe.*

27. M. Gerhards, A. Grajczyk and W. Klingler, 'Programmangebote und Spartennutzung im Fernsehen 1998', *Media Perspektiven* 8 (1999), pp.390 400.

28. Ibid.

29. For the US, see D.H. Weaver and G.C. Wilhoit, *The American Journalist: A Portrait of US News People and their Work* (Bloomington, IN: Indiana University Press, 3rd edn. 1996). For an international comparison see Weaver and Wei Wu (eds.), *The Global Journalist.* For comparisons between German and British journalists, see R. Köcher, 'Bloodhounds or Missionaries: Role Definitions of German and British Journalists', *European Journal of Communication* 1 (1986), pp.43–64; F. Esser, 'Editorial Structures and Work Principles in British and German Newsrooms', *European Journal of Communication* 13 (1998), pp.375–405. For work on journalists in Germany, see K. Schoenbach, D. Stuerzebecher and B. Schneider, 'Oberlehrer und Missionare? Das Selbstverständnis deutscher Journalisten', in F. Neidhardt (ed.), *Öffentlichkeit, öffentliche Meinung, soziale Bewegungen* (Opladen: Westdeutscher Verlag 1994); W. Donsbach, 'Redaktionelle Kontrolle im Journalismus: Ein internationaler Vergleich', in W.A. Mahle (ed.), *Journalisten in Deutschland. Nationale und internationale Vergleiche und Perspektiven* (Munich: Ölschläger 1993); W. Donsbach, 'Das Verhältnis von Journalismus und Politik im internationalen Vergleich', in *Bürger fragen Journalisten* (ed.), *Medien in Europa* (Erlangen: TM Verlag 1993); K. Schoenbach, D. Stuerzebecher and B. Schneider, 'German Journalists in the Early 1990s: East and West', in Weaver and Wei Wu (eds.), *The Global Journalist*, pp.213–27.

30. H.A. Semetko, 'The Media', in L. LeDuc, R.G. Niemi and P. Norris (eds.), *Comparing Democracies. Elections and Voting in Global Perspective* (Thousand Oaks, CA: Sage 1996).

31. C.H. de Vreese, 'Public Broadcasting in Transition: News, Elections and the New Market Place' (paper presented at the Annual Convention of the Association of Education in Journalism and Mass Communication, New Orleans, LA, August 1999).

32. Ibid.

33. Interview with Jonathan Baker, Editor, *BBC Nine o'Clock News*, 23 Sept. 1999, by Claes de Vreese.

34. Interview with Gary Roger, *Editor Channel 5 News*, 27 Sept. 1999, by Claes de Vreese.

35. J.G. Blumler (ed.), *Communicating to Voters. Television in the First European Parliamentary Elections* (London: Sage 1983).
36. K. Siune, 'The Campaigns on Television: What was Said and who Said it', in Blumler (ed.), *Communicating to Voters*, pp.226–7.
37. The four-year research programme is funded by grants from the Dutch National Science Foundation (NWO) to Holli A. Semetko, Klaus Schoenbach and Cees van der Eijk.
38. B. Maartenson, 'Between State and Market: The Economy in Swedish Television News', in N.T. Gavin (ed.), *The Economy, Media and Public Knowledge* (London: Leicester University Press 1998), p.122.
39. J. Corner, 'Television News and Economic Exposition', in Gavin (ed.), *The Economy, Media and Public Knowledge*, p.55.
40. Fundesco/AEJ Annual Report, *The European Union in the Media 1995*.
41. P. Norris, *A Virtuous Circle: Political Communications in Post-industrial Democracies* (Cambridge: Cambridge University Press 2000).
42. Ibid.
43. H.A. Semetko and K. Schoenbach, *Germany's 'Unity Election': Voters and the Media* (Cresskill, NJ: Hampton Press 1994); P. Norris *et al.*, *On Message: Communicating the Campaign* (London: Sage 1999); H.A. Semetko, M. Scammell and T. Nossiter, 'Media Coverage of the 1992 British General Election Campaigns', in A. Heath, R. Jowell and J. Curtice (eds.), *Labour's Last Chance? The 1992 Election and Beyond* (Aldershot: Dartmouth 1994); H. de Vries and P. van Praag, 'De inhoud van het campagnenieuws', in K. Brants and P. van Praag (eds.), *Verkoop van de politiek. De verkiezings-campagne van 1994* (Amsterdam: Het Spinhuis 1995).
44. H.A. Semetko, 'The News Agenda', in Norris *et al.*, *On Message*, pp.73–8.
45. U.M. Krüger and T.Z. Schramm, 'Fernsehwahlkampf 1998 in Nachrichten und politischen Informationssendungen', *Media Perspektiven* (5/1999), pp.222–36; M. Schneider, K. Schoenbach and H.A. Semetko, 'Kanzlerkandidaten in den Fernsehnachrichten und in der Wählermeinung: Befunde zum Bundestagswahlkampf 1998 und früheren Wahlkämpfen', *Media Perspektiven* (5/1999), pp.262–9.
46. Semetko, 'The News Agenda', pp.73–8.
47. J. Brukx and C.H. de Vreese, *Het NOS Journaal & de verkiezingen van 1998: Visies op verkiezingsberichgeving* (Internal research report, Dutch Broadcasting Association, Hilversum, The Netherlands 1998).
48. J. Andersen *et al.*, *Vaelgere med omtanke. En analyse af folketingsvalget 1998* (Aarhus: Systime 1999).
49. H.A. Semetko and P.M. Valkenburg. 'Framing European Politics: A Content Analysis of Press and Television News', *Journal of Communication* 50 (2000), pp.93–109. This research was supported by a grant from the Royal Dutch Academy of Sciences (KNAW) to Holli A. Semetko and Patti M. Valkenburg.
50. P.M. Valkenburg, H.A. Semetko and C.H. de Vreese, 'The Effects of News Frames on Readers' Thoughts and Recall', *Communication Research* 26 (1999), pp.550–69.
51. This is in stark contrast to the US, where television news has been blamed for encouraging viewers to attribute responsibility for social problems such as poverty to the individual rather than the system or the government. S. Iyengar, *Is Anyone Responsible? How Television Frames Political Issues* (Chicago, IL: University of Chicago Press 1991).
52. Semetko and Valkenburg, 'Framing European Politics'.
53. Ibid.
54. Valkenburg *et al.*, 'The Effects of News Frames on Readers' Thoughts and Recall'.
55. In a singular and exceptional study linking media coverage about the European Union to public opinion, it was reported that a press, persistently sceptical towards the new currency, had damaged early confidence in the euro. Monthly fluctuations in the direction of the news coverage of that issue were related to changes of public support for the new currency. Yet in contrast to that rather issue-specific public opinion, an effect of the news coverage on more general attitudes towards the EU was not found – although the tone of the news about the EU was modestly, but consistently, negative; see Norris, *A Virtuous Circle*.
56. B. Cohen, *The Press and Foreign Policy* (Princeton, NJ: Princeton University Press 1963), p.13.

57. M.E. McComhs and D.L. Shaw, 'The Agenda-setting Function of Mass Media', *Public Opinion Quarterly* 36 (1972), pp.176–84.
58. For an overview see J.W. Dearing and E.M. Rogers, *Agenda-setting* (Thousand Oaks, CA: Sage 1996).
59. G.E. Lang and K. Lang, 'Watergate: An Exploration of the Agenda-building Process', in G.C. Wilhoit and H. DeBock (eds.), *Mass Communication Review Yearbook 2* (Beverly Hills, CA: Sage 1981), pp.447–68.
60. de Vreese, 'Public Broadcasting in Transition'.
61. S. Iyengar and D.R. Kinder, *News that Matters. Television and American Opinion* (Chicago, IL: The University of Chicago Press 1987); S. Iyengar and A. Simon, 'News Coverage of the Gulf crisis and Public Opinion. A Study of Agenda-setting, Priming, and Framing', *Communication Research* 20 (1993), pp.365–383; J.A. Krosnick and D.R. Kinder, 'Altering the Foundations for Support for the President through Priming', *American Political Science Review* 84 (1993), pp.173–90.
62. Z. Pan and G.M. Kosicki, 'Framing Analysis: An Approach to News Discourse', *Political Communication* 10 (1993), pp.59–79.
63. R. Entman, 'Framing: Toward Clarification of a Fractured Paradigm', *Journal of Communication* 43 (1993), pp.51–8; T. Gitlin, *The Whole World is Watching* (Berkeley, CA: University of California Press 1980), p.7; E. Goffmann, *Frame Analysis* (New York: Harper & Row 1974); W.R. Neuman, M.R. Just and A.N. Crigler, *Common Knowledge* (Chicago, IL: University of Chicago Press 1992) p.63; G. Tuchman, *Making News: A Study in the Construction of Reality* (New York: Free Press), p.iv.
64. Valkenburg *et al.*, 'The Effects of News Frames on Readers' Thoughts and Recall'.

Backbenchers Learn to Fight Back: European Integration and Parliamentary Government

TAPIO RAUNIO and SIMON HIX

Supporters of parliaments are bound to feel dejected by academic interpretations of the impact of European integration on parliamentary government in the domestic arena in Europe. According to the so-called 'standard version' of the 'democratic deficit', the development of the European Union (EU) has led to an erosion of parliamentary control over executive office-holders. At the national level, so the argument goes, legislatures have lost both constitutionally and politically. Constitutionally, a wide array of policy competencies has shifted to the European level, and the allocation and delegation of executive, legislative and judicial powers at that European level are decided by a collective agreement between the national governments. Moreover, these agreements are usually presented as a 'take-it-or-leave-it' package to national parliaments, where the only options for domestic legislatures are to accept the constitutional bargains without amendment or to reject the packages and plunge the EU into constitutional crisis. Constitutional bargains between member state governments have only twice been rejected by national parliaments. In 1954, the French National Assembly failed to ratify the plan for a European Defence Community, and in January 1986 the Danish Folketinget rejected the Single European Act (SEA), only for the will of the parliamentary majority to be overturned by a consultative referendum held in February that year.

Politically, in the control of European-level executive powers and in the adoption of legislative acts at the EU level, neither domestic parliaments nor the European Parliament (EP) are sovereign bodies. In the collective exercise of executive and legislative powers by the EU governments, the increased use of qualified-majority voting in the Council effectively removes the ability of national parliaments to force governments to make *ex ante* commitments before taking decisions at the European level. Also, despite its increased post-Amsterdam status, the powers and legitimacy of the EP are not full compensation for the loss of power of national parliaments. Moreover, through the centrality of technical expertise in the EU policy-process, the true winners of European integration have been bureaucrats and organised private interests at all levels of government and not directly elected parliamentarians – the traditional holders of legitimacy in the European system of parliamentary government.

But how far is this gloomy picture true? This study examines one central aspect of this analysis: the impact of European integration on parliamentary government in the 15 EU member states. In line with the other contributions to this volume, the dependent variable in this study is the process of continuity/change in domestic parliamentary government, with the latter defined here as the position of the national parliament in the political system and, in particular, the ability of the legislature to hold the government accountable for its actions. In the following section, we review the existing literature and present the dominant 'deparliamentarization' thesis. Next, the discussion focuses on developments in domestic legislative–executive relationships that are unrelated to the process of European integration, and the usual argument that the powers of European parliaments have generally been in decline since the Second World War. The analysis then turns to the specific impact of European integration. We show that notwithstanding the transfer of constitutional, executive and legislative powers to the European level, the overall impact of European integration on parliamentary government in the domestic arena has actually been rather modest. Despite some cross-country variance, a fairly distinctive pattern of institutional and political convergence in legislative–executive relations emerges. However, this is only weakly related to the process of European integration. As a result, the standard 'deparliamentarization' thesis needs to be qualified. While the executive branch – the Prime Minister, individual cabinet ministers, regulatory agencies, and bureaucrats – has strengthened its leverage in agenda-setting, policy preparation and implementation, the parliaments have also improved their position through more effective overall scrutiny of government, particularly better access to information. In fact, in some countries, European integration has been a catalyst in the re-emergence of parliaments. Legislatures, alarmed by governmental autonomy resulting from integration, have started to invest more resources in holding executive office-holders accountable on EU-related as well as non-EU-related matters. We discuss some theoretical assumptions that might explain this development, before drawing together the various strands of the discussion in a brief conclusion.

THE 'DEPARLIAMENTARISATION' THESIS

The dominant view in the academic and non-academic literature on democracy and European integration is that the latter poses a difficult challenge, if not a direct threat, to the former. The most pessimistic accounts see the equation as an insoluble dilemma. There is almost universal agreement among political scientists, including both integration and legislative scholars, that power has shifted further to the executive at the expense of parliaments and that traditional mechanisms of parliamentary accountability have been weakened. National legislatures have seen their position weaken both formally – through erosion of sovereignty – and politically, as the executives and the civil servants dominate decision-making on EU issues to a greater extent than on domestic matters. At the European level, the EP is only gradually gaining powers normally held by national parliaments and – despite the extended application of the co-decision procedure introduced by the Amsterdam Treaty – it is still far from becoming an equal partner with the Council of Ministers in Community legislation.[1]

A good example of this line of reasoning is provided by Joseph Weiler *et al.*, who argue that:

> the volume, complexity and timing of the Community decisional process makes national parliamentary control, especially in large member states, more an illusion than a reality. In a majority decision environment, the power of national parliaments to affect outcomes in the Council of Ministers is further reduced. The EP does not offer an effective substitution ... So Union governance results in a net empowerment of the executive branch of the states.[2]

Constitutionally, the issue is relatively straightforward. Powers that previously were under the jurisdiction of national legislatures have been shifted upwards to the European institutions, with monetary policy, agriculture, fisheries, internal market, external trade, and segments of environmental and consumer legislation the most important policy areas in this respect. Second, the ability of parliaments to control their governments on European matters is relatively poor, resulting from the use of qualified-majority voting and particularly from the superior administrative resources of the executive. While Council decision-making is still primarily based on mutual adjustment in search of compromises, national legislatures are to an increasing extent no longer able to veto legislation directly (regulations) or indirectly (directives) applicable across the 15 member states. However, national legislatures have themselves voluntarily conceded these powers, thereby signalling that the benefits accruing to member states from integration outweigh the losses to national parliamentary sovereignty.[3]

More developed arguments stress the political dynamics of the EU decision-making system. The 'intergovernmentalist' school of integration theorising, which stresses the primacy of member state governments, argues that the national executives have used the European institutions in a two-level game to strengthen their autonomy *vis-à-vis* other national actors, primarily the representative bodies. The dominant position of domestic governments in both national and European politics, combined with the constant interaction and policy co-ordination between the two levels, reduces the influence of parliaments at all stages of the decision-making process. According to Moravcsik, EU institutions shift the balance of domestic initiative and influence:

> by according governmental policy initiatives greater domestic political legitimacy and by granting them greater domestic agenda-setting power ... the institutional structure of the EC strengthens the initiative and influence of national governments by insulating the policy process and generating domestic agenda-setting power for national politicians.[4]

While the relationship between national executives and supranational organs varies between policy sectors, and depends on decision rules – such as unanimity versus qualified-majority voting and the type of legislative procedure used – governments, and not legislatures, are the national bodies striking bargains at the European level.[5] Through their regular participation in the work of the Council, cabinet ministers, civil servants and member states' permanent representatives develop an extensive network of contacts with both fellow governments and the other EU institutions. Obviously it is open to debate to what extent governments actually control the legislative process, as both the drafting and implementation of bills are primarily done in the hundreds of Commission and Council working groups, with the implementation committees usually referred to as comitology committees. In such a 'murky world of committees and expertise', national civil servants often possess considerable autonomy.[6] Even when the respective bureaucrats operate under tight instructions from the government, national parliaments are *de facto* excluded from the process. At the domestic level, governments defend policies agreed in the European Council and the Council of Ministers, presenting national legislatures often with a *fait accompli*, as the political cost of unravelling Council decisions, which frequently are complex package deals, is usually very high.

Notwithstanding such behaviour from national governments, the systemic features of the decisional process seem to favour the executive branch and insulate the representative institutions. Community decision-making is characterised by heavy sectorisation, manifested by the policy independence enjoyed by Commission Directorates-General, sectoral Councils, and EP committees; this sectoral autonomy is then replicated at the national level. Studying the impact of EU membership on member states, Wolfgang Wessels and Dietrich Rometsch recognised some common patterns in domestic decision-making across the Union:

> decentralisation and flexibility, strong sectorisation, high administrative co-ordination and low parliamentarisation ... Thus national parliaments – to a varying degree – lost in decision-making competencies in all member states, whereas the national governments, with the help of the bureaucracy, could strengthen their position and extend their scope of competencies.[7]

Politically, EU membership has been argued to reduce further the policy autonomy of the member states and their parliaments. Especially the single market and the criteria for Economic and Monetary Union (EMU) have narrowed the policy options available to national governments. While the potential stability brought by the EMU may actually increase the financial means available to national executives to carry out redistributive measures, the growing harmonisation of fiscal and economic policies curtails the ability of leftist governments to defend or strengthen the welfare state. Such loss of autonomy can be only partially compensated by European-level regulation, as social and economic redistributive policies are still largely decided by the member states.[8]

In addition, the development of market regulation instruments at the European level has facilitated the delegation of regulatory policies to independent agencies in the domestic arena. The delegation of the harmonisation of product and process standards in the single market to the Commission and the various EU regulatory agencies, and the setting of common competition and state aids rules in the single market, have gone hand in hand with the emergence of regulatory agencies in the domestic arena in Europe. As public industries are privatised, as independent central banks are established in preparation for EMU, and as new technical, control and product approval functions are delegated to private bodies, quasi-autonomous agencies take on many of the traditional functions of political executives or parliamentary bodies. In this multi-level 'regulatory state' final policy outputs are shaped more by the decisions of 'independent' bodies than the traditional 'politicised' or 'majoritarian' processes of parliamentary government.[9]

In sum, integration seems to impose on national parliaments a political environment where not only have the legislatures lost constitutionally, with power delegated upwards to European institutions, but also politically, as member states are involved in a political system where policies that strongly diverge from the status quo are to an increasing extent no longer feasible. And most importantly, national executives have strengthened their position at the expense of legislatures. From a parliamentary point of view, the conventional wisdom thus paints a rather bleak picture. However, to what extent is this alleged 'deparliamentarisation' a result of the unique process of European integration? We first examine changes in legislative–executive relations *independent* of integration in the member states before turning to the specific changes that have resulted from the process of European integration.

THE STORY INDEPENDENT OF EUROPEAN INTEGRATION: THE DECLINE OF PARLIAMENTS IN EUROPE?

Comparative studies of parliaments have sought to categorise legislatures with respect to their powers and overall standing in the political system. Since legislatures and national political systems vary quite significantly, the resulting typologies have been rather crude, serving more as indicators of influence than as exact approximations of their powers. Furthermore, the operationalisation of parliaments' influence is highly problematic, as quantitative indicators, such as the ability of the legislature to get its amendments accepted or the use of parliamentary questions, tell us rather little and such activity can in fact also be interpreted as a sign of institutional weakness. Stronger legislatures often do not have to rely on such measures, as they can influence the content of the bills before they are introduced in parliament. Such anticipatory behaviour is arguably particularly pronounced in countries with minority or Rikerian minimum winning coalition cabinets. Jean Blondel measured power as 'viscosity' – meaning the ability of the chamber to influence initiatives emanating from the executive.[10] In a more developed model, Michael Mezey proposed two yardsticks: the ability of the legislature to modify and veto policy proposals, or even to balance or substitute the executive's agenda with that of its own; and the support enjoyed by parliaments among the elites and the public, with the latter particularly relevant for the long-term stability of the legislature.[11] These analyses, based mainly on evaluations from the 1960s and 1970s, classified the European legislatures as exercising, all things considered, a rather modest influence on policy-making. Legislatures were portrayed as reactive rather than active, that is, reacting to and approving initiatives coming from the executive. More recent comparative projects led by Norton have arrived at a similar conclusion. The Italian Camera dei Deputati and the German Bundestag are normally ranked as the most efficacious parliaments, followed by the Scandinavian ones and the Dutch legislature. The British House of Commons, the Irish Oireachtas, the Spanish and Portuguese legislatures, and the French Assemblée Nationale are located at the weaker end of the spectrum. Not only have the respective country rankings remained largely unaltered, but there appears to have also been relatively little change in the overall influence of the parliaments.[12] If anything, their position has become weaker.

Modernisation and the imperative of party government have been identified as the two main factors reducing parliamentary influence. When combined, they arguably make control of the executive branch more an illusion than a reality. The 'modernisation' thesis claims that the sheer complexity, technical knowledge, and sectorisation characteristic of modern decision-making make representative bodies ill-suited to exercise any effective influence on governments; in turn, the latter rely heavily on the policy expertise of the civil servants. To put it bluntly, states operate increasingly like large firms, with emphasis on technical expertise, managerial top-down decision-making, and wide use of specialised agents operating under the respective ministries. Legislatures resemble shareholders' meetings, with the board of directors briefing them on government operations. In this situation, legislatures are largely left with their 'one core defining function: that of giving assent to measures that, by virtue of assent, are to be binding on society'.[13]

Perhaps the starkest interpretation is offered by Svein Andersen and Tom Burns, who view modern societies moving towards post-parliamentary governance, wherein legislatures are 'undergoing systematic erosion'.[14] Legislatures do make a significant contribution, but basically just through legitimating decisions made elsewhere. Parliaments simply do not possess the knowledge and technical expertise required of modern governance. Governments make extensive use of specialised agents and bureaucracy, which, in turn, base their decisions on information gathered independently and from various interest groups. Both policy initiation and actual implementation are delegated downwards to the various non-elected actors, as well as upwards to international and supranational institutions. As Andersen and Burns argue:

there is a growing divergence between the normative model of popular sovereignty and the actual practices of contemporary governance dominated by special issue and interest organisations ... Monitoring, overview, investigation, deliberation, decision-making is far beyond the capacity of a parliament (and its membership), no matter how large, how capable, how well organised, how specialised.[15]

Poorly equipped to monitor day-to-day legislation, parliaments, according to Andersen and Burns, should focus on long-term developments and constitutional questions, thus introducing overall coherence and legitimacy to the political system. While the modernisation thesis is correct in pointing out the limits of parliamentary control, the problem with this and similar interpretations is that they lack empirical data and tend to assume a glorious parliamentary past. That the latter in reality never existed has been confirmed by the above-mentioned comparative studies on legislatures.

Effective management requires, in turn, strong government. The member states have in the past decades moved towards a more executive-oriented system, with a powerful Prime Minister in charge of a cabinet, whose ministers have considerable autonomy in their respective policy fields. As Anthony King pointed out, the executive–legislative relationship must not be portrayed as one between two separate institutions, but as a more complex phenomenon, with significant variation across countries.[16] The government–opposition dimension cuts across the institutional divide, and is arguably the more significant of the two. As Philip Norton notes, 'what is remarkable about the legislatures is not their power to say no to government but rather their reluctance to employ that power.'[17] Since government survival depends on the confidence of the parliamentary majority, cohesive party groups provide the necessary means for providing that support. Instead of the whole parliament as an institution criticising the executive, checking the government takes place largely within parties, for example, through weekly meetings between government parties' parliamentary groups and the party leaders, including the ministers.[18] In member states with cohesive, disciplined parties – such as Austria, Denmark, Finland, Germany, Great Britain, Spain and Sweden – the executive and parliament are often so intertwined that measuring their independent influence in decision-making is, at best, very difficult.

The shift towards a more executive-directed system is clearest in policy initiation. As Norton points out: 'The effect has been to confirm or to shift the onus for formulating – or "making" – public policy onto government. Whatever the formal status of the legislature, the principal measures of public policy emanate from the executive.'[19] The resources available to parliaments vary, but in all member states the government, by virtue of its sheer size, enjoys a huge informational advantage over the legislature. Parliaments can at least partly remedy the situation through cost-effective legislative institutionalisation. As legislatures are in control of their own Standing Orders, they can implement changes that improve their ability to check the government. Research has shown that extensive use of committees facilitates stronger scrutiny. Committees with jurisdiction paralleling executive departments, small and stable membership and amendment rights, are especially well equipped to exercise control.[20] Committees organise hearings with government representatives, summon evidence from other relevant actors, and thereby gradually improve their ability to scrutinise legislative initiatives. Thus, legislatures with strong committees, such as the Italian Camera dei Deputati and the German Bundestag, are normally ranked as the most powerful in Europe. Of the weaker parliaments, the British House of Commons and the Irish Oireachtas have both started to make more use of committees in order to gain increased control over the government.[21]

With modest influence over domestic legislation, analysts have underlined the importance of legislatures contributing to regime legitimacy and stability. Parliaments and regular elections provide MPs and the electorate with a public forum for airing grievances. This is indeed a very important function. Representatives are subject to more intensive lobbying by interest groups than before.[22] Similarly, contacts between citizens and their MPs have become more extensive. However, public support for parliaments seems to be in decline. Strict party discipline, the representation of special interests, and the MPs' alleged pursuit of self-interest attract most criticism from the citizens. Moreover, citizens may to an increasing extent feel that national institutions, particularly representative bodies, are no longer capable of delivering the goods, as real power is seen to lie elsewhere: central banks (including the European Central Bank), large multinational companies, government and the EU.[23]

National parliaments can also transfer power downwards to regional and sub-national actors. Some member states have undergone significant constitutional reforms. In 1993, Belgium became a federal state, following a gradual, piecemeal process, which began in the 1960s. This federalisation was necessitated by the growing rifts between the two main linguistic communities, the Flemish and the French speakers, and had nothing to do directly with European integration. Power was delegated downwards to the regions and linguistic communities, thus reducing the competence of the national bicameral legislature. At the same time, the co-equal status of the two houses was abolished, and the Chambre des Représentants became the dominant house.[24] In Finland, the powers of the President were recently reduced, as the new constitution, which entered into force in 2000, strengthens the position of the Eduskunta and the government. This change was partly accelerated by EU membership, as the constitution was already amended in 1994 in order to make the parliament and the government the main institutions handling European matters. In the UK, the devolution started by the Labour government that came to power 1997 has transferred significant powers to the Northern Irish, Scottish and Welsh legislatures.

Having outlined the main developments in parliamentary government that have occurred independently of the process of European integration, let us now examine what impact, if any, European integration has had on domestic parliamentary government.

EUROPEAN INTEGRATION AND DOMESTIC PARLIAMENTARY GOVERNMENT: A CATALYST FOR TIGHTER SCRUTINY

Parliaments are mainly reactive institutions, casting rather modest influence on policy initiatives coming from the executive. In such a government-led environment, their legitimising function has arguably assumed greater importance than before. The technicality of most legislation, strong party government, and increasing globalisation and international commitments have all been argued to limit the real influence of parliaments, no matter how extensive their formal powers may be. The British House of Commons is the most often cited example in this respect. We argue in this section that integration is but one element in this process, and has not *alone* had any significant impact on domestic executive–legislative relations. Integration has also led to a positive spill-over, as parliaments have sought to strengthen their constitutional and political position *vis-à-vis* their governments.

Notwithstanding transfer of power to the European Union, the impact of integration on parliament–executive relations appears to have been modest. For example, in Spain, 'EC membership has not resulted in an excessive disequilibrium in the distribution of powers' between the *Cortes* and the government, and 'it is therefore difficult to evaluate whether membership has affected parliamentary custom'.[25] In Denmark, executive–legislative relations have not changed significantly because of membership.[26] The impact appears to have been strong in Portugal, and has gone hand in hand with the evolution towards a stable democratic country. Before and after accession into the Community in 1986, the Portuguese Constitution was gradually amended to bring it closer to that of the other member states. Amendments linked to the Maastricht Treaty in 1992 enhanced the role of the parliament in auditing the government and improved executive–legislative relations. As Jose Magone argues:

> In general, it can be observed that the Portuguese MPs are playing an important role in enhancing the influencing ability of its national Government. Executive–legislative relations have improved substantially since 1992. The European integration process seems to be a challenge to modernise and further democratise the present Portuguese political system.[27]

Considering the lack of empirical studies on this topic, we shall here focus on certain cross-national developments: the strengthened position of the Prime Minister, the increased workload of the parliaments, the growing relevance of the EU as a source of policy initiatives, and enhanced overall scrutiny of government through the establishment of European Affairs Committees (EAC).

With the partial exception of Italy, strong party government is the norm throughout the EU. The majority of cabinets stay in office for the whole electoral term, with cohesive party groups of the government parties providing the necessary parliamentary support. This executive dominance is strengthened by the EU, where national governments are the key decision-makers. Prime Ministers (and/or Presidents from Finland and France) form the European Council, which largely sets the political agenda and takes the most important decisions. The summits are highly publicised events and, apart from carrying enormous political weight, raise the profile and leadership of the heads of government. As the agendas of the summits include issues from virtually all policy sectors, ranging from the development of the Common Foreign and Security Policy (CFSP) to discussing the abolition of the sale of duty-free goods, Prime Ministers have a significant role in co-ordinating national EU policies. Cabinet ministers participate in the Council of Ministers, which is the main legislative organ of the EU. Thus, European obligations, including the Council presidency, encourage government stability. For example, in Italy, the goal of joining EMU among the first countries from the start of 1999, and the necessary economic austerity needed to meeting the convergence criteria, explain to a large extent the move towards a more prime ministerial form of government since 1992. Parliaments have tried to balance this through tighter scrutiny over government; the move towards committee-based organisation is seen also in adaptation to integration through the establishment of EACs.

However, the institutionalisation of committees is primarily explained by domestic developments, not by European integration.

One obvious consequence resulting from EU membership is the increase in the workload of the legislatures. The transfer of powers to the European level does not exclude national parliaments from the decision-making process, as the Council is composed of national ministers who are accountable to their legislatures. Scrutiny of Community legislation, implementation of directives and debates on European issues all take time and impose an additional burden on the national MPs, whose priority is domestic, not European, legislation. Parliaments and ambitious, re-election-seeking MPs may also find integration matters frustrating. The ability of an individual representative to influence European legislation is close to zero, and to become informed about Community legislation requires more effort than on domestic issues. However, improved knowledge of European matters is crucial, particularly due to the interconnectedness of domestic and European agendas and legislation. The number of issues handled and the number of laws enacted by parliaments have both increased as a result of EU membership. Hans Hegeland has calculated that during the legislative year 1997/98, 1,098 EU documents were submitted to the standing committees of the Swedish Riksdag, with the Foreign Affairs and Agriculture Committees receiving 60 per cent of the total. The House of Commons is estimated to receive around 900 EU documents per year.[28]

The EU is increasingly relevant for national parliaments in terms of policy initiation. Apart from Community directives, an increasing share of domestic legislation originates in the Commission or the Council. The EU and EMU, in particular, thus not only set limits to what is politically and economically feasible, but also serve as forums for policy diffusion. For example, in 1983–94 about 20 per cent of all Bundestag legislation originated at the European level.[29] It is very probable that the situation is more or less the same in other member states. Agenda-setting and policy initiation are, therefore, not only in the hands of the government; the executive's room for manoeuvre is also to an increasing extent influenced by European policy choices. This point is emphasised by Vivien Schmidt, who argues that:

> between court decisions, policy recommendations, standardisation procedures, or business and regional access and influence, the EU has in many different ways diminished the autonomy of national governments in policy formulation, limited their flexibility in policy

implementation, and reduced their control over national constituencies.[30]

Similarly, international rules agreed upon in the World Trade Organisation and other intergovernmental bodies have come to an increasing extent to regulate, or deregulate, the economic and particularly external trade policies of individual countries. Supranational EU legislation is the most extensive example of such norms that guide the behaviour of its member states. Thus, national legislatures operate in an environment where external trade and foreign policies are to a large extent decided elsewhere. While some MPs may lament this loss, it can also be seen as a positive development, reducing the legislatures' workload and enabling them to focus on matters in which they possess formal and *de facto* authority, such as education, taxation, culture, and social and health policies.

When entering the EU, a member state accepts not only all existing and future Community legislation, but also the primacy of EC law over national law. Under current institutional rules, a single national legislature can veto all treaty amendments, and thereby halt the integration process, but no single parliament can alter the existing system, nor indeed even make any formal initiatives to that end. As Michael Newman summarises:

> the EU is structurally embedded into the domestic systems. However, this inter-penetration alters the parameters for parliaments, which have traditionally sought to control their governments. For they are now operating in a situation where the source of legislation is partially external, and where they cannot legally bring about any alteration in the *acquis* or even promote alternative policies or laws which would conflict with those of the EU.[31]

The single market project and the increasing regulatory activities of the EU institutions have also resulted in an exponential growth in lobbying at the European level. In the domestic context, lobbying is primarily targeted at governments, particularly so in European matters where most legislation is decided by the Council. Commission, Council and the EP receive to an increasing extent information from supra/transnational companies or interest groups, which often simultaneously lobby member state governments.[32] This two-route lobbying strategy is not really open to national parliaments. Multilateral contacts between national parliaments, for example through the six-monthly Conference of the European Affairs Committees (COSAC), or party-based ties between national MPs and Members of the European Parliament (MEPs), have basically remained as channels for exchange of information, not for regular policy co-ordination. Findings of an elite survey from 1996 showed that national MPs had very low rates of contact with the various EU institutions.[33] This increases informational asymmetries to the detriment of parliaments, as the whole process of policy-making, from sketching preliminary drafts of legislative proposals to actual implementation, is heavily dominated by civil servants. For example, in the Nordic countries, integration has strengthened the role of civil servants, who appear to have become more important at all stages in decision-making.[34] To counteract such dominance by the executive branch, the House of Commons, Danish and Finnish parliaments, and the French Senat have established offices in Brussels in order to obtain relevant information and to provide channels of communication between the national parliament and the EU institutions. Apparently, national MPs also favour increasing interparliamentary co-operation. An elite survey from 1996 reported that almost two-thirds of MEPs and MPs favoured joint committees to examine EU matters and joint committee meetings. The majority of MPs also support stronger links between themselves and the commissioners.[35]

Regarding EU decision-making, therefore, national parliaments possess very limited influence. Alarmed by this executive dominance, all member state legislatures have established special EACs, whose task is to co-ordinate parliamentary scrutiny of European matters and to monitor the government representatives in the Council.[36] The main function of the EACs is to influence and control national decision-making on individual pieces of EC legislation. Member state governments have the obligation to submit to national parliaments Commission legislative proposals that fall within the competence of the legislatures. In most countries, legislatures have also the right to receive documents on the preparation of international agreements between the EU and third parties, co-operation in Justice and Home Affairs (JHA) and CFSP matters, Green and White papers, the proposal for the annual EU budget, and other Commission consultation documents. The government informs the parliament of its position, and the legislature scrutinises the cabinet position. It is essential that parliament is kept up-to-date, as the initiatives are often quite significantly amended by the Council and the EP. The extent to which legislatures delegate European matters downwards to specialised standing committees varies between countries. The system is most developed in Finland, where the standing committees of the Eduskunta must, according to the law, process all bills and are, therefore, routinely involved in scrutinising European legislation. But in the majority of parliaments the committees remain marginalised in European

TABLE 1
EUROPEAN AFFAIRS COMMITTEES IN MEMBER STATE LEGISLATURES

Member State	Parliament	Name of Committee	Est.	MPs (%)	Frequency of Meetings	Mandating Power
Austria	Nationalrat	Hauptausschuß	1994	15.8	Twice a month	Strong
	Bundesrat	EU-Ausschuß	1995	25.0	No regular meetings	Weak
Belgium	Chambre des Représentants/Sénat[1]	Comité d'avis fédéral chargé de questions européennes	1985	6.7/14.1 (+10 MEPs)	Once a month	Weak
Denmark	Folketinget	Europaudvalget	1972	9.5	Once a week	Strong
Finland	Eduskunta	Suuri valiokunta	1995	12.5	Twice a week	Moderate
France	Assemblée Nationale	Délégation de l'Assemblée Nationale pour l'UE	1979	6.2	Once a week	Weak
	Sénat	Délégation du Sénat pour l'UE	1979	11.2	Once a week	Weak
Germany	Bundestag	Ausschuß für Fragen der Europäischen Union	1991	5.9 (+14 MEPs)	Once a week	Moderate
	Bundesrat	EU-Ausschuß	1957	26.1	Every three weeks	Strong
Greece	Vouli Ton Ellinon	Epitropi Evropaikon Ypothesseon	1990	7.0 (+10 MEPs)	No regular meetings	Weak
Ireland	Dáil Éireann/Seanad Éireann	Joint Committee on European Affairs	1995	8.4 / 8.3	Once every two weeks	Weak
Italy	Camera dei Deputati	Commissione Politiche dell'Unione Europea	1990	7.6	Regularly, even 2-3 times a week	Weak
Luxembourg	Senato della Repubblica	Giunta per gli Affari della Comunità europea	1968	7.4	No regular meetings	Weak
	Chambre des Députés	Commission des Affaires étrangères et communautaires	1989	18.3	On occasion of important Council meetings	Weak
Netherlands	Tweede Kamer	Algemene Commissie voor EU-Zaken	1986	16.7	Once a week	Weak
	Eerste Kamer	Vaste Commissie voor Europese Samenwerkings-organisaties	1970	14.7	About twice a month	Weak
Portugal	Assembleia da Republica	Comissão de Assuntos Europeus	1987	11.7	Once a week	Weak
Spain	Congreso de los Diputados/Senado	Comisión Mixta para la Unión Europea	1985	6.6 / 6.2	Once a week	Weak
Sweden	Riksdagen	EU-nämnden	1994	4.9	Once a week	Moderate
United Kingdom	House of Commons	Select Committee on European Legislation	1974	2.5	Once a week	Moderate
	House of Lords	Select Committee on the European Communities	1974	1.6	Twice a month	Weak

Note: In several member states the name, composition, and powers of the EACs have undergone substantial changes during EC/EU membership. The frequency of meetings column refers to periods when the legislature is in session. The MPs column reports the share of members represented in the EACs. For Belgium, Ireland, and Spain, where a joint committee has been established by the two houses, separate figures are provided for each chamber.
[1] In Belgium, the lower house established an EAC in April 1985 and the Senate in March 1990. The two committees were combined in October 1995.

Sources: European Parliament, *De särskilda utskotten för EU-frågor vid medlemsstaternas och medlemsstaternas och ansökarländernas parlament* (Generaldirektoratet för utskott, kommittéer och delegationer, September 1998); Bergman, 'National Parliaments and EU Affairs Committees'; and data compiled by the authors.

issues. Before Council meetings, the EACs receive the agendas of the meetings as finalised by Coreper, together with government memoranda. The responsible minister then appears, if requested, in person before the Committee, and the MPs have the opportunity to put questions to the minister, after which the EAC decides if there is a majority in favour or against the government position. After the Council meeting, the minister reports back to the Committee, appearing in person if so required to give an account of the meeting. The same procedure applies more or less to monitoring European Council meetings and Intergovernmental Conferences.

The Austrian Nationalrat and the Finnish Eduskunta turned pre-existing committees into an EAC. Of the bicameral parliaments, the Belgian, Irish and Spanish legislatures have joint committees of the two chambers (see Table 1). The average size of a lower house EAC is 7.4 per cent of all representatives.[37] Members of the European Parliament are represented in the Committees in the Belgian federal parliament, the German Bundestag, and Greek and Irish legislatures. In Belgium and Greece, they have the same rights as national MPs, full voting rights included. In Bundestag, MEPs do not have the right to vote, and in Ireland MEPs can attend the meetings without special invitation, but possess no voting rights.[38] There is notable variation in the frequency of Committee meetings, with the EACs of the British, Danish, Dutch, Finnish, French, German, Italian, Portuguese, Spanish and the Swedish legislatures meeting on a weekly basis when the parliament is in session. Considering that the Council of Ministers holds around 100 meetings per year, it is reasonable to assume that the more often the EACs meet, the better positioned they are to control their ministers. All EACs have jurisdiction over the first (EC) pillar of the Union. Approximately half of the Committees have the right to handle second pillar (CFSP) and third pillar (JHA) issues. In other parliaments, CFSP issues are usually handled by the Foreign Affairs Committee.

The EACs of the Austrian Nationalrat and the Danish Folketinget have the right to issue binding voting instructions to government representatives. The German Bundesrat has the power to issue binding instructions in matters that fall under the exclusive competence of the Länder. Both chambers of the Dutch parliament and the Italian parliament have the right to issue binding instructions in third pillar matters. The strong mandating position of the Danish Europaudvalget *vis-à-vis* the national government has aroused both admiration and criticism outside Denmark. To what extent the EACs make use of their mandating power is a matter requiring further investigation. In practice, such mandating is bound to be selective, as parliaments do not have the information and resources of the executive. For example, in Austria, the Hauptausschuß has made quite limited use of its strong constitutional powers to mandate the government, selecting for deliberation and issuing opinions only in a very small number of cases. Second, excessively tight voting instructions may be counterproductive, as Council decisions are often complex package deals, involving considerable last-minute bargaining between the governments.[39] Even when the minister acts as the agent of the legislature, that is, on the basis of parliament's instructions, the possibility for shirking is always present due to informational asymmetries. However, the strong mandating position acts as an important pre-empting mechanism, encouraging governments to engage in a wider consultation and negotiation process than might otherwise be the case.

While the establishment of EACs shows that there is substantial convergence in organisational adaptation, the main difference between the legislatures lies in their level of activity. Comparative research indicates that the variation is primarily explained by two factors: the role of the parliament in the political system of the member state, and public and party opinion on European integration. The key variable has been argued to be the executive–legislature relationship, with the parliament controlling the government to the same extent in European matters as it does in the context of domestic legislation. Similarly, the contentiousness of the European dimension is important, with countries where integration issues produce divisions within parties and among the public adopting tighter scrutiny mechanisms.[40]

Integration has also led to constitutional amendments that have strengthened the ability of the legislature to control the executive. The transposition of directives into domestic legislation, particularly in the context of the Single Market project, was an unwelcome reminder of the erosion of national sovereignty. In several member states, constitutional amendments were introduced in the wake of the Maastricht Treaty in order to improve parliamentary scrutiny on European questions.[41] In Germany, for example, the Basic Law was amended in December 1992, giving the Bundestag and the Bundesrat better access to information on European issues.[42] In Portugal, following Maastricht, monitoring integration was extended to all standing committees, and Assembleia's competence to monitor European issues was enshrined in the Constitution. According to a further law (20/94), the government is obliged to present an annual report on integration, which is then debated by all the committees and finally by the whole chamber.[43] In France, Article 88 of the Constitution was amended to give the parliament stronger rights over information on European legislation.[44] Improved access to information on European matters has been the norm throughout the Union, and this has already in some countries begun to spill over to domestic legislation as well. In Ireland, O'Halpin points out that more powerful scrutiny by Oireachtas on EC issues 'has coincided with changes in the pattern of domestic politics, with the emergence of coalitions as the dominant model of government and with a modest strengthening of the legislature's powers of oversight and enquiry through specialist committees such as the JCFA'.[45] In Finland, the tight scrutiny mechanism adopted to monitor the government on European matters has spilled over to other committees, with ministers appearing in person in the specialised committees much more frequently than before. Thus, integration has benefited the overall scrutiny of government behaviour.

Moreover, EU membership means that national parliaments participate, through their government, in a decision process that produces binding laws applicable in the 15 member states, the European Economic Area (EEA) countries, and to a growing extent, in the east and central European membership applicant states. Previously, legislatures played only a secondary role in foreign policy issues, and their influence was mainly restricted to ratifying international treaties negotiated by the executives. The opposition parties were even more marginalised. While ratification was often accompanied by critical debates, parliaments had little, if any, say over the substance of the agreements.[46] Now the situation has changed, and at least potentially national parliaments can wield considerably more influence than before. National legislatures, through their governments, can seek to influence EC legislation, which then becomes the norm throughout the 15 member states. This applies especially to routine Community legislation, where the cleavage lines vary. Matters are not simply decided on the most often mentioned integration/anti-integration or neo-liberalism/ interventionism dimensions; other dimensions, too, have become increasingly significant. In such a multidimensional political space, member state governments, and thereby parliaments, can accordingly seek to gain outcomes close to their ideal points, especially when qualified-majority voting is applied in the Council.

In conclusion, all things considered, the impact of integration on domestic parliamentary government has been modest. Constitutionally, the situation has naturally changed dramatically, as considerable powers have been shifted to the European level. Apart from such deepening of integration, which all member state legislatures have supported or at least grudgingly consented to, any weakening of parliamentarism is only partly attributable to the European Union. Von Beyme is right to emphasise the changed role of national legislatures: decisions are *de facto* taken in informal discussions between sectoral policy experts, especially in corporatist countries, and between heads of government, for example in the European Council. The main function of parliaments is to act as the formal framework in which decisions reached elsewhere are accepted or ratified. The legislature thus remains sovereign, but has seldom any impact on the contents of the issues.[47] Evidence indicates that integration has mainly accentuated already existing trends rather than acted as a catalyst for change. Integration has, therefore, reinforced changes that were already taking place. Parliaments have recently sought to balance this strong executive dominance through tighter overall government scrutiny. Such efforts have at least in part been undertaken in response to integration, as legislatures have recognised the need to reassert themselves in European matters in order to gain more influence over domestic politics.

THEORETICAL ANALYSIS: PARTY COMPETITION AND INFORMATION IN THE EUROPEAN PARLIAMENTARY-GOVERNMENT MODEL

The above analysis and empirical findings point to an interesting anomaly. First, most general legislative scholars contend that European parliaments have been in decline *vis-à-vis* executives since the 1950s. Second, several leading scholars of European integration argue (without testing the arguments on empirical evidence) that European integration has contributed to the process of strengthening executives against parliaments. But, surveying the empirical evidence, we find that this is simply not the case. Instead, controlling for the general decline of parliaments against executives, one could argue that in the area of EU affairs, since the beginning of the 1990s, parliaments have actually made some important gains against governments. This argument is summarised in Figure 1.

For a variety of reasons – such as the expansion of the size of the executive, the increasingly technical nature of contemporary legislation, the increased organisational power of party leaderships over parliamentary rank-and-file members – the control of the executive by parliaments has generally declined since the 1950s. This has occurred independently of the process of European integration – as is shown by the upper trend-line in Figure 1. Whether deliberately or unintentionally, European integration has involved the delegation of executive, legislative and judicial powers in an ever-increasing list of public policies to a new political centre – away from domestic parliamentary scrutiny and party competition.

FIGURE 1
THE IMPACT OF EUROPEAN INTEGRATION ON PARLIAMENT-EXECUTIVE
RELATIONS

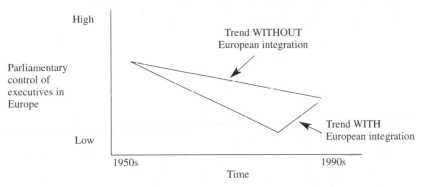

However, in the 1990s, parliaments began gradually to fight back. Across Europe, European Affairs Committees emerged, with a wide political mandate to scrutinise the legislative, executive and constitutional actions of national political and administrative executive office-holders at the European level. The result is that at the end of 1990s it was almost impossible to differentiate between the general decline of parliaments and the decline of parliaments as a result of the process of European integration – in Figure 1, the lower trend-line finishes at almost the same point as the upper trend-line.

But, how can this be explained? The key is the role of 'information' in the process of party competition in the European model of parliamentary government. The role of information has recently become a mainstay of theories of legislative competition in the United States Congress – starting from the theoretical assumptions proposed by Keith Krehbiel.[48] Traditional models of legislative behaviour and organisation in the US assumed that to gain re-election, legislators must secure legislative outputs that promote or protect the interests of their constituents and supporters.[49] As a result, legislators join committees that cover policy areas related to their constituents' concerns.[50] For example, legislators from rural areas try to gain positions of power on the agriculture committee. Against this view, Krehbiel contends that legislators also have important informational requirements: in order to know what positions to take in the legislative process to secure efficient policy outcomes or to promote the interests of their constituents. As a result, against the theory of legislative behaviour and organisation based on the idea that legislators aim to 'gain from exchange', the informational model sees legislative competition as a mix of common and competing informational requirements.

The European context of parliamentary government and electoral competition and legislative–executive relations controlled by powerful party organisations, interests and ideologies is very different. However, similar theoretical arguments can be applied. The traditional conceptualisation of parliamentary government is somewhat similar to the gains-from-exchange theory of congressional politics. Either to gain votes, or to secure political office, or to promote policy goals for their own sake, political parties need to secure policy outputs from the legislative and executive processes to promote and protect the interests of their constituents.[51] Where parties can form one-party governments, they usually do not need to compromise on their electorate promises. However, where coalition government is the norm – as is the case in most member states – party elites become involved in similar sorts of policy exchanges that occur in the US Congress.

But information is also key to the European parliamentary government process. A central element of the 'parliamentary decline' thesis is that governments have dominated parliaments because they have more access to information in the policy process than opposition parties or backbench parliamentarians. This is particularly pertinent in regard to parliamentary scrutiny of government actions in EU affairs – where EU actions are often highly technical, and national ministers and bureaucrats have a virtual monopoly of information and technical expertise. In other words, the argument that European integration has reduced the power of parliaments against executives is implicitly an application of a Krehbiel-type analysis: that the political actors with more access to quality information can use this to gain advantage in the electoral arena.

However, parliaments have secured gains from governments in the area of EU affairs precisely because it has been in the interests of parliamentarians to reduce the information gap. As in the creation of certain committees in the US Congress, the driving force behind the creation of EACs have been legislators with common informational requirements, rather than the need to engage in vote-trading. In particular, realising that an information gap has been emerging in the area of EU affairs, opposition parties were eager to use EACs to gain access to European documents at early stages in the EU policy process and also to force ministers and bureaucrats to explain their actions in the European arena. This information can then be used in the process of domestic party competition – in the preparation of party policy positions on European issues in party manifestos and other policy documents.[52] In addition, EACs have often been filled with independently minded backbench parliamentarians from governing parties. Isolated from party leaderships, these politicians can use their committee membership to gain access to information about their party elites' actions, which they can use to their advantage in internal party disputes and competition for leadership positions.

Internal party divisions over Europe facilitate such parliamentary assertiveness. As Mezey notes, 'no matter how many parties are functioning, when party discipline decreases, the power of the legislature increases'.[53] Based on the traditional societal cleavages well established in political science literature, and with the left–right dimension forming the dominant structure of competition in each EU member state, national parties have often faced serious internal fragmentation on integration matters. Considering the broad, cross-party pro-European consensus in the majority of member states, and the lack of congruence between elites and the electorate, the more Eurosceptical national MPs in particular can benefit from the situation. There is indeed some preliminary evidence that opposition MPs as well as more Eurosceptical members from government parties have been particularly active in the EACs. In the EU-*nämnden* of the Swedish Riksdag in 1995–96, the Moderate Party, which was in opposition, and the Left Party and the Green Party, both of which are highly critical of the EU, were, according to the verbatim records, far more active than the ruling Social Democrats.[54] The same applies to the EACs of the British House of Commons and the French National Assembly, where the more Eurocritical MPs have been most active in European questions.[55]

CONCLUSION

Overall, the ability of parliaments to control executives has declined since the 1950s, and the process of European integration is certainly one of the reasons why this has happened – providing executives with an arena for action away from domestic parliamentary scrutiny, and a monopoly on information in an ever larger portfolio of public policies. However, when looking empirically at the impact of the European integration on parliamentary government in Europe, we find that during the 1990s most parliaments in Europe established institutions and mechanisms that forced governments to explain their EU policies and actions in the European arena to parliaments. The driving force behind this partial reassertion has been the desire by non-governing parties and backbench parliamentarians to redress the 'information gap' between governing elites and the parliamentary rank-and-file.

Despite such improvements, the 1996 elite survey showed that the overwhelming majority of parliamentarians throughout the Union thought that national parliamentary scrutiny of EU decision-making was too weak and should be strengthened.[56] At the same time, national MPs thought that the European Parliament should have more influence on EU decision-making than national legislatures, with only the Swedish MPs ranking the institutions in the opposite order.[57] The responses indicate that while MPs are dissatisfied with domestic parliamentary supervision, the majority of them also feel that controlling EU decision-making is primarily a job of the EP. Moreover, national MPs are also broadly pro-European, favouring further transfer of competencies to the European level.[58] National parliaments find themselves in a structurally awkward situation: their input is piecemeal, consisting primarily of scrutinising individual pieces of European legislation, and their main job is domestic, not EU, politics.

However, efficient scrutiny of European matters is significant also in terms of national legislation, as the policy choices adopted at the European level increasingly affect and constrain member states' domestic politics. Detailed scrutiny of EU issues, therefore, contributes to supervision on domestic matters and reduces the informational advantage of the executive. On the other hand, parliaments that do not invest resources in European questions also undermine their ability to check on the government on domestic matters.

NOTES

We are grateful to the other project participants for their insightful comments. We are particularly indebted to Roger Scully for his perceptive criticisms of our earlier draft. Erik Damgaard, Cristina Leston-Bandeira, Wolfgang Müller, Georgios Trantas and Luca Verzichelli provided valuable information on country-specific developments.

1. See J. Coultrap, 'From Parliamentarism to Pluralism: Models of Democracy and the European Union's "Democratic Deficit"', *Journal of Theoretical Politics* 11 (1999), pp.107–35; B. Kohler-Koch, 'Die Europäisierung nationaler Demokratien: Verschleiß eines europäischen Kulturerbes?', in M.T. Greven (ed.), *Demokratie – eine Kultur des Westens?* (Opladen: Leske + Budrich 1998) pp.263–88; C. Lord, *Democracy in the European Union* (Sheffield: Sheffield Academic Press 1998); W. Merkel, 'Legitimacy and Democracy: Endogenous Limits of European Integration', in J.J. Anderson (ed.), *Regional Integration and Democracy: Expanding on the European Experience* (Lanham, MD: Rowman & Littlefield 1999), pp.45–67; M. Newman, *Democracy, Sovereignty and the European Union* (London: Hurst & Company 1996); K. Neunreither, 'The Democratic Deficit of the European Union: Towards Closer Cooperation between the European Parliament and the National Parliaments', *Government and Opposition* 29 (1994), pp.299–314; M.P. Smith, 'Democratic Legitimacy in the European Union: Fulfilling the Institutional Logic', *Journal of Legislative Studies* 2 (1996), pp.283–301; M. Telò (ed.), *Democratie et Construction Européenne* (Brussels: Editions de l'Université de Bruxelles 1995); J.H.H. Weiler, U.R. Haltern and F.C. Mayer, 'European Democracy and Its Critique', *West European Politics* 18 (1995), pp.4–39;

B. Wessels and R.S. Katz, 'Introduction: European Parliament, National Parliaments, and European Integration', in R.S. Katz and B. Wessels (eds.), *The European Parliament, the National Parliaments, and European Integration* (Oxford: Oxford University Press 1999), pp.3–18; S. Williams, 'Sovereignty and Accountability in the European Community', *Political Quarterly* 60 (1990), pp.299–317; and D. Wincott, 'Does the European Union Pervert Democracy? Questions of Democracy in New Constitutionalist Thought on the Future of Europe', *European Law Journal* 4 (1998), pp.411–28.

2. Weiler *et al.*, 'European Democracy and Its Critique', p.7.
3. See T. Raunio, 'Always One Step Behind? National Legislatures and the European Union', *Government and Opposition* 34 (1999), pp.180–202.
4. A. Moravcsik, 'Preferences and Power in the European Community: A Liberal Intergovernmentalist Approach', *Journal of Common Market Studies* 31 (1993), pp.473–524.
5. There is a rapidly growing theoretical and empirical literature on the autonomy of national executives and supranational institutions in EU decision-making. See, for example, S. Hix, *The Political System of the European Union* (Basingstoke: Macmillan 1999); J. Peterson and E. Bomberg, *Decision-Making in the European Union* (Basingstoke: Macmillan 1999); and W. Sandholtz and A. Stone Sweet (eds.), *European Integration and Supranational Governance* (Oxford: Oxford University Press 1998).
6. Wincott, 'Does the European Union Pervert Democracy?', p.413. On the role of committees and comitology, see, for example, R. Dogan, 'Comitology: Little Procedures with Big Implications', *West European Politics* 20 (1997), pp.31–60; R.H. Pedler and G.F. Schaefer (eds.), *Shaping European Law and Policy: The Role of Committees and Comitology in the Political Process* (Maastricht: EIPA 1996); and W. Wessels, 'Comitology: Fusion in Action. Politico-Administrative Trends in the EU System', *Journal of European Public Policy* 5 (1998), pp.209–34.
7. W. Wessels and D. Rometsch, 'Conclusion: European Union and National Institutions', in D. Rometsch and W. Wessels (eds.), *The European Union and Member States: Towards Institutional Fusion?* (Manchester: Manchester University Press 1996), pp.329 and 362. Also see K. Hanf and B. Soetendorp (eds.), *Adapting to European Integration: Small States and the European Union* (Harlow: Longman 1998); and T. Bergman and E. Damgaard (eds.), *Delegation and Accountability in European Integration: The Nordic Parliamentary Democracies and the European Union* (London: Frank Cass 2000).
8. The effect of integration, and especially the Single Market and the EMU, on the future of the social democratic welfare state has attracted much academic interest. See for example F.W. Scharpf, 'Economic Integration, Democracy and the Welfare State', *Journal of European Public Policy* 4 (1997), pp.18–36.
9. See, especially, G. Majone, 'The Rise of the Regulatory State in Europe', *West European Politics* 17 (1994), pp.78–102; and G. Majone, *Regulating Europe* (London: Routledge 1996).
10. J. Blondel, 'Legislative Behaviour: Some Steps Towards a Comparative Measurement', *Government and Opposition* 5 (1970), pp.67–85.
11. M. Mezey, *Comparative Legislatures* (Durham: Duke University Press 1979).
12. See P. Norton (ed.), *Parliaments in Western Europe* (London: Frank Cass, 2nd edn 1997); and P. Norton (ed.), *Parliaments and Governments in Western Europe* (London: Frank Cass, 2nd edn. 1998).
13. P. Norton, 'Introduction', in Norton (ed.), *Parliaments and Governments in Western Europe*, p.xi.
14. S.S. Andersen and T. Burns, 'The European Union and the Erosion of Parliamentary Democracy: A Study of Post-parliamentary Governance', in S.S. Andersen and K.A. Eliassen (eds.), *The European Union: How Democratic Is It?* (London: Sage 1996), p.227.
15. Ibid., pp.244–5.
16. See A. King, 'Modes of Executive-Legislative Relations: Great Britain, France and Germany', *Legislative Studies Quarterly* 1 (1975), pp.11–34.
17. P. Norton, 'Conclusion: Do Parliaments Make a Difference?', in Norton (ed.), *Parliaments and Governments in Western Europe*, p.192.
18. See K. Heidar and R. Koole (eds.), *Parliamentary Party Groups in European Democracies: Political Parties Behind Closed Doors* (London: Routledge 2000).

19. P. Norton, *Parliaments and Governments in Western Europe*, p.5.
20. See I. Mattson and K. Strøm, 'Parliamentary Committees', in H. Döring (ed.), *Parliaments and Majority Rule in Western Europe* (Frankfurt: Campus 1995), pp.249–307.
21. See E. O'Halpin, 'A Changing Relationship? Parliament and Government in Ireland', in Norton (ed.), *Parliaments and Governments in Western Europe*, pp.123–41; and P. Norton, 'Old Institution, New Institutionalism? Parliament and Government in the UK', in ibid., pp.16–43.
22. See P. Norton (ed.), *Parliaments and Pressure Groups in Western Europe* (London: Frank Cass 1999).
23. See P. Norton (ed.), 'Parliaments and Publics', *Parliamentary Affairs* 50/3 (1997, special issue).
24. See L. de Winter, 'Parliament and Government in Belgium: Prisoners of Partitocracy', in Norton (ed.), *Parliaments and Governments in Western Europe*, pp.97–122.
25. C. Closa, 'Spain: The Cortes and the EU – A Growing Together', in P. Norton (ed.), *National Parliaments and the European Union* (London: Frank Cass 1996), pp.145, 147. See also L.M. Maurer, 'Parliamentary Influence in a New Democracy: The Spanish Congress', *Journal of Legislative Studies* 5 (1999), pp.24–45.
26. E. Damgaard and A.S. Nørgaard, 'The European Union and Danish Parliamentary Democracy', in Bergman and Damgaard (eds.), *Delegation and Accountability in European Integration*.
27. J. Magone, 'The Portuguese Assembleia da República: Discovering Europe', in Norton (ed.), *National Parliaments and the European Union*, p.162. For a contrary argument that EU membership has facilitated executive dominance in a country lacking deep-rooted democractic or parliamentary traditions, see A. Barreto, 'Portugal: Democracy through Europe', in J.J. Anderson (ed.), *Regional Integration and Democracy: Expanding on the European Experience* (Lanham, MD: Rowman & Littlefield 1999), pp.95–122.
28. H. Hegeland, 'Den svenska riksdagen och EU', in K.M. Johansson (ed.), *Sverige i EU* (Stockholm: SNS Förlag 1999), pp.95–112; The House of Commons, *The European Scrutiny System in the House of Commons* (November 1998).
29. K. von Beyme, 'Niedergang der Parlamente: Internationale Politik und nationale Entscheidungshoheit', *Internationale Politik* 53 (1998), pp.21–30.
30. V.A. Schmidt, 'European Integration and Democracy: The Differences Among Member States', *Journal of European Public Policy* 4 (1997), p.142.
31. Newman, *Democracy, Sovereignty and the European Union*, p.189.
32. See for example S.S. Andersen and K.A. Eliassen, *Making Policy in Europe: The Europeification of National Policy-Making* (London: Sage 1993); and J. Greenwood, *Representing Interests in the European Union* (Basingstoke: Macmillan 1997).
33. See R.S. Katz, 'Role Orientations in Parliaments', in Katz and Wessels (eds.), *The European Parliament, the National Parliaments, and European Integration*, pp.61–85.
34. See Bergman and Damgaard (eds.), *Delegation and Accountability in European Integration*.
35. See B. Wessels, 'Institutional Change and the Future Political Order', in Katz and Wessels (eds.), *The European Parliament, the National Parliaments, and European Integration*, pp.213–28.
36. See T. Bergman, 'National Parliaments and EU Affairs Committees: Notes on Empirical Variation and Competing Explanations', *Journal of European Public Policy* 4 (1997), pp.373–87; D. Judge, 'The Failure of National Parliaments', *West European Politics* 18 (1995), pp.79–100; F. Laursen and S.A. Pappas (eds.), *The Changing Role of Parliaments in the European Union* (Maastricht: EIPA 1995); Norton (ed.), *National Parliaments and the European Union*; Raunio, 'Always One Step Behind?'; E. Smith (ed.), *National Parliaments as Cornerstones of European Integration* (London: Kluwer Law International 1996); and M. Wiberg (ed.), *Trying to Make Democracy Work: The Nordic Parliaments and the European Union* (Stockholm: Gidlunds 1997).
37. In November 1999, including upper chambers, 514 out of 7,363 MPs/senators sat in the EAC: 358/4,831 in the lower chambers, and 156/2,532 in upper chambers.
38. EACs in some member state legislatures also utilise MEPs' policy expertise by arranging hearings. Specialised standing committees have also to a varying degree invited MEPs seated

in the corresponding committee in the EP to appear before the committee. However, the limitations of such interparliamentary co-operation are obvious: the work of an MEP is a full-time job, and, more importantly, MEPs are not accountable to their national legislatures. During the 1990s, national parties started to make more use of their MEPs, and this party-based co-ordination offers a potentially cost-effective way to learn about EU developments, especially about forthcoming legislation. After all, national parties are in control of candidate selection in Euroelections, and MEPs thus have a career incentive to participate in the work of domestic party organs when so required.

39. For example, in Austria the minister can deviate from the instructions of the Hauptauschuß only in the case of 'compelling reasons concerning foreign or integration policy'. According to article 142(2)c of the Austrian constitution, a minister or other government representative who does not act in the Council according to the instructions of the EAC or to the common position of the provinces can be brought to trial before the constitutional court by a simple majority of the plenary session of the Nationalrat or by majority decisions in Land parliaments. At the beginning of Austrian EU membership, the Hauptauschuß issued very detailed instructions to the ministers, but the Committee now formulates its positions in a more flexible manner as tight guidelines were seen to undermine the bargaining power of the ministers. See P. Luif, 'Austria: Adaptation through Anticipation', in Hanf and Soetendorp (eds.), *Adapting to European Integration*, pp.122–42.

40. See Bergman, 'National Parliaments and EU Affairs Committees'; J. Fitzmaurice, 'National Parliaments and European Policy-making: The Case of Denmark', *Parliamentary Affairs* 76 (1976) pp.281–92; Judge, 'The Failure of National Parliaments', in Norton (ed.), *National Parliaments and the European Union*; R. Pahre, 'Endogenous Domestic Institutions in Two-Level Games and Parliamentary Oversight of the European Union', *Journal of Conflict Resolution* 41 (1997), pp.147–74; and Raunio, 'Always One Step Behind?'.

41. For information on constitutional changes in the member states, see F. Laursen and S. Vanhoonacker (eds.), *The Ratification of the Maastricht Treaty: Issues, Debates and Future Implications* (Maastricht: EIPA 1994); and Norton (ed.), *National Parliaments and the European Union*.

42. T. Saalfeld, 'The German Houses of Parliament and European Legislation', in Norton (ed.), *National Parliaments and the European Union*, pp.12–34.

43. C. Leston-Bandeira, 'Relationship between Parliament and Government in Portugal: An Expression of the Maturation of the Political System', in Norton (ed.), *Parliaments and Governments in Western Europe*, pp.142–66.

44. F. Rizzuto, 'The French Parliament and the EU: Loosening the Constitutional Straightjacket', in Norton (ed.), *National Parliaments and the European Union*, pp.46–59.

45. E. O'Halpin, 'Irish Parliamentary Culture and the European Union: Formalities to be Observed', in Norton (ed.), *National Parliaments and the European Union*, p.134.

46. Von Beyme, 'Niedergang der Parlamente'.

47. Ibid.

48. K. Krehbiel, *Information and Legislative Organization* (Ann Arbor, MI: University of Michigan Press 1991).

49. See D.R. Mayhew, *Congress: The Electoral Connection* (New Haven, CT: Yale University Press 1974).

50. K. Shepsle and B. Weingast, 'The Institutional Foundations of Committee Power', *American Political Science Review* 81 (1987), pp.85–104.

51. See, for example, K. Strøm, 'A Behavioural Theory of Competitive Political Parties', *American Journal of Political Science* 34 (1990), pp.565–98.

52. On the other hand, granting the opposition a larger role in European matters, especially on more important issues such as Treaty amendments, can also effectively remove the issue from party competition as all the main parties share the responsibility for the policy choice. See M. Maor, 'The Relationship between Government and Opposition in the Bundestag and House of Commons in the Run-Up to the Maastricht Treaty', *West European Politics* 21 (1998), pp.187–207.

53. M. Mezey, 'Parliament in the New Europe', in J. Hayward and E.C. Page (eds.), *Governing the New Europe* (Cambridge: Polity Press 1995), p.205.

54. D.A. Christensen, 'Europautvala I Danmark, Sverige, og Norge: Sandpåströningorgan eller politiska muldvarpar?', *Nordisk Administrativt Tidsskrift* 2 (1997), pp.143–62.

55. V. Miller and R. Ware, 'Keeping National Parliaments Informed: The Problem of European Legislation', *Journal of Legislative Studies* 2 (1996), pp.184–97; and Rizzuto, 'The French Parliament and the EU', pp.56–7.

56. An elite survey carried out in 1996 asked MPs and MEPs, using a scale from 1 (too much) to 7 (too little) whether their national parliament 'is exercising too much or too little supervision over the positions of the [country] government in the Council of Ministers of the European Union?'. The averages were 5.35 for MEPs and 5.22 for MPs, showing that there is a broad consensus on the inefficiency of domestic control. Among the national sub-sets of MPs, the range was from 4.18 in Spain to 5.90 in Greece. Basically those respondents who are generally satisfied with how democracy works in their own country are also more satisfied with parliamentary scrutiny of EU matters. MPs from Austria, Denmark, Finland, France and the UK were not included in the survey. See R.S. Katz, 'Representation, the Locus of Democratic Legitimation and the Role of the National Parliaments in the European Union', in Katz and Wessels (eds.), *The European Parliament, the National Parliaments, and European Integration*, pp.21–44.

57. The same survey also asked the MPs and MEPs the following question: 'Some people regard the European Parliament as the democratic heart of the Union, because democratic legitimacy of the Union can only be based on a supranational parliament. Others say that this is a wrong ambition because the legitimacy of the Union is already based on the national parliaments'. The respondents were again asked to place their opinions on a scale from 1 (EP) to 7 (national parliaments). The averages were 3.04 for MEPs and 3.57 for MPs. Among the national sub-sets of MPs the range was from 3.13 in Spain to 5.50 in Sweden. See Katz, 'Representation'.

58. See Katz and Wessels (eds.), *The European Parliament, the National Parliaments, and European Integration*; and H. Schmitt and J. Thomassen (eds.), *Political Representation and Legitimacy in the European Union* (Oxford: Oxford University Press 1999).

The Positioning of EU Judicial Politics within the United Kingdom

DAMIAN CHALMERS

Any lawyer can, at best, be ambivalent about the study of judicial politics. The treatment of courts 'as one governmental agency among many – as part of the ... political process rather than as a unique body of impervious legal technicians above and beyond the political struggle'[1] suggests a supreme disinterest in the epistemic foundations of law. This heavy instrumentalisation, by reducing courts to simple agents of the political process, can offer little instruction in the grammar codes of legal knowledge, processes and discourse. Yet it is the internalisation of these by participants that forecloses certain options and provides a certain resistance to, and therefore autonomy from, outside pressures – in essence, those very legal qualities that lead political or other actors to resort to law. For this author, at least, ambivalence is not synonymous with dismissal. The autonomy of the political system imposes external constraints upon the operation of the law and, whilst the judicial system may be autonomous, it is not autarkic. It will often be used instrumentally by political actors. Indeed, a feature of the legal system is that it is particularly vulnerable to these outside pressures. For its quest for formal and functional effectiveness leads not just to a concern with the problem of compliance, but also to a desire to 'perfect', and therefore be sensitive to, the properties of the political processes, domestic and European Union (EU), that it regulates. The insights offered by judicial politics lie precisely on this apex in its strong focus upon the process of negotiation and adjustment between the judiciary, other agencies of government and the wider political sphere.

Judicial politics studies have a particular strong resonance in the case of the judicial system of the EU. The dependence of the European Communities' (EC) legal system upon a variety of national governmental agencies for its implementation, enforcement and much of its application has led to concerns about its formal effectiveness; at the same time, its relatively inchoate and 'young' nature has rendered it particularly vulnerable to charges of being excessively disruptive. These structural features have been exacerbated by the activities of the European Court of Justice (ECJ). It has both developed relationships with national courts and litigants that, in functional terms, have acted as surrogate policy processes at the expense of national governments,[2] and, through its constitutionalist case law, placed itself at the centre of all debates about the civil and political identity of the Union. These have raised expectations about the capability of EC law to exert compliance and about the demands in terms of liberal values that can be exerted by it,[3] whilst, at times, testing the limits of its acceptance by national government agencies and judges.

It is unsurprising, therefore, that a rich literature in judicial politics has developed. The debate centres around three themes. There are, first, theses that revolve around *institutional politics*. These focus on the motivations and behaviour of national courts. On one side of the divide there are arguments which attribute a calculative frame on the part of the national courts. The possibilities offered by EC law for rent-seeking versus other arms of government,[4] other branches of the judiciary[5] or simply the opportunities it provides to advance personal policy preferences[6] have, it is claimed, influenced national judicial reception of it. They also include arguments which suggest that the high acceptance of EC law by national judges can be attributed to no prior calculations on the part of national courts, but is rooted in notions of judicial identity[7] or the absorption of fairly pliant norms into local contexts.[8]

The second theme centres upon *interest group politics*. If national courts and the ECJ are seen as 'supplying EC law', these theories suggest that it is policy elites that provide the demand for EC law.[9] The invocation of EC law, therefore, depends upon the organisation of resources at a national level,[10] the presence of repeat litigators[11] and the extent to which litigants are excluded by other policy processes.

The third theme links the invocation of EC law less explicitly to a narrow institutional context. Instead, it draws a correlation between the level of acceptance and application of EC law and the level of *transnational activity*.[12] Correlations are, therefore, made between the levels of preliminary references and receptiveness to EC law by national law, on the one hand, and levels of intra-EC trade, on the other.

These themes follow patterns that permeate the broader judicial politics debate.[13] Yet, as theories, they share a unique attribute. None have been thoroughly tested. The bulk of the Court's 'constitutionalising' has national courts at its epicentre, as it locates itself in their duties to apply EC law independently of and over national law. In like vein, national courts have acted as interlocutors of the ECJ, through their reference of questions of EC law and enforcement of rulings, in virtually all those areas where its judgments have encroached in substantive policy terms on national government autonomy. Any analysis of the depth and contribution of judicial politics to EU integration must, therefore, use national courts as its principal laboratory. The evidence used for all the above, however, has been scant and unrepresentative. It includes the largely irrelevant case law of the ECJ itself;[14] the very occasional 'seminal' judgments from higher courts accepting or resisting the formal invocation of EC law;[15] those minority of judgments referred to the ECJ from national jurisdictions[16] or interesting, but unextrapolable, case studies.[17]

Even to focus on reported cases, as this study does, in its examination of all reported judgments in the UK between 1971 and 1998 in which EC law was addressed by national judges, has a *faute de mieux* quality.[18] It will not capture extra-judicial legal activity nor will it capture the intensity of the British judicial contribution to European integration, as the overwhelming number of cases, particularly in the lower courts, are not reported, and many of those reported are, in reality, representative actions, whose results will be used to resolve a number of other actions. Moreover, as it is complexity, novelty and legal significance which tend to lead to judgments being reported, these cannot be unquestioningly correlated to the broader category of non-reported judgments.[19] Two studies in the United States have given empirical weight to the intuitive suspicion that because of the nature of the cases reported, judges there tend to be more aware of their role in the policy-making process.[20] In cases involving EC law, where the question of integration is a central binary code of the policy-making process, one would, therefore, both expect a higher proportion of references and refusals to refer from reported cases. One would also expect a higher percentage of judgments to be reported that are either explicitly 'positive' or 'negative' about EC law. This might be through giving or refusing to give it *de iure* supremacy, granting significant (or rejecting) institutional authority to the decisions of the Commission or ECJ, or judgments that considerably extend the ambit of substantive provisions of EC law or severely restrict or distinguish them.

Nevertheless, a study of reported cases has a representative value in two senses. First, it is indicative of the spread of litigation. If anything, such a study is likely to understate the proportion of litigation in EC law's most heavily litigated areas. For the areas where EC law has been most heavily invoked – tax, social security, labour and immigration – are legal domains which tend to be dominated at first instances by quasi-judicial bodies –

employment tribunals, immigration adjudicators, social security commissioners, VAT tribunals – whose decisions are only rarely reported. Second, a study of reported decisions does capture the amplificatory effects of judicial activity. That is to say, it will capture that level of judicial activity that provokes responses in significant legal and non-legal milieus. This is partly because all decisions that carry doctrinal weight on anything other than interlocutory matters, symbolic importance or far-reaching effects on economic or political activity will be reported. It is also important because the act of reporting, by bringing the decision to the attention of legal and other communities, generates those circulatory effects likely to provoke a reaction.

A quantitative analysis of those British cases in which EC law is invoked shows that the bulk of such activity is very narrowly focused. It is narrow not just in the sectors of EC law it covers. It is also narrow in that it covers very few private disputes, and it is narrow in terms of the ideological readjustments that it has provoked. All this, in institutional terms, contributes to understanding why the judicial application of EC law has not provoked more tensions. The threat suggested to administrative autonomy through judicial empowerment has been limited. Moreover, insofar as most EC law is, in practical terms, not judicially enforceable, it has instead been used to augment administrative capacity through its development of administratively applied norms and networks.

Those areas that were litigated tend to be intensively litigated. This piece examines the reaction to judicial developments of both the British administration and the wider public sphere. It finds that, contrary to some assumptions, litigation was not some form of policy-making by stealth. There is a high level of coverage and debate in at least some of the areas that were most intensively litigated. The central variables are twofold. The first is the extent to which the area is dominated by elite competition and political cleavages. The second is the extent of ECJ involvement, either actively through the preliminary reference procedure, or passively through invocation of its case law by domestic courts. Comment and debate, normally adverse, increased in proportion to the extent of this involvement. The reason for this seems to be that the ECJ offers an opportunity structure for 'outsider' elites who have been denied satisfaction in domestic fora. Once a judgment has been made, it is relatively easy, because of the decision trap, for the latter to block amendments to EC legislation with the consequence that there is heavy polarisation between EC and domestic law.

The third feature that this analysis picks up is how British courts have positioned themselves within these wider processes. It finds that in addition to the traditional constraints mentioned in the literature, which circulate around questions of judicial incentives and judicial identities, there are a number of further features derived from the institutional environment – going to perceptions of what the courts were meant to do – that influence judicial behaviour. There is no evidence that the judiciary is concerned to protect particular central spheres of British political and legal life from EU intrusion. Resistance is, however, marked where EC law restricts domestic institutions' capacity to secure conformity in British society whether that conformity takes the form of securing those conditions that sustain and stabilise private relationships and private autonomy or whether it takes the form of protecting those institutions, such as criminal or immigration law, which are taken to sustain a common collective consciousness.

THE CONUNDRUM OF THE JUDICIAL REVISITING OF THE BRITISH CONSTITUTIONAL SETTLEMENT

The application of EC law in UK courts cannot be equated to a form of best-level analysis that involves a simple shift in allegiances from the periphery to the centre by the national courts. It involved a transformation in the relationships the judiciary enjoyed with other arms of government, with the central institutions of civil society and within the judiciary itself.

First, EC law reversed the hierarchy between the British judiciary and the other arms of government. The British constitutional settlement had traditionally been one within which, as the sovereign, parliament sat at the apex, and courts, whilst having extensive powers in the private law field, had limited ones in public law. They had no powers of legislative review and applied only a weak measure of review over administrative acts, which allowed considerable administrative discretion.[21] By requiring national courts to disapply administrative or legislative acts that conflicted with it, EC law gave national courts sweeping new powers of legislative and administrative review, which placed them at the apex of the constitutional settlement. Furthermore, the new measure of review, that of compliance with EC law, seemed to enable them to intervene sweepingly and more intensively in previously untouched areas of governmental activities.

Second, EC law required British courts to mediate a fundamentally different relationship between individual and state. Its monarchist and hereditary trappings aside, the approach of the British constitutional settlement to legal and political life has always been strongly republican in nature. The legitimacy of the hegemony of a majoritarian institution such as parliament lay in its being the most representative body to enact a corpus of laws best suited to the conditions and mores of British society. The strongly collectivist nature of this vision accords priority to the legal system as a whole in which it mediates between plural interests and in which individual rights enjoy an essentially derivative role.[22] Similarly, politics becomes measured by its success in securing collective goods, with individual measures being reviewed against their contribution towards that.[23] The EC Treaty, by contrast, was centred around a series of economic freedoms whose ideological foundations were based upon the liberal vision of private autonomy.[24] Within the liberal vision, these principles enjoy a transcendental and prior status to any collective settlements. Legal priority is thus given to subjective rights. Likewise, a more self-limiting vision of politics is taken within which as much space as possible is preserved for autonomous behaviour by private individuals.

Third, the application of EC law undermined internal judicial hierarchies. Whilst the division of labour within British courts is not as strong as in some jurisdictions, specialised courts exist in, *inter alia*, the fields of labour law, immigration, tax and intellectual property, and only the higher courts – the High Court, the Court of Appeal and the House of Lords in England and Wales – have powers of judicial review. The system of precedent imposes powerful hierarchies within the system by obliging lower courts to follow prior decisions of higher courts on materially identical questions. EC law subverts these by robbing higher courts of their privileges *vis-à-vis* the other arms of government in granting powers of judicial review or legislative review to any body which, acting under governmental supervision, contains quasi-judicial procedures to determine EC rights.[25] Powers usually reserved for the higher courts[26] are not merely granted to all other courts, but also to statutory bodies that often contain lay members and enjoy a hinterland status somewhere between government agency and judiciary.[27] EC law also undercuts the authority of higher courts over lower courts by enabling the latter to refer points to the ECJ and give authority to ECJ rulings on points materially identical to those already decided by higher national courts.[28]

Fourthly, EC law brought unprecedented administrative intervention into the legal institutions of civil society. Historical sociologists have observed how the development of modern notions of political sovereignty contributed to the development of capitalist economies by enabling the economic sphere to be separated from the political sphere and, through centralised laws, giving political backing to those private property rights that are the mainstay of a capitalist economy.[29] This was done in many European jurisdictions through the development of civil codes. An 'abeyance' emerged in the British constitutional settlement whereby although parliament had formal sovereign powers, in practice it seldom trespassed on the autonomy of the common law.[30] This allowed the British courts a property over the origins and development of the legal institutions of private law society not enjoyed to the same extent by their counterparts elsewhere. In this, as the roots of the common law lay embroiled in custom, they came to act as central fora for societal self-learning experimentation[31] in such a way that it was perhaps easier for British commentators to claim that the common law acted as a mirror for the ethics of British society.[32] To be sure, the autonomy of these institutions became subject to increasing legislative and executive intrusion from the end of the nineteenth century onwards.[33] Yet EC law still represented a drastic intrusion on the considerable residual autonomy of these institutions. On the one hand, EC competition law interfered in an unprecedented manner with the exchange function of contract.[34] On the other, EC regulation in fields such as health and safety, environment and consumer law intruded far more intensively than prior British legislation into the risk allocation functions performed by both contract and tort law. These intrusions threatened to generate radical new elisions, dislocations and complexities in the hitherto relatively monolithic institutions of contract and tort.[35]

The picture sketched above of the British constitutional settlement is a simplistic and static one, which has encountered substantial change since 1973.[36] Even allowing for this, the constitutional resettlement required was not only considerable, but encountered three further pressures that all militated in favour of the status quo. First, the resettlement of power brought about by the application of EC law is essentially redistributive in nature. That is to say that no 'win–win' scenarios exist, as any empowerment of one institutional actor is at the expense of another. Moreover, subject to what will be said below, it is not even possible to locate a constituency that can anticipate clear institutional benefits from the application of EC law. In all instances, the forms of institutional gain brought by EC law had to be set off against corollary restrictions on autonomy and forms of disempowerment. The eventual 'winners' and 'losers' would depend upon unpredictable modalities of application of EC law; for example, would more opportunities for judicial review arise than opportunities for administrative intervention. Furthermore, whilst it was not possible to identify future 'winners', it was possible to identify one clear 'loser', the British Parliament and its surrounding constituency, which seem to be disempowered under any scenario through the possible extension of either executive or judicial power.

Second, the British constitutional settlement was, on its face, explicitly structured against this revision. A feature of parliamentary sovereignty is that parliament cannot formally tie the hands of its successors, and thereby curb its own powers.[37] This rendered the application of EC law particularly vulnerable, as all EC law, whether adopted prior or subsequent to accession, takes formal legislative effect within the UK by virtue of section 2(1) European Communities Act 1972. Any EC legislation was thus in the unique situation that its application was threatened not merely by subsequent parliamentary action, but also by parliamentary measures that preceded it, but took effect after 1 January 1973. This possibility of challenge could either be mounted generally, as happened with the Private Member's Bill curbing the ECJ's powers suggested by Ian Duncan-Smith in 1996, or, where there was not a sufficient constituency, more specifically by bringing in legislation that expressly contradicted individual pieces of EC legislation.[38] To be sure, such actions would provoke a crisis with other member states, but this would only provoke immediate costs for the executive. Whilst the executive, through the governing party, usually has had a strong grip on parliament, where the executive's influence was weak, as was the case of the 1992–96 Major government, the likelihood of such a danger increased.

The third obstacle to revision was the traditionalist approach taken to accession. The European Communities Act 1972 only anticipated membership as having significant repercussions for relations between the executive and the legislature through its conferral by section 2(2) European Communities Act of sweeping quasi-legislative powers on the executive to implement, through Orders in Council, EC obligations – normally Directives – that had themselves been negotiated by the executive. In all other respects, its impact was perceived as marginal. Most notably, in the application of Community law, courts were to be confined by section 2(4) European Communities Act to their traditional role of interpreting administrative and legislative acts rather than reviewing them, which sought to resolve potential conflicts between EC law and parliamentary statutes by requiring the latter to be 'construed' in the light of the former.

Pre-existing conceptions of the constitutional settlement also informed judicial practice through the 1970s and 1980s in a number of ways. In several judgments strong deference was made to the prerogatives of the other arms of government and the need for judicial reserve. This was most marked in the approach of the courts to conflicts between EC law and parliamentary statute. These were to be interpreted away under the fiction that section 2(4) was merely an extension of the practice of interpreting

British statutes in the light of its international treaty obligations.[39] It was also present in a number of judgments that emphasised the traditional balance of powers between the judiciary and other arms of government.[40] Similarly, there was a strong emphasis on preserving judicial hierarchies. Industrial tribunals were prevented from applying EC law until 1979.[41] Whilst there were isolated instances of lower courts invoking decisions of the ECJ at the expense of those given by higher national courts,[42] they continued to consider themselves generally bound by decisions of the latter on points of EC law.[43] There was also evidence that lower courts felt that referrals to the ECJ should normally be the prerogative of the higher courts.[44] Similarly, EC law was not considered as ousting the exclusive jurisdiction of certain courts to decide certain forms of dispute, even if this excluded other courts from applying EC law.[45] Finally, British courts were equally protective about their hegemony over the common law. EC competition law was not envisaged as creating any new forms of private action,[46] and British courts were reticent to treat as privileged, in private law disputes before them, legal advice given to undertakings in preparation for competition hearings before the Commission.[47]

On its face, this makes the change brought about in the *Factortame* saga all the more dramatic.[48] Famously, the highest court in the UK, the House of Lords, accepted the supremacy of EC law and, with it, the power for British courts to review legislative measures for their compliance with EC law. Since then, as a matter of legal doctrine, the formal supremacy of EC law has been entrenched in British law. There has been the occasional act of defiance. British courts have departed – temporarily – from the ECJ on the legal effects of Directives[49] and, more recently, have noted that the ECJ cannot, as EC law currently stands, rule generally on the compatibility of national administrative action with fundamental rights norms and on treaties entered into by the UK prior to EC accession.[50] Yet these latter judgments are relatively isolated and have their precursors in similar judgments given by national courts in other EU jurisdictions.[51] More broadly, the study carried out also attempted to measure covert resistance, where EC law was not explicitly challenged, but devices were used to distinguish its application to a case in hand.[52] These made up only 98 cases, nine per cent of the total – a small number. These tended to be slightly higher, in proportionate terms, in the early years, suggesting that not only has judicial resistance increased as a consequence of the more onerous formal duties imposed by *Factortame* or EC law's increasing incursion into new fields of policy, but that some process of socialisation took place. This is to be contrasted with the number of rulings that can be characterised as positive.

These were ones that either applied the case law of the ECJ directly to the factual circumstances or referred the matter to the ECJ,[53] as these implicitly accept the interpretative authority of the ECJ to the case in hand or in some other way were positive about the application of EC law (for example, changed legal aid rules to accommodate EC complaints, accepted the exclusive jurisdiction of EC law, interpreted EC law very widely, relaxed rules of standing). These do not include simple interpretations of EC provisions, but still number 559, a figure that is over five times that of the 'restrictive' cases (see Table 3).[54]

EC LAW AND THE CONSTITUTIONAL RESETTLEMENT OF ADMINISTRATIVE RATHER THAN JUDICIAL POWER

The conundrum as to the acceptance and application of EC law, given that it seems to posit, in a truly revolutionary manner, both the judiciary and the liberal principles contained in EC law at the apex of the British constitutional settlement, becomes less opaque when one looks at the actual praxis. The study found 1,088 cases reported in which a question of EC law or British accession to the EU was addressed by a British judge.[55] These concerned 1,205 areas of EC law (see Table 2). As would be expected, the bias in reporting led to the majority of reported cases involving the higher courts. In addition to the higher courts set out – the High Court and Court of Appeal of England of Wales, and the House of Lords – the senior courts of Northern Ireland and Scotland accounted for 17[56] and 34[57] cases respectively. There were six judgments which concerned none of these jurisdictions – two from the Isle of Man, two from the Channel Islands and two involving the Privy Council.[58] In addition to the two lower courts mentioned, the Employment Appeal Tribunal and the VAT and Duties Tribunals, other courts or judicial bodies who figured prominently were the Crown Court (15 cases), the Immigration Appeals Tribunal (12), Employment Tribunals (19), Magistrates (27) and the Social Security Commissioner (26). The provisions invoked most frequently were EC Treaty provisions, 880 times.[59] Directives were invoked 581 times and Regulations 214 times. In addition, international agreements signed by the EC were invoked 12 times before British courts.

The most striking feature of these statistics was the narrow focus of litigation. It was narrow, first, in the sectors it covered: 659 out of 1,205 areas fell within just five bands – taxation, sex discrimination, free movement of goods, free movement of persons (excluding issues of service provision and establishment) and intellectual property. This narrowness was

TABLE 1
COURTS IN WHICH EC LAW WAS INVOKED

Year	High Court	Court of Appeal	House of Lords	Employment Appeals Tribunal	VAT and Duties Tribunal	Other
1971	0	1	0	0	0	0
1972	1	1	0	0	0	0
1973	3	1	0	0	1	0
1974	1	2	0	0	0	4
1975	5	0	1	0	0	6
1976	1	2	0	1	0	3
1977	8	4	1	1	0	9
1978	1	3	1	1	0	1
1979	5	3	0	2	0	10
1980	3	7	0	0	2	4
1981	6	1	1	1	3	3
1982	4	3	0	0	2	7
1983	6	0	3	3	2	6
1984	8	7	0	0	0	5
1985	4	5	3	2	8	6
1986	8	5	1	2	3	4
1987	11	2	0	3	4	2
1988	11	9	4	0	6	13
1989	10	6	5	4	3	10
1990	11	10	1	1	12	8
1991	14	6	4	6	7	10
1992	12	6	2	4	22	7
1993	21	10	1	7	22	5
1994	26	11	1	14	15	6
1995	30	16	2	16	17	10
1996	36	27	3	20	18	27
1997	31	29	3	11	24	16
1998	49	37	8	17	13	22
Total	**326**	**214**	**45**	**116**	**184**	**203**

exacerbated by 68 of the free movement of goods cases being centred exclusively around Articles 28–30 EC. If one includes the social security cases within this group, as these centred exclusively either upon Regulation 1408/71 EEC and its amending legislation, which deals with the social security entitlements of migrant workers, or Directive 79/7/EEC, which curbs the sex discriminatory effects of social security schemes, one arrives at a situation in which 61 per cent of the litigation falls within these narrow areas of EC law. Similarly, in the case of Directives – so pivotal to central domains of EC law such as the single market, environment, labour and consumer law – five Directives alone account for 426 instances, 73 per cent of the total, in which Directives are reported to have been invoked before British courts.[60] Conversely, in the field of the environment, in which there are over 200 pieces of EC legislation, one finds only 39 cases, of which 31

TABLE 2
THE CENTRAL FIELDS OF LITIGATION*

Year	No. of Cases	Taxation	Sex Discrimination	TUPE	Free Movement of Goods	Free Movement of Persons	Environment	Intellectual Property	Social Security	Competition	Agriculture	Fisheries	Transport	External Relations	Pharmaceuticals	Freedom of Establishment	Freedom to Provide Services	Public Procurement	Immigration	Criminal
1971	1	0	0	0	0	0	0	0	0	0	0	0	0	0	0	0	0	0	0	0
1972	2	0	0	0	0	0	0	1	0	1	0	0	0	0	0	0	0	0	0	0
1973	5	1	0	0	1	0	0	2	0	2	0	0	0	1	0	0	0	0	0	0
1974	7	0	0	0	0	0	0	0	3	1	0	0	0	0	0	1	0	0	0	0
1975	12	0	0	0	1	2	0	2	4	2	0	0	0	0	0	0	0	0	0	0
1976	7	0	1	0	0	1	0	0	3	1	0	0	0	0	0	0	0	0	0	0
1977	20	0	1	0	3	2	0	2	7	0	5	0	0	0	0	0	1	0	0	1
1978	7	0	3	0	1	1	0	0	0	1	0	0	0	0	0	1	0	0	0	1
1979	20	0	4	0	0	5	0	2	9	0	1	1	0	1	0	0	1	0	0	1
1980	16	4	0	0	3	1	0	2	2	0	1	0	1	1	0	0	0	0	0	4
1981	15	4	0	0	1	1	0	0	0	2	2	2	2	1	0	0	0	0	1	1
1982	16	2	2	2	3	2	0	1	3	3	2	0	3	0	0	0	0	0	0	3
1983	20	2	2	0	1	3	0	1	1	0	2	0	2	0	0	0	0	0	0	3
1984	20	2	3	2	3	4	0	1	1	3	3	1	2	1	0	0	0	0	0	1
1985	26	8	3	2	4	2	0	2	4	1	2	1	2	0	0	0	0	0	0	2
1986	23	5	3	2	2	2	0	0	0	1	3	3	0	0	0	0	0	0	0	3
1987	22	6	3	0	4	1	0	0	1	1	3	3	4	0	0	0	0	0	0	7
1988	43	9	9	1	2	3	0	4	6	6	4	3	2	0	0	2	0	0	0	2
1989	38	8	7	1	12	2	0	2	7	4	5	1	0	0	0	0	0	0	1	2
1990	44	12	14	2	2	1	1	2	7	2	2	2	3	1	1	0	0	0	0	8
1991	47	8	7	2	7	3	3	1	3	3	3	1	1	0	0	1	0	2	1	4
1992	54	26	9	0	9	0	0	2	0	7	3	2	3	3	1	0	0	1	0	3
1993	66	24	9	5	2	1	2	3	4	6	6	2	0	3	0	2	1	2	3	2
1994	74	20	13	10	6	3	2	8	0	7	7	0	4	5	1	2	0	3	0	8
1995	91	29	13	8	3	4	6	13	3	7	4	2	0	8	1	0	0	0	1	6
1996	131	31	25	11	6	7	5	11	3	12	2	1	3	1	3	2	3	1	3	6
1997	113	32	12	7	3	4	8	16	3	9	6	0	0	7	3	0	4	2	5	5
1998	148	39	21	10	5	4	12	2	2	4	2	0	1	1	3	1	0	0	2	3
Total	**1088**	**272**	**164**	**65**	**84**	**59**	**39**	**80**	**76**	**86**	**68**	**25**	**33**	**31**	**13**	**12**	**10**	**11**	**17**	**76**

* 'Immigration' refers to cases concerning third country nationals in which Article 39 EC was not invoked. Other headings invoked not included on the table were: Company Law (total of 7); Redundancies and Rights of Employees in Case of Insolvency (8); Privileges of the European Parliament (2); Education (2); Budget (2); State Aids (5); Consumer Law (6); Public Undertakings (1); Public Procurement (11); Insurance (6); Broadcasting (1); Banking (1); Structural Funds (1); Social Fund (1); Health and Safety in the Workplace (3); Commercial Agents (8); Justice and Home Affairs (1); Free Movement of Capital and Monetary Policy (3). In some cases it was artificial to state that a dispute revolved around one area rather than another. In such cases, 127, the cases were treated as falling into two areas. Also included in the survey were eight judgments that concerned issue of accession or ratification of the Treaty. There were also one that dealt with the ECJ rulings on fundamental rights and one with those on legitimate expectations. Neither concerned any substantive provision of EC law. Purists might object to these ten judgments being included in the survey, but they were included as all centred upon judicial attitudes to the EC integration process. Finally, although not in a heading in its own right, cases that involved criminal sanctions are posted.

were in the period 1995–98. EC consumer guarantees, another area of British law substantially remodelled by EC intervention, have only been invoked six times. Perhaps most interesting, however, is that of the single market, the field of law that is both seen to have regenerated the EC and contributed significantly to centrifugal pressures. Although 59 judgments can be attributed to legislation adopted as part of, or ancillary to, the 1988–93 Single Market Programme,[61] 29 of these judgments concerned Directive 89/104/EEC on the harmonisation of trademarks; eight concerned public procurement and eight concerned Directive 92/12/EC on the harmonisation of excise duties. Aside from these three areas, one is left with only 14 judgments. In the period 1994–98, they accounted for only 2.5 per cent of all recorded judgments.

EC judicial involvement is also narrow in another sense. Direct intervention in private disputes is very limited. The majority of cases involves litigation against the state's exercise of its administrative or fiscal powers or criminal cases: 647 cases involve litigation against the state in this former capacity and a further 76 cases centre around a criminal prosecution. Of the remaining 355 cases, which involve either private disputes or actions against public bodies where the latter are acting in a transactional capacity, 229, that is, 64 per cent, concern two discrete areas, sex discrimination legislation and protection of workers in the case of transfer of ownership of undertakings (TUPE).

The above does not necessarily mean that EC law has not had an effect on these other spheres of social interaction. It does suggest that these, most notably the market-place, have an autonomy relatively unperturbed by the traditional apparatus of legal enforcement, the judiciary. Certainly less so

TABLE 3
THE APPLICATION OF EC LAW

	EC Treaty	Directives	Regulations	Success	Failure	Apply ECJ	Positive	Restrictive	P.Refs	P.Refs Ref'd
1971	0	0	0	0	0	0	0	0	0	0
1972	1	0	0	0	1	0	0	0	0	0
1973	4	1	1	2	3	2	1	0	0	2
1974	4	0	3	5	2	0	1	1	0	2
1975	7	2	4	3	8	0	3	2	2	2
1976	4	0	3	2	5	1	0	3	1	0
1977	7	2	13	10	7	7	1	2	8	0
1978	6	0	0	4	3	0	0	1	3	1
1979	9	5	11	10	9	1	1	2	9	1
1980	10	3	5	7	5	1	0	1	6	3
1981	10	6	4	4	11	2	0	1	4	1
1982	9	2	9	6	8	3	1	5	5	0
1983	14	10	7	9	8	2	1	1	7	2
1984	17	9	6	13	7	0	2	1	8	2
1985	23	14	3	14	11	3	1	3	9	2
1986	15	10	8	14	8	4	0	3	9	1
1987	18	9	4	13	9	2	3	3	7	1
1988	38	15	6	13	30	4	1	8	15	5
1989	29	17	10	18	16	5	3	1	12	1
1990	36	23	7	15	23	6	6	3	8	2
1991	38	21	10	19	24	10	1	3	17	4
1992	48	36	7	31	23	9	6	3	14	4
1993	62	42	2	30	32	20	4	11	10	5
1994	62	49	13	36	30	24	1	7	23	7
1995	78	59	16	43	41	26	1	6	21	6
1996	108	74	17	65	61	42	5	12	18	15
1997	94	70	24	53	43	30	3	7	18	5
1998	129	102	21	67	50	51	3	9	24	12
Total	**880**	**581**	**214**	**506**	**478**	**254**	**49**	**98**	**258**	**86**

Note: The first three columns indicate the central provisions (EC Treaty articles/Regulations/Directives) invoked in British courts. The next two indicate whether the party claiming the EC legal right was able to assert that right successfully or not (Success/Failure). In many cases this was difficult to tell, notably in the case of references back to British courts from the ECJ or in interlocutory hearings. This is the reason for this figure being less than 1,088. The next column details the number of cases in which an ECJ ruling was central to the *ratio decidendi* of the British court (Apply ECJ). The next two columns consider whether positive or negative comments about EC law were made by the British court (Positive/Restrictive). The final two columns show the number of Preliminary References given and refused (P.Refs/P.Refs Refused). The 'Positive', 'Apply ECJ' and 'P'Ref' columns are all, for obvious reasons, mutually exclusive. The figure of 258 references differs from the 269 given by the ECJ: nine of those reported by the ECJ involved the Judgments Conventions, which were outside this study. Despite exhaustive studies, the other two could not be found. Certainly, neither of them led to judgment by the ECJ. In addition, the year given differs from those given by the ECJ. This is because this study took the date as that when the order was made by the British court and not when it is marked as received by the ECJ.

than in purely domestic contexts, where one finds private law actions making up the overwhelming majority of non-criminal actions. If this is right, then where EC law is used to govern private transactions, its centre of gravity is absorbed into the 'global law beyond the nation-state', that a number of commentators have observed.[62] This consists of the panoply of norms generated through standard form contracts, codes of conduct, systems of arbitration, and participation in organisations such as United Nations Commission on International Trade Law (UNIDROIT) and International Institute for the Unification of Private Law (UNICITRAL) in which the transnational, mega-law firm has become both the central laboratory and player for both the enactment and elaboration of these norms.[63]

The third manner in which judicial involvement has been limited is that it has not led, directly at least, to any constitutional resettlement around constitutive liberal freedoms. This manifests itself most clearly in the limited impact of the 'economic freedoms' on judicial practice. If there are any constitutive principles that anchor the EC polity, the provisions on free movement of goods, capital, services, establishment and persons surely count among them.[64] All have been interpreted, albeit to varying degrees, to prohibit not merely protectionist measures, but also to act as constitutive 'economic due process' provisions, which put limits on the level of administrative intervention in the market-place.[65] Yet, for all this, there has been no liberal resettlement within the UK. There are only 169 instances of these being invoked in British cases. Taken as a whole, their rate of successful invocation is below average and they account for only 39 out of 506 instances, eight per cent, in which litigants have successfully invoked EC law.

THE PUZZLE OF THE IMPLEMENTATION OF EC LAW IN THE UNITED KINGDOM

European Community law's acceptance may have been facilitated by its 'threat' to administration's domestic capabilities being relatively isolated. Yet a corollary of this is that it becomes proportionately harder to argue that it is the involvement of judicial networks that has contributed to the embeddedness of EC law and to the endurance of the EU.[66] For the judicial stick does not seem, in practice, to be present to beat and cajole the administration into transposing, applying and enforcing EC law. The puzzle gets deeper as the performance of the British government, when measured by a number of indicators, has been pretty obedient. The early 1990s witnessed a significant growth in the amount of secondary legislation that national governments were required to implement. Notwithstanding this, the Commission lodged and successfully won only seven enforcement actions against the British government in the whole of the 1990s.[67] This level of compliance is reflected in Commission reports on transposition of directives at both a general[68] and at a sector-specific level.[69] It is also manifested in a willingness of the British administration to reform laws to comply with adverse Commission opinions.[70]

Undoubtedly, one variable is the formal pull of the law. There are costs to the breach of any law in the tag of lawlessness that attaches to the perpetrator and, as a feature of all law is that it lends itself to obedience for its own sake, law also has certain inductive effects.[71] These have been reinforced by the approach to transposition of the British government adopted in July 1999. Whilst individual ministries are, of course, responsible for implementation of directives (or in some cases regulations) that fall within their policy umbrella, they are all now subject to the Guidelines offered by the Cabinet Office in its 'Checklist for the Transposition of European Legislation'.[72] On their face, these seem to advance administrative discretion by not 'framing' transposition as a formal legal venture. Transposition is to be done within the context of the ministers choosing from a series of policy options presented before them. The option chosen must include, as one of its goals, the minimisation of regulatory costs. This discretion is qualified, however, by the requirement that an assessment must be made of the legal risks of the adoption of a particular option. This analysis does not address the question of whether the option breaches EC law, but the more strategic one of what is the risk of litigation and the seriousness of the costs of litigation. Whilst ostensibly highly calculative in nature, the reality is that the Guidelines are likely to reinforce compliance by ministries by making them highly risk-averse. If a challenge is mounted on legal grounds not only will that have to be addressed in the courts, but, administratively, the ministry will be deemed within Whitehall to have 'miscalculated' its legal risk analysis. An additional administrative cost is, therefore, added to non-compliance, that of breach of guidelines issued by one of the most powerful units in British government.

The second factor that generates administrative compliance with EC law is its heavy normativity. Normativity, in this context, means the establishment of some common denominator, which seeks to stabilise and standardise behaviour (normalisation) through reference not to some external standard but to 'the characteristics or attributes of the things, activities, facts or populations to which it is to be applied'.[73] Directives on mutual recognition, for example, set out acceptable standards for goods, professionals or services and so on. The normative qualities of law are most typically contrasted with its coercive qualities that are manifested most strongly through the judicial enforcement of its sovereign authority. To be sure, in any legislation there is a balance and tension between these two qualities. It would appear, however, that in the case of EC law, with whole swathes in practical terms unaffected by the coercive capabilities of the 'sovereign legal order' set up by the ECJ, its normative qualities are heavily predominant. This is hardly surprising. Scharpf has observed that the fractured public sphere of the EU renders any form of input-oriented legitimacy problematic, as the absence of a collective identity provides no basis for losers or minorities to accept majoritarian or explicitly redistributive measures. The legitimating devices of the EU have, therefore, always been more heavily output-oriented, namely couched in terms of its ability to solve problems that have proved intractable elsewhere.[74]

Within such a regime, a feature of law is that it is never an isolated artefact but incorporates itself into a 'continuum of apparatuses ... whose functions are the most part regulatory'.[75] The role of law is not merely to set out and formalise the norm in question. It also, in Foucault's words, 'effects distributions [of power] around the norm'.[76] The formal and general authority of law is used to set out the standards and the forms of knowledge that will be used to adjudge whether a particular course of conduct is appropriate and the institutions that will carry out that adjudication.

This has important institutional consequences as to whom EC law is empowering and disempowering. For EC law is engaged, primarily, in the politics of recognition through its formalisation of authority, justification of intervention and valorisation of activities. A feature of EU legal integration is, therefore, that it has not led, on any significant scale to the 'emergence of regulatory gaps', disempowering the ability of states to regulate at a domestic level,[77] but has *become directly involved in the capacity-building of national administrations*. In particular, a variety of empirical studies suggest that it has either been used to empower pre-existing centres of administration or as a cipher for a more sweeping centralisation and rationalisation of administrative power. Neil Fligstein and Iona Mara-Drita's pioneering study of single market legislation found that it tended to contour the nooks and crannies of the pre-existing EU political economy.[78] In the single market programme, the creation of new rules of exchange, through the 'New Approach to Harmonisation', tended to be concentrated in high-export industries. In other industries, there was a greater concentration on preserving existing governance structures whose autonomy was protected through the device of mutual recognition, which provided for a horizontal network of contacts between national administrative centres with very little external steering done by any of the supranational authorities.[79] More directly within the UK, in areas as diverse as broadcasting,[80] regulation of food stuffs,[81] competition,[82] environmental protection[83] and policing,[84] implementation of EC Directives was no more than a catalyst or contributor to a broader process of reform, which in all cases led to the establishment of new centralised regulatory institutions or the formalisation and consolidation of existing central ones.

To argue, *simpliciter*, that administrations developed and implemented EC law because it increased their power is too crude. For it detaches the question of narrow institutional rents too abruptly from the broader tasks of problem-solving and policy-making that inevitably pervades implementation. This capacity-building rather takes place against a backdrop in which powerful, wider frames of administrative problem-solving have led, since the nineteenth century, to a specialisation and extension of government.[85] In this, the development of EC law coincides not merely with the extension of government but also its elaboration. Yet there is a catch. For this can lead to implementation generating internecine administrative tensions. Offe has observed how the development and specialisation of administration has brought with it an internal pluralisation and fragmentation of the state apparatus. Administrative units/sub-units develop their own autonomous pathologies of rent-seeking, problem-solving and clientelism, which bring them more often than not in competition with other administrative sub-units.[86] The implementation of EC law reinforces this in that it does merely elaborate national administrative power, but, by seeking to adjust or 'perfect' existing regulatory processes, it redistributes that power through creating new divisions, designations and specialisations. Some of the central tensions provoked by EC law and, in institutional terms, some of the most likely foci of resistance are likely to arise from this administrative adjustment.

Case studies have, therefore, illustrated how administrative sub-divisions, operational practices and centre–periphery tensions have in some jurisdictions increased the administrative costs of implementing EC law and generated bureaucratic rents, constituencies and pathologies opposed to its implementation.[87] The problems have been less within the UK because of the traditional hegemony of central governmental institutions.[88] It is also tempting to speculate that it has been facilitated by the proliferation of centralised agencies – such as the agencies regulating the utilities, the Environment Agency and the Financial Services Authority – in the 1980s and 1990s whose position has been consolidated by the conferral of new tasks under EC law. Despite occasional tensions within central government,[89] it has, therefore, been relatively simple for British governments to implement and transpose EC law as both the administrative costs and bureaucratic rents opposing such implementation have been less than in states with highly federalised or devolved systems of government.

Be that as it may, it is possible to speculate – no more than that – that there is a form of administrative adjustment that has provoked as much resistance in the UK as elsewhere. In particular, the implementation of EC law has led increasingly to a 'governmentalisation of government' within the UK. The introduction of mechanisms such as audit, review by administrative unit by another, and deliberative procedures review have increasingly subjected government, within a purely domestic context, to the same processes of external management and review as that to which it subjects private citizens. To be sure, this is a feature of our age,[90] but as it goes to the heart of what is government and who governs, one would anticipate resistance from vested interests. Such resistance would not manifest itself at the formal level of transposition, but is more likely to manifest itself at the moment of review or management (for example, at the moment of application).[91]

POLITICAL REACTION TO JUDICIAL POLITICS IN THE UNITED KINGDOM

Judicial activity might be tightly focused, but that does not make it any less intense within this zone of activity. Reported cases constitute a fraction of the judicial activity that took place. In 1998, five decisions of the Employment Appeal Tribunal were reported on TUPE, yet judicial statistics indicate that the tribunal gave 28 judgments in this area.[92] More generally, one finds that in the fields of sex discrimination and VAT, areas dominated by EC law, the Employment Appeal Tribunal and the VAT and Duties Tribunals received 99 and 2,797 cases respectively.[93] As both bodies are appellate bodies, this is obviously a fraction of the number of cases decided.[94] Even those reported often mask representative actions or generate overwhelming harmonised responses. The *Foster* case, which found that enforced differential ages of retirement for men and women by British Gas violated Directive 76/207/EEC, the Equal Treatment Directive, was brought upon behalf of 400 women and resulted in an £8.48-million settlement by the employer.[95] Similarly, the *Johnston* case, uncovering sex discrimination in the Royal Ulster Constabulary, was brought on behalf of 310 police women and resulted in a settlement of around £1 million.[96] The lifting of the cap on compensation in sex discrimination cases in *Marshall (No. 2)* led to, according to different estimates, the Ministry of Defence having to settle between 4,500 and 5,500 cases at a cost of around £18 million.[97] It has also led to a general intensity of judicial activity in this area. From 1995 to 1996, there was a more than 200 per cent increase in the size of the awards and out-of-court settlements offered to victims.[98] More recently, the decision of the ECJ[99] that part-time workers had a right to participate in occupational pension schemes led, through the organisation of key trade unions such as UNISON, to 40,000 cases being lodged against employers in industrial tribunals.[100] Finally, one could point to the ripple effects of this activity. The effects of the *Barber* judgment in its requirement of the equalisation of occupational pension entitlements was costed by the government, prior to subsequent qualification by the ECJ of that judgment's effects, at £50 billion.[101]

Neo-functionalist writers have argued that the impact of this is softened by the law acting as a 'mask for politics'.[102] By this it is meant that the activities of courts are less widely reported than those of legislatures and the general, universalist language of law assuages the ideological and practical implications of legal decisions, whilst its arcanity obfuscates what is at stake. Against this it may be noted that the strong asymmetries of information enjoyed by courts and the necessity for them to impose 'win–lose' solutions results in a greater likelihood of seemingly inconsequential decisions having the unanticipated consequence of adversely affecting influential or broad constituencies significantly. An apparently trifling dispute about a bus pass, for example, had implications for the charges that could be imposed by public transport networks on 1.5 million Britons, with corollary significant knock-on effects on the planning and financing of these networks.[103]

Be that as it may, the 'impact' of judicial application of EC law within the domestic public sphere was measured through analysis of press coverage of judicial application,[104] domestic and ECJ, of those areas of EC law whose incidence in terms of reported case-load was highest (and therefore impact most intense).[105] These four areas were sex discrimination, taxation, safeguarding of employee rights in the event of transfer of undertakings (TUPE), and intellectual property (see Table 4).

Table 4 shows a very high level of reporting of sex discrimination litigation (a notable feature of which was high levels of tabloid reporting, as opposed to comment, of decisions), a reasonably high level of reporting of TUPE decisions, little reporting of VAT decisions and no reporting of intellectual property decisions. Whilst it may be possible to argue in the latter two sectors that judicial application has shielded policy development

TABLE 4

MEDIA REPORTING OF JUDICIAL APPLICATION OF EC LAW IN THE UK

	National Court	ECJ	Report[1]	Comment	Editorial	Positive	Negative	Tabloids	Other[2]	Total No. Items
Sex Discrimination										
1988	4	0	5	0	0	0	0	0	1	5
1989	1	1	2	2	0	0	0	0	0	4
1990	5	4	11	3	0	1	1	0	2	14
1991	5	4	10	2	1	0	2	0	1	13
1992	0	8	10	3	0	0	1	0	1	13
1993	9	11	21	2	1	0	4	3	1	24
1994	13	15	34	14	5	3	8	9	5	53
1995	12	16	50	8	0	0	6	10	21	57
1996	10	14	27	8	0	2	2	8	5	35
1997	7	10	19	4	2	1	2	3	3	25
1998	3	7	11	7	1	1	1	1	1	18
Total	69	90	200	51	10	8	27	34	41	261
Taxation										
1988–98	4	4	1				1	1		5
Safeguarding of Employee Rights in the Event of Transfer of Undertakings (TUPE)										
1988–98	7	4	24	7	1	0	8	1	9	30

Notes:

[1] These do not refer to law reports published in newspapers. These were omitted for the same reason as the *Financial Times*, and that they are not really evidence of a 'political' reaction. Reports here reported to where newspapers deemed a judgment sufficiently newsworthy to be covered as a legal or political event.

[2] These were reports of decisions of the ECJ that were invoked in non-judicial settings.

from the glare of public scrutiny and debate, as a general argument, this view does not seem to run.

More interesting are the differences in the levels of reporting between the different sectors. The difference between taxation and sex discrimination is particularly striking. Fiscal matters go right to the heart of the question of sovereignty in the submission to financial obligations they impose on a populace.[106] Debates about Directive 77/388/EEC, the Sixth VAT Directive, which is by far and away the most heavily litigated fiscal instrument go also to the heart of government capability. With the increasing reliance for government revenue on indirect taxation, the Sixth VAT Directive determines what can be taxed, who is taxed and, to a considerable degree, the level of taxation on VAT, the central form of indirect taxation.[107] It is also too simplistic to put it down to differing levels of 'public interest' on one over the other or differing levels of legal complexity. A feature of tax cases is that their consequences can be represented fairly simply, for example, 'X decision results in the Exchequer losing Y amount of money' or 'A decision results in consumers not having to pay tax on B goods or services'. There has, for that matter, been considerable public debate within the UK over the Commission proposal for a withholding tax on savings.[108] Analysis of the litigation and the reports suggest that there are three variables that influence the amount of coverage a matter receives.

EC Law as a Direct or Indirect Source of Rights

It is possible that the formal salience of EC law influences domestic reaction. The mechanism of indirect effect is used heavily as vehicle of EC legal rights where EC law has been successfully invoked in the fields of taxation (46 instances), intellectual property (14 instances) and TUPE (10 instances). That is to say, individuals gain their rights through national law being interpreted in the light of EC law. By contrast, there is a low incidence in the case of sex discrimination (only seven instances) which relies far more heavily upon the direct application of EC provisions. Indirect effect is a less stark instrument than the other sources of individual rights, direct effect and state responsibility.[109] It does not emphasise the autonomy and precedence of the EC legal order over the national one. Instead it stresses mutual adjustment and co-ordination between the two within a heterarchical framework. Not only is consonance suggested between the aims of the two legal orders, but the national legal system appropriates responsibility for the decision. The decision is not something 'externally' foisted upon national law by EC law, but rather something for which there is joint responsibility.

The Imposition of Private Duties and Costs

There seems to be a resistance within the UK to the judicial application of EC law regulating private relationships. This manifests itself in part in a high level of judicial resistance to applying EC law provisions that cut across private legal relations. It shows itself more broadly in the reaction of the press to the two areas where there is heavy involvement by EC law in the judicial regulation of private relationships, TUPE and sex discrimination, and where EC law is, in both quantitative and proportionate terms, frequently successfully invoked. In the reporting and comment upon sex discrimination litigation, adverse comments grouped in the following manner: 37 reported upon the general regulatory costs of compliance (as distinct from the individual compensation awarded); seven reported on the costs to the taxpayer from changes in the welfare regime brought about by rulings; five approached it from a centre–periphery perspective, namely that there did not seem good grounds why this should have anything to do with the EC; and five were critical because judgment conflicted with received notions about how to regulate questions of gender or sexual orientation. A similar premium upon private autonomy is present in the reporting of TUPE: seven reports were critical of the costs or difficulties its judicial development had placed upon the transfer of business; two were critical of there being an EC dimension; and seven argued that the lack of clarity of the Directive was hampering planning by business.

The ECJ and Its Case Law

A greater prominence of the ECJ and its case law tends to lead to increased comment and criticism. In the field of sex discrimination, where EC law had been successfully invoked, it was possible to identify 35 cases where the case law of the ECJ was determinative (47 per cent). The equivalent figures were 61 for taxation (33 per cent), five for intellectual property (22 per cent) and 20 for TUPE (56 per cent). Next to this must be placed the number of referrals to the ECJ, which, both proportionately and quantitatively, is led quite some way by the sex discrimination field.

To be sure, the *habitus* of the ECJ, locked away in its remote, gloomy, supranational corridors in Luxembourg, is more geared towards acting as an external policing agent than national courts with their formal or informal proximities to national administrations. This possibly leads the ECJ to challenging existing national taboos and conventions more readily.[110] Furthermore, resistance might be provoked by the ECJ representing the most stark personification of the exteriority of EC law to national law. Yet, if this were so, one would have expected comment to focus on more narrow centre–periphery institutional questions.

There are two more central reasons for resistance. First, the logics underpinning the majority of cases referred to Luxembourg are very different from those running through the majority of cases decided by British courts. The latter will often be concerned with resolution of a dispute that is confined to a narrow set of factual circumstances in which the interests are often not strongly generalisable and where the remedy sought is often pecuniary in nature.[111] A feature of a heavy proportion of the cases referred to Luxembourg, by contrast, is that they dabble fairly explicitly in judicial politics. Litigation is brought by or concerted by organised interests

– quangos, NGOs, organised industrial interests – and the remedies sought are a bid to determine the content of the law rather than pursuit of some form of compensation. In this, ECJ judgments represent an outcome of a process in which politics is very much a form of elite competition centred around 'decision of the exception'. For matters are only litigated – and considerable expense discharged – because of the dissatisfaction of the domestic interest in question with the legal status quo. Not only is the domain litigated, therefore, naturally contentious, but, going to Europe, as part of a two-level game, is inevitably a consequence of that interest being unable to be met through domestic opportunity structures.[112]

There is a second reason that explains domestic reaction, particularly in situations, such as that in the case of TUPE, where there have been very few references, but heavy reliance upon ECJ case law. A structural feature of fields heavily regulated by ECJ case law is that their strong reliance upon a single, centralised, non-specialised judicial institution leads them to be, in terms of regulatory design, highly inflexible. It is not simply that the ECJ will suffer from asymmetries of information and representation in its regulation of local labour markets and that a single regime will be insensitive to sectoral and geographical variations.[113] The problem derives from an institution such as the ECJ being unable to monitor and steer a sector sufficiently intensely. As a court it is only able to react in an *ad hoc* manner to those cases brought before it. More uniquely, in any area, the number of cases it decides, in absolute terms, is never that high. The consequence is that not only does ECJ case law inevitably tend to throw up more questions than answers, but that any shift in the case law will be perceived as imposing quite dramatic shifts in pre-existing working practices. In the case of TUPE, therefore, relatively subtle shifts in the reasoning in just two ECJ cases, three years apart, led to huge shifts in expectations, and corollary uncertainty, about the circumstances in which there was a transfer of an undertaking and employee protection activated.[114]

Notwithstanding all this, is it possible to point to the litigation process having a considerable autonomy from these political pressures? Pollack, in particular, has observed how the thresholds required for agreement in EC legislative procedures and intergovernmental conferences (IGCs) impose high costs and difficulties for member states seeking to obtain legislative amendments.[115] Legislative amendments being the central tool available to administrations to police the ECJ, the corollary of this is that the difficulties in obtaining these give a corresponding autonomy not just to the ECJ, but also to all other actors participating in the judicial application of EC law. For a decision of a high-ranking domestic court will be as difficult to curb as that of the ECJ, and can be perceived by the British government as equally significant. Thus, the decision that prompted the British government to pressurise the Commission to revise the TUPE Directive was a decision of the Employment Appeal Tribunal in 1993 holding that the Directive did apply to public services contracted out through privatisation.[116] These arguments would appear to apply with particular force to the practice of British courts. A feature of the majority of rulings is that they concern either EC Treaty Articles or Directives adopted in the 1970s.[117] Not only has this length of time given these areas of law time to develop autonomous path-dependencies of their own, but they all require either an intergovernmental conference or a unanimity vote in the Council to amend.

Institutional constraints have considerable persuasive effect in explaining 'constitutional interpretation', the autonomy of judicial interpretation of EC Treaty articles. In this instance, the central obstacle is not the unanimous agreement of other governments that must be obtained but rather the narrow timeframe within which this must be done. In practice, IGCs cannot be used to reverse decisions of four or five years standing. For, as parties will have had to adjust their positions to comply with these decisions, there would necessarily be considerable costs to reversal of those decisions. In practice, IGCs have, therefore, only been used to clarify decisions that appeared in a relatively narrow window before the IGC.[118]

The position is different with secondary legislation. Here tomorrow belongs to opposing governments, as they have indefinite periods to secure amendment of legislation. Furthermore, the legislative thresholds confer only a limited autonomy on the judicial sphere. It seems even a unanimity requirement in the Council will in some circumstances not prevent frequent amendment. By the end of 1999, the Council had amended the Sixth VAT Directive, Directive 77/388/EEC, 16 times.[119] For a decision trap to emerge it seems that a further requirement is that the area is one in which there is also relatively strong elite competition. In the case of TUPE, the 1994 Commission proposal to amend the Directive was stalled for a number of years, despite having the support of UNICE, and the British, Italian, French and German governments. In part, this was certainly because the British Trade Union Congress saw the existing version as hugely beneficial and successfully lobbied the Danish and Swedish governments and the European Parliament, both independently and with the ETUC, to oppose any amendment.[120] This opposition by the unions reduced following the *Süzen* judgment when it became clear that the Directive could cut both ways.[121] A similar situation exists in the field of sex discrimination, where women's organisations have not merely taken advantage of the opportunity structures offered by the ECJ, but have created a powerful lobby in Brussels and a few national capitals which enables them to entrench those gains.[122]

All this creates a form of decision trap that results in strongly exacerbated tensions in areas where there are both elite competition and a significant number of ECJ judgments. Opportunity structures are not merely available to 'outsider' elites that are not available domestically, but the nature of the decision-making structures in Brussels makes it relatively easy to protect those gains. This leads to a reterritorialisation of difference, where one elite will have hegemony in those areas regulated wholly in the domestic sphere, whilst an opposing one will have hegemony in those areas regulated by EC law. These institutional structures not only exacerbate centre–periphery tensions on grounds of ideological difference, but reinforce those tensions through providing incentives for the respective elites to engage heavily in turf-protection.

JUDICIAL TENSIONS IN THE APPLICATION OF EC LAW

The Patterning of Judicial Behaviour by the Institutional Environment

The generalistic, reductivistic assumptions of statistics within which each case is given an equal value and treated as possessing (or not) a limited series of attributes render them unsuited in many ways to producing acute insights into particular judicial preferences or storylines. And in this respect the case study is a far more productive form of analysis. Notwithstanding this, entry into litigation is entry into an organisational process with highly defined properties, which, in turn, will generate homologies of its own. There is a consensus in the EC judicial politics literature that judicial behaviour does not fit in some neat, universalistic model of institutional design, but, in Moe's words, is a 'unique structural reflection of its own politics'.[123] Analysis has approached this, however, in quite discrete supply and demand terms. On the supply side, there is a burgeoning literature that recognises that the formal and informal resources that inform judicial autonomy also structure attitudes to preliminary references and reception of EC law – be they formal legal rules, either procedural or substantive; notions of judicial identity; patterns of recruitment; understanding of intra-judicial relations, relations with other arms of government or with civil society.[124] More recently, from a demand side, it has been observed how general variations between jurisdictions concerning the patterns in the quantity and distribution of litigation affect the development of EC law in these different jurisdictions.[125]

All these are important structural constraints. Yet, by being treated as simply an external constraint on the output of judicial behaviour, they fail to account for the nature of the dialectic between each other that is generated through the process of litigation and adjudication and how these processes themselves frame and transform that dialectic. No account is taken of what cultural institutionalists label 'the institutional environment', the series of 'rational myths' that condition and enable behaviour, 'rational in that they specify in a rulelike way how certain activities are to be conducted to achieve a given objective, mythical in that the rules "work" because and only to the extent, they rest on widely shared beliefs'.[126] The feature of such belief-systems is that they not only act as important autonomous forms of organisation. As they frame how organisations perceive the nature of their tasks, measure their success in performing those tasks and enter into relations with their parties, success and legitimacy are measured in areas characterised by strong institutional environments by the extent to which organisations conform to these 'rational myths'. This, in turn, leads to strong convergences in behaviour.

The central form of institutional environment that patterns judicial behaviour is that the judge must enter into a *quintessentially legal relationship* with the parties who come before the court. Legal structures will determine who and what appears before the court and when. Legal structures will also determine the triangular relationship between the court and the parties during litigation, and finally the outcome will have to be expressed and reasoned in legal terms. At a very general level, these condition judicial behaviour and limit options. In particular, law contains a number of structures that condition judicial decision-making. These include abstraction – law refers to generic sets of situations – and comprehensiveness – no constraints will be recognised, formally, on legal authority other than those imposed legally. The need for law to stabilise expectations also leads any legal decision to couch itself by reference to past practice and to be non-falsifiable. That is to say that where there is a deviance between a legal norm and behaviour, it is the latter that is to be regarded as legally at fault. Furthermore, the requirement upon judges to couch decisions using binary legal/illegal distinctions precludes them from reaching certain outcomes, such as constructing negotiated settlements.

Institutional Capabilities for Conformity as the Central Constraint on Reception of EC Law

The above are all very general, however. There are structures that condition the attitudes of British judges towards application of EC law far more specifically. The first of these is, unsurprisingly, the legal doctrine itself, be it substantive or procedural. It may come as a surprise to some of the judicial politics literature, but a feature of judicial identity is that judges are there to apply the law! Within the context of European integration this can cut both ways, as this could involve not merely applying EU legal rules, but also national ones that might conflict with these. Under such a scenario, one would expect national judicial resistance to the reception of EC law to be higher where it is challenging pre-established domestic laws. This has not really happened simply because there is a convergence in UK and ECJ legal doctrine that in cases of conflict EC law should take precedence. Applying the law, therefore, means applying EC law. Notwithstanding this, divergence between EC law and British law has generated some resistance at the edges, which has manifested itself in two ways. In a number of cases, most notably sex discrimination, but also in other fields, there was an unwillingness to 'distort' national law through interpreting it in the light of subsequent directives.[127] In addition, there was not one example, despite it being legally possible, of a directive being invoked in a British court, where no national legislation was in place. In some instances, the latter was not conformant to EC law, but its presence seemed almost to be a precondition to litigation.

A far more powerful centrifugal pressure, and one that seemed to be central to explaining variations in judicial behaviour across different sectors, was that there was a greater resistance to the application of EC law wherever it was perceived as disrupting the capacity of the central institutions within the British political economy to secure societal conformity. This requires a word of explanation. A central feature of law is that it both seeks to stabilise the expectations and govern the conduct of its subjects. With the emergence of liberal political economy it has contributed to securing two broad forms of conformity. On the one hand, adjudication helps sustain repressive conformity. This assumes a 'collective consciousness is present through the language and practices that each individual shares'.[128] It seeks to sustain this by making 'the members of the group bind themselves even more to the type of collectivity and stress their mutual similarities'.[129] This is done either through punishment or through the exclusion of those who are clearly not part of the group. In practical terms, it leads to law being concerned with the protection of the administrative apparatus' interests[130] and of central symbols or practices, for example, criminal law, immigration law, laws on blasphemy and obscenity. On the other hand, law helps to sustain restitutionary conformity. Derived from the division of labour, this 'disposes individuals exercising different occupations and playing different roles to find cohesion among themselves'.[131] In this instance, the function of law is to provide rules of mutual dependence (for example, property rights, contract law, recognition of the privileges of professional associations), which allow activities to develop in a patterned and regular manner despite this diversity.[132] In protecting each type of conformity, national law is drawn into a network of relationships with those other institutions that contribute to this conformity. Correspondingly, in applying the law, judicial identity becomes suffused into identification with protection of these institutions. As this association exists essentially at the level of a belief-system, the formal process of giving precedence to EC law cannot displace it. The consequence is that there is a greater unreceptiveness to application of EC law where it disrupts these institutions' capabilities to ensure conformity.

In the case of repressive conformity, this is revealed in the apparently paradoxical treatment of the 76 cases involving criminal sanctions by British courts in this period. EC law was invoked successfully 43 times. These figures conceal a stark dichotomy, however. Where EC legislation is being used to extend the state 'monopoly of violence' by providing further bases for criminalising behaviour – most notably in the field of transport, but also in the fields of fisheries, agriculture, taxation and environment – there are, out of 50 cases, 40 instances of EC law being successfully invoked. This is very different from the scenario where EC law acts in a deregulatory manner by threatening to prevent a state from applying criminal sanctions on the grounds that these breach EC law. In only three out of 26 cases was EC law being successfully invoked. These figures suggest that there is no core of national competencies upon which courts will not let EC law intrude.[133] There is a positive view to EC law where it builds up the state's capacity to secure repressive conformity and extend sanctions, even if this is at the cost of allowing EC law to determine the normative content of that conformity. There is, however, an extremely resistant approach to EC law and the ECJ where, in narrow institutional terms, EC law hinders the capacity to impose not just sanctions, but collective ties. There is further evidence for this hypothesis in the figures on free movement of persons. The overwhelming majority of the former (40 out of 59) concern rights of entry, circulation and residence within the UK rather than questions of employment or non-discrimination – the question of entry into the national society. A feature of the application of this area of law is a high number of restrictive judgments, a low number of referrals and, given that this area involves a substantial legal regime which grants substantial rights to the EC migrant, a much lower rate of success than either the sex discrimination or TUPE cases (see Table 5).

TABLE 5
PATTERNS OF ACCEPTANCE OF CENTRAL AREAS OF EC LAW

	Successfully invoked	Unsuccessfully invoked	Success rate (%)	'Restrictive' judgments	No. of references	Reference refused	Percentage of reported cases referred
Tax	185	70	0.725	17	34	21	0.125
Sex Discrimination	74	65	0.532	19	49	7	0.299
TUPE	36	27	0.571	4	1	0	0.015
Free Movement of Goods	13	48	0.213	7	31	10	0.369
Free Movement of Persons	16	37	0.302	15	19	10	0.322
Environment	8	28	0.222	6	6	5	0.154
Intellectual Property	23	34	0.404	3	9	10	0.113
Social Security	34	39	0.466	1	33	3	0.434
Competition	14	50	0.219	5	5	2	0.058
Agriculture	33	24	0.579	2	40	6	0.588
Fisheries	11	12	0.478	1	16	2	0.640
Transport	26	6	0.813	3	8	4	0.242
External Relations	15	6	0.714	2	8	2	0.226
Pharmaceuticals	9	3	0.750	0	7	1	0.538
Freedom of Establishment	7	5	0.583	0	6	0	0.500
Freedom to Provide Services	3	5	0.375	1	1	2	0.100
Public Procurement	4	6	0.400	0	3	1	0.273
Immigration	2	12	0.143	0	4	0	0.235

Note: TUPE = Safeguarding of Employee Rights in the Event of Transfer of Undertakings

This distribution cannot be put down to the powerful imagery that forms the background to that legislation which secures repressive conformity, for a similar pattern emerges in the case of legislation securing restitutionary conformity. In this instance, there is a very clear dichotomy between legislation that overlaps and supplements enduring private legal relationships and that legislation which cuts across and disrupts these relations. Sex discrimination legislation and TUPE are examples of the former. They build and consolidate the contract of employment. Both have relatively high levels of being successfully invoked. There is a steady pattern of references in the case of sex discrimination and a high deference to the case law of the ECJ in the case of both. One therefore finds, once again, that there is no hallowed turf of British private law upon which British judges will not let EC law intrude. This attitude stands in marked contrast to the attitude of British judges to EC competition and environment law. Competition law, as an area, cuts across private contracts by rendering them unenforceable. It diminishes the steering capacity of the institution of contract and had a correspondingly low rate of being successfully invoked.

In the case of environmental law, the majority of the decisions concerned challenges to public authority 'development consents' granting permission for some private development. The judicial challenge was, in substantive terms, therefore, concerned with thwarting private initiatives and curbing the exercise of private property rights. A feature of this area was that on every point it scored lowly. There was a low success rate of invocability, a high rate of refusals by British courts to refer, and a higher than average number of 'restrictive' judgments.[134]

CONCLUSION

In the absence of comparative analysis, there are dangers in extrapolating the British experience to offer insights on the practice in other jurisdictions. At the risk of over-extension it is possible to indicate where it might have some resonance. For, in as fragmented and decentralised a process as litigation, particularly before many tribunals with low entry costs, it is difficult to believe that the British experience on the narrow application of EC law is unique. The heavy normativity of EC law is likely to be a pan-European feature and offers explanations for governmental acceptance of the EC legal order and also suggests a re-evaluation of how EC law should be critiqued by legal academics. It is likely, by contrast, that there are many features of British political reaction to ECJ case law that are esoteric. The disposition of the press and the grip that the 'European' issue has over one of the main political parties are themselves distinguishing features. As for the logics that have underpinned British judicial reception of EC law and patterns of references, patterns of litigation will of course vary. But there is nothing in the British experience to suggest that the broad features determining judicial behaviour in the light of these patterns will be too different, notably the absence of fit between references to the ECJ and broad application of EC law in national courts.

If that is so, there are two implications for the debate about the nature of the Union judicial system that will take place in the forthcoming Intergovernmental Conference. The first concerns the debate about European constitutionalism. The constitutional norms of EC law beloved of legal scholars are applied in such limited scenarios that to demand a European constitution, taking them as one's starting point is to argue for the exception becoming the rule. It involves such a radical transformation in the nature of the EU that it simply beggars belief to argue for this as some form of extension of existing processes.[135] Instead, advocates for such a cause would be better advised to explain why it should be the EU, rather than other more cosmopolitan settings, be they global, such as the UN bodies, or genuinely pan-European, such as the OSCE or Council of Europe, that is the appropriate setting for such arrangements.

The second concerns the preliminary reference procedure. Currently, it is creaking under the number of references – a problem that will be exacerbated by enlargement.[136] The UK experience suggests that not only are the majority of references hugely unrepresentative of the type of litigation that involves British courts day in day out, but that EC law is successfully applied by British courts in areas where there are very references. Moreover, it appears that it is above all the structure of the reference system rather than any judicial bias on the part of the ECJ that leads to so many judgments being a source of dissension. It is clearly unrealistic to suppose that judicial politics can ever be separated from the application of EC law. But there would be much to be said for most of it taking place within the domestic judicial sphere – attitudes to the ECJ will be less polarised, difficult judgments will be easier to reverse, and the problem would be seen as being as much a responsibility of the national legal system as the EU one. This could be simply achieved by only allowing national courts of last resort to refer.[137]

NOTES

There have been a number of debts accumulated in this article. Thanks go to Karen Alter, Matt Gabel, Simon Hix, Erik Jones, Imelda Maher, Gillian More, and Alec Stone Sweet, as well as the London EU Group.

1. M. Shapiro, *Law and Politics in the Supreme Court* (New York: Free Press 1964), p.15.
2. K. Alter, 'Who are the "Masters of the Treaty"?: European Governments and the European Court of Justice', *International Organization* 52 (1998), pp.121 and 125.
3. Most notably J. Weiler, *The Constitution of Europe* (Cambridge: Cambidge University Press 1998).
4. J. Weiler, 'A Quiet Revolution: The European Court of Justice and Its Interlocutors', *Comparative Political Studies* 26 (1994), pp.510 and 523; W. Mattli and A.-M. Slaughter, 'The Role of National Courts in the Process of European Integration: Accounting for Judicial Preferences and Constraints', in A.-M. Slaughter, A. Stone Sweet and J. Weiler (eds.), *The European Court and National Courts: Doctrine and Jurisprudence* (Oxford: Hart 1998), pp.253 and 259–61. It should be noted that neither of these authors, nor any author for that matter, has argued that this is the sole, or even predominant, factor influencing national judicial attitudes towards EC law. In their most recent work, these authors catalogue a number of factors, which will have varying degrees of pull in different cases. These include judicial self-understanding; cross-fertilisation of ideas and concepts between courts; the broader national and European political contexts; the deployment of national courts by litigants; the impact of different legal cultures, and, lastly, the biases of individual judges. J. Weiler, A.-M. Slaughter and A. Stone Sweet, 'Prologue – The European Court of Justice', in Slaughter *et al.* (eds.), *The European Court and National Courts*.

5. K. Alter, 'Explaining National Court Acceptance of European Court Jurisprudence: A Critical Evaluation of Theories of Legal Integration', in Slaughter *et al.* (eds.), *The European Court and National Courts*.

6. J. Golub, 'The Politics of Judicial Discretion: Rethinking the Interaction between National Courts and the European Court of Justice', *West European Politics* 19 (1996), p.360.

7. D. Chalmers, 'Judicial Preferences and the Community Legal Order', *Modern Law Review* 60 (1997), p.164.

8. I. Maher, 'Community Law in the National Legal Order: A Systems Analysis', *Journal of Common Market Studies* 36 (1998), p.237.

9. A.-M. Burley and W. Mattli, 'Europe Before the Court: A Political Theory of Legal Integration', *International Organization* 41 (1993), p.47; W. Mattli and A.-M. Slaughter, 'Revisiting the European Court of Justice', *International Organization* 52 (1998), p.177.

10. K. Alter, 'The European Union's Legal System and Domestic Policy: Spillover or Backlash?', *International Organization* 54 (2000), p.489; K. Alter and J. Vargas, 'Explaining Variation in the Use of European Litigation Strategies: EC Law and UK Gender Equality Policy', *Comparative Political Studies* 32 (2000), p.452; L. Conant, 'Europeanization and the Courts: Variable Patterns of Adaptation among National Judiciaries', in J. Caparaso, M. Cowles and T. Risse (eds.), *Europeanization and Domestic Structural Change* (Ithaca, NY: Cornell University Press 2000).

11. C. Harlow and R. Rawlings, *Pressure Through Law* (London: Routledge 1992), pp.268–87; R. Rawlings, 'The Eurolaw Game: Some Deductions from a Saga', *Journal of Law and Society* 20 (1993), p.309.

12. J. Golub, *Modelling Judicial Dialogue in the European Community: The Quantitative Basis of Preliminary References to the ECJ*, RSC 96/58 Working Paper (Florence: European University Institute 1996); A. Stone Sweet and T. Brunell, 'The European Court and the National Courts: A Statistical Analysis of Preliminary References', *Journal of European Public Policy* 5 (1998), p.66; A. Stone Sweet and J. Caparaso, 'From Free Trade to Supranational Polity: The European Court and Integration' in W. Sandholtz and A. Stone Sweet (eds.), *European Integration and Supranational Governance* (Oxford: Oxford University Press 1998).

13. For a summary of the main lines of argument, see E. Ringquist and C. Emmert, 'Judicial Policymaking in Published and Unpublished Decisions: The Case of Environmental Litigation', *Political Research Quarterly* 52 (1999), p.7.

14. G. Garrett, 'International Cooperation and Institutional Choice: the European Community's Internal Market' *International Organization* 46 (1992), p.533; G. Garrett, 'The Politics of Legal Integration', *International Organization* 49 (1995), p.171; G. Garrett, R. Keleman and H. Schulz, 'The European Court of Justice, National Governments and Legal Integration in the European Union', *International Organization* 52 (1998), p.149; Burley and Mattli, 'Europe Before the Court'; Mattli and Slaughter, 'Revisiting the European Court of Justice'.

15. For example Slaughter *et al.* (eds.), *The European Court and National Courts*.

16. Stone, Sweet and Brunell, 'The European Court and the National Courts'.

17. Rawlings, 'The Eurolaw Game', p.309; Alter and Vargas, 'Explaining Variation in the Use of European Litigation Strategies'.

18. Almost all reported cases involving EC law are passed on to the Registry of the ECJ. The author is particularly grateful to Jacqueline Suter who provided a list of these judgments, which acted as the starting point for this research. The following law reports were then scanned: *British Company Cases, Common Market Law Reports, Current Law, European Commercial Cases, European Current Law, European Law Reports, European Trade Mark Reports, Environmental Law Reports, Fleet Street Reports, Immigration Appeal Reports, Incorporated Law Reports of England and Wales, Industrial Case Reports, International Legal Procedure, Intertax, Law Reports of Jersey, Lloyds Law Reports, Manx Law Reports, Northern Ireland Law Reports, Reports of Patents and Design, Weekly Law Reports, Scots Law Times, Session Cases, Simon's Tax Cases, Times Law*

Reports, Trading Law, Value Added Tax Tribunals Reports. In the case of judgments that involved more than one court, either because of appeal or reference, the judgment was given only a value of one and the decision of the final court taken. If a fresh matter was litigated between the parties, however, it was treated as a separate judgment. This happened in only two cases.

19. On the UK, see B. Atkins, 'Interventions and Power in Judicial Hierarchies: Appellate Courts in England and the United States', *Law and Society Review* 24 (1990), p.71; B. Atkins, 'Data Collection in Comparative Judicial Research: A Note on the Effects of Case Publication upon Theory Building and Hypothesis Testing', *Western Political Quarterly* 45 (1992), p.783.

20. In the one study this led to more employee-friendly judgments than in non-reported cases. In the other, it led to more severe environmental penalities. See, respectively, J. Donohue and P. Siegelman, 'The Changing Nature of Employment Discrimination Litigation', *Stanford Law Review* 43 (1989), p.983; Ringquist and Emmert, 'Judicial Policymaking in Published and Unpublished Decisions', p.7. Also see, for a general study confirming this, C. Rowland and R. Carp, *Politics and Judgment in Federal District Courts* (Lawrence: University of Kansas Press 1996).

21. There were essentially three tests. On the one hand, there was the two-fold test famously set out in *Associated Provincial Picture Houses v. Wednesbury* [1948] 1 KB 223. A measure would be illegal, on the one hand, if it was *ultra vires*. In particular, it took account of a factor or failed to take account of a failure that was precluded by statute. It would also be illegal if it was unreasonable, namely 'so absurd that no sensible person could ever dream that it lay within the powers of authority'. On the other, the doctrine of natural justice emerged in the 1960s to impose certain requirements of procedural justice, *Ridge v. Baldwin* [1964] AC 40. None of these tests applied a stringent test of substantive review. This has changed in the last 25 years with a plurality of tests emerging, whose intensity will depend upon the nature of the measure reviewed. For more on this, see P. Craig, *Administrative Law* (London: Sweet and Maxwell, 4th edn. 1999), ch. 12 *et seq*.

22. J. Habermas, *Between Facts and Norms* (Cambridge: Polity 1996), pp.270–72.

23. Ibid., p.298.

24. The irony is that the ECJ applies a measure of review to national action that is quintessentially liberal in nature, namely is the measure in question excessively restrictive of the economic freedom in question, Case 104/75 *Officier van Justitie v. De Peijper* [1976] ECR 613. It applies, however, a far more lenient, republican version to review of EC institutions' actions merely considering whether the measures were 'manifestly unsuitable', Case C-22/94 *Irish Farmers Association v. MAFF* [1997] ECR I-1809. Being only able to review national measures for their compatibility with EC law, it is the former test that national courts have to apply, however. Case 314/85 *Firma Fotofrost v. HZA Lübeck Ost* [1987] ECR 4199.

25. Case 246/80 *Broeckmeulen v. Huisarts Registratie Commissie* [1981] ECR 2311; Case C-24/92 *Corbiau v. Administration des Contributions* [1993] ECR I-1277.

26. In England and Wales powers of judicial review are only given to the High Court, Court of Appeal and House of Lords.

27. Examples include Employment Tribunals, Value Added Tax and Duties Tribunals, Immigration Appeals Tribunals, Social Security Commissioners.

28. Case 146/73 *Rheinmühlen v. Einfuhr-und Vorratstelle Getreide* [1974] ECR 139

29. R. Brenner, 'The Agrarian Roots of European Capitalism', in T. Aston and C. Philpin (eds.), *The Brenner Debate: Agrarian Class Structure and Economic Development in Pre-Industrial Europe* (Cambridge: Cambridge University Press 1985), pp.284–99; A. Giddens, *The Nation-State and Violence* (Cambridge: Polity 1985), pp.148–52.

30. M. Foley, *The Silence of Constitutions* (London: Routledge 1989), ch. 2.

31. W. Murphy, *The Oldest Social Science? Configurations of Law and Modernity* (Oxford: Oxford University Press 1997), pp.81–100. One author thus saw the emergence of the common law in the thirteenth century as designed to preserve 'the harmony of the free

landowning class'. R. van Caenegem, *The Birth of the English Common Law* (Cambridge: Cambridge University Press, 2nd edn. 1988), p.97.

32. H. Collins, 'European Private Law and the Cultural Identity of Member States', *European Review of Private Law* 3 (1995), p.353.

33. P. Atiyah, *The Rise and Fall of Freedom of Contract* (Oxford: Oxford University Press 1979), chs. 17–22.

34. The exchange function deals with the price at what a good or service could be sold. There had been monopolies and restrictive practices legislation in the UK since 1948. There was also legislation protecting against exorbitant pricing. A feature of this legislation, however, was weak administrative powers, R. Whish, *Competition Law* (London: Butterworths, 3rd edn. 1993), pp.170–74, and considerable judicial discretion, J. Adams and R. Brownsword, 'The Unfair Contract Terms Act: A Decade of Discretion', *LQR* 104 (1988), p.94.

35. T. Wilhelmsson, 'Integration as Disintegration of National Law', in H. Petersen and H. Zahles, *Legal Polycentricity: Consequences of Pluralism in Law* (Aldershot: Dartmouth 1995); H. Schepel, 'Legal Pluralism in Europe', in P. Fitzpatrick and J. Bergeron (eds.), *Europe's Other: European Law between Modernity and Postmodernity* (Aldershot: Ashgate 1997); G. Teubner, 'Legal Irritants: Good Faith in British Law or How Unifying Law Ends Up In New Divergences', *Modern Law Review* 61 (1998).

36. The courts began to engage far more extensively in judicial review from the mid-1980s onwards. The Human Rights Act 1998, by subjecting all administrative and, to a more qualified extent, legislative action to review against the norms set out in the European Convention on Human Rights and Freedoms has anchored the British constitutional settlement around certain liberal, constitutive principles safeguarding private autonomy. The onset of the regulatory state in Britain has also considerably reduced the ambit and autonomy of the common law. With the possible exception of the latter (and even there many of the interventions were wholly domestic in nature), the direct contribution of the EC to these broader developments was inconsiderable. The Labour Party in its 1996 Manifesto did not resort to any arguments based on EC law to justify the Human Rights Act 1998. J. Straw and P. Boateng, 'Labour's Plans to Incorporate the ECHR', *European Human Rights Law Review* 1 (1997), p.94. If EC law were to have been a vehicle for judicial empowerment, it would have involved, from an early stage, a high incidence of *ex parte* judicial review actions. For these give access to the administrative law remedies of *certiorari* and *mandamus*, which enable courts to compel other government agencies to act or desist from acting. In fact, in the early years these were far and few between. It was only after the judiciary repositioned itself, in disputes that did not involve EC law, *vis-à-vis* the other arms of government that the incidence of such actions involving EC law increased. The figures for such actions in the cases analysed were the following: 1977-2, 1980-1, 1982-2, 1984-4, 1985-1, 1986-8, 1987-4, 1988-4, 1989-4, 1990-4, 1991-9, 1992-4, 1993-14, 1994-17, 1995-20, 1996-20, 1997-18, 1998-27.

37. 'If the act of parliament will positively enact a thing to be done which is unreasonable, I know of no power that can control it ... for that were to set the judicial power above that of the legislature' (Blackstone's Commentary 1765, Vol. I, p.91). More recently see *British Railways Board v. Pickin* [1974] AC 765.

38. Most recently see the Food Labelling Bill introduced by Stephen O'Brien, and backed by the National Farmers Union, on 15 Dec. 1999. Clause 2 will require all food imports to be labelled with their State of origin, a piece of draft legislation that quite clearly breaches Article 28 EC, the provision on free movement of goods. <accessed 20 February 2000>.

39. *Garland v. BREL* [1983] 2 AC 751.

40. *Processed Vegetables Growers Association v. CCE* [1974] 1 CMLR 113, *Applications des Gaz v. Falks Veritas* [1974] 2 CMLR 75; *National Insurance Commissioner Decision No CS 8/76* [1977] 1 CMLR 1.

41. See *Sparkes v. Insurance Officer* [1977] CMLR 2 317 which overruled two prior rulings to the opposite effect, *Amies v. ILEA* [1977] ICR 308, *Snoxell v. Vauxhall Motors* [1977] 3 WLR 189.

42. *Kenny v. Insurance Officer* [1978] 1 CMLR 181.
43. *British Ten Pin Bowling Association v. CCE* [1989] 1 CMLR 561.
44. *Burton v. British Rail Board* [1981] 3 CMLR 100.
45. *Jensen v. Corporation of the Trinity House of Deptford* [1982] 2 CMLR 218.
46. *Valor International v. Application des Gaz* [1978] 1 CMLR 30.
47. *Hasselblad v. Orbinson* [1984] 3 CMLR 679; *Hasselblad v. Hodes* [1985] 3 CMLR 664.
48. *R. v. Secretary of State for Transport ex parte Factortame (No 1)* [1990] 2 AC 85; *R v. Secretary of State for Transport ex parte Factortame (No 2)* [1991] AC 603.
49. *Duke v. GEC Reliance* [1988] AC 618; *Finnegan v. Clowney* [1990] AC 407.
50. *R. v. MAFF ex parte First City Trading* [1997] 1CMLR 250; *R. v. Secretary of State for the Environment, Transport and Regions ex parte IATA* [1999] 1 CMLR 1287. These were both given by the same judge, Justice Laws, a former Treasury Devil (lawyer appointed to represent and defend the government), but the former has now been reaffirmed in *Marks and Spencer v. CCE* [1999] 1 CMLR 1152.
51. On Directives, see *Minister of the Interior v. Cohen Bendit* [1980] 1 CMLR 543, *Re VAT Directives* [1982] 1 CMLR 527. On the 'limited powers' of the ECJ see *Brunner v. European Union Treaty* [1994] 1 CMLR 57, *Carlsen v. Rasmussen*, judgment of the Danish Constitutional Court of 6 April 1998.
52. To merely equate resistance with the unsuccessful application of EC law is far too broad. The author looked instead for explicit devices used by national courts. These were explicit refusal by UK courts either to accept EC law, particular pieces of legal doctrine or the institutional authority of the EC institutions. A second more common category was ECJ case law was distinguished by being confined to narrower contexts than the one in hand. The third was where a narrow interpretation of legislation was taken, which ignored ECJ decisions on the matter or interpreted a provision in a manner that was less integrationist than subsequent decisions. The above inevitably involved an element of judgement on the part of the author. Insofar as it was clear that resistance was not great, the study has a bias towards exaggerating the level of resistance through the methodology used which can omit some cases and its reliance upon reported cases.
53. If a matter was referred, it was treated as not falling in any of the other 'positive' categories to avoid double counting. The number for references is 256, as there were two references in which the reference was restrictively received by the referring court *R. v. Secretary of State for the Home Department ex parte Santillo* [1981] 1 CMLR 569; *R. v. Secretary of the State for the Home Department ex parte Gallagher* [1996] 2 CMLR 951.
54. These were rulings that either explicitly accepted the authority of EC law or the supranational institutions (e.g. EC Commission Decisions), applied ECJ case law, interpreted national law in the light of EC law or adopted interpretations of EC legislation that were more integrationist than or subsequently adopted in ECJ decisions. These were taken subsequently from references to Luxembourg. It is possible that the number is exaggerated not just from the reliance upon reported decisions, but also as in some cases this did not result in successful invocation of EC law. Nevertheless, given the precedential effects of such decisions (i.e. they were not neutral as to future action) it seemed appropriate to include them.
55. Litigation involving the Convention on Jurisdiction and Enforcement of Judgments in Civil and Commercial Matters 1968 (Brussels Convention) and subsequent Judgments Conventions were not included in this study. Although the UK acceded to the Brussels Convention in 1982 and this does allow for references to the ECJ, the legal structures for these conventions is different from that of the TEU.
56. Of these, five were decided by the High Court and 12 by the Court of Appeal. One of the cases decided by the House of Lords came from Northern Ireland.
57. Twelve were decided by the High Court of the Justiciary and 22 by the Court of Session. Two of the cases decided by the House of Lords were appealed from Scottish courts.
58. Some Commonwealth countries elect to use this body, whose members are made up of House of Lords judges, as a court of final appeal.

59. More than one provision could be invoked in the same case.

60. These are Directive 76/207/EEC-75; Directive 77/187/EEC-65; Directive 77/388/EEC-228; Directive 79/7/EEC-29, and Directive 89/104/EEC-29.

61. This was treated broadly in terms of the subject-matter and legislation adopted in 1993 was considered because of the lag in the legislative programme.

62. B. de Sousa Santos, *Toward a New Common Sense: Law, Science and Politics in the Paradigmatic Transition* (London: Routledge 1995), ch. 5; G. Teubner, 'Breaking Frames: The Global Interplay of Legal and Social Systems', *American Journal of Comparative Law* 45 (1997), p.149.

63. On this 'lex mercatoria', see C. Schmitthoff, *Export Trade: The Law and Practice of International Trade* (London: Stevens 9th edn. 1990); H.-J. Mertens, 'Lex Mercatoria: A Self-Applying System Beyond Law', in G. Teubner (ed.), *Global Law without a State* (Aldershot: Dartmouth 1997). On the role of the law firm, see Y. Dezalay and G. Garth, *Dealing in Virtue: International Commercial Arbitration and the Construction of a Transnational Legal Order* (Chicago, IL: University of Chicago Press 1996).

64. E. Mestmäcker, 'On the Legitimacy of European Law', *Rabels Zeitschift* 56 (1994); E. Streit and W. Mussler, 'The Economic Constitution of the European Community: From "Rome" to "Maastricht"', *European Law Journal* 1 (1995), C. Ball, 'The Making of a Transnational Capitalist Society: The Court of Justice, Social Policy and Individual Rights under the Community's Legal Order', *Harvard International Law Journal* 37 (1996).

65. M. Poiares Maduro, *We the Court: The European Court of Justice and the European Economic Constitution* (Oxford: Hart 1998), pp.61–88.

66. Cf. Weiler, 'A Quiet Revolution', p.510; A.-M Slaughter and L. Helfer, 'Toward a Theory of Effective Supranational Adjudication', *Yale Law Journal* 107 (1997), p.273.

67. During that time it also brought one unsuccessful action, Case C-300/95 *Commission v. United Kingdom* [1997] ECR I-2629, and the number might rise to eight if the Court follows the Opinion of Advocate General Alber in Case C-359/97 *Commission v. United Kingdom*, Opinion of 27 Jan. 2000.

68. At the end of 1998, the UK had notified implementing measures for 1,402 out of 1,455 of the directives applicable within its territory, 96 per cent, see EC Commission, *XVIth Report on Monitoring the Application of Community Law*, COM (99) 301 final, 103.

69. At the end of 1999, in the field of the single market the UK was estimated by the Commission to have implemented 97 per cent of the Directives. Only Sweden, Finland, Denmark and Spain had better records, <accessed 22 February 2000>.

70. 497 letters of formal notice – the first formal stage of an enforcement action – were brought against the UK in the period 1994–98 out of an EU total of 5,695. This was a below average number, but the most striking feature was how few were eventually referred to court. Only six were referred to court, 1.2 per cent, against 355 for the whole of the EU, 6.2 per cent, see EC Commission, *XVIth Report on Monitoring the Application of Community Law*, COM (99) 301 final, Table 2.1.

71. A separate, but similar argument is that compliance might be induced through national officials belonging to the same epistemic communities as the EC legislators, P. Haas, 'Compliance with EU Directives: Insights from International Relations and Comparative Politics', *Journal of European Public Policy* 5 (1998), pp.30–33. This might indeed have some pull. The difficulty with knowledge-based arguments is that even on their own terms the discourse-coalition literature has shown how particular time-space contexts will mould cognitive and communicative understandings of particular 'discursive frames', so that, in the treatment of causation, it becomes increasingly problematic to analogise discursive frames across varying contexts. On 'discourse coalitions', see M. Hajer, *The Politics of Environmental Discourse* (Oxford: Oxford University Press 1995), pp.66–72.

72. These are now on the web. See *http://www.cabinet-office.gov.uk/regulation/1999/europe/transposition.htm*

73. M. Dean, *Governmentality: Power and Rule in Modern Society* (London: Sage 1999), p.120.

74. F. Scharpf, *Governing in Europe: Effective and Democratic?* (Oxford: Oxford University Press), pp.7–16.

75. M. Foucault, *History of Sexuality: Volume One* (Harmondsworth: Penguin 1984), p.144; Dean, *Governmentality*, pp.118–20.

76. Ibid., p.144.

77. Cf. F. Scharpf, 'Negative and Positive Integration in the Political Economy of European Welfare States', in G. Marks *et al.* (eds.), *Governance in the European Union* (London: Sage 1996).

78. N. Fligstein and I. Mara-Drita, 'How to Make a Market: Reflections on the Attempt to Create a Single Market in the European Union', *American Journal of Sociology* 102 (1996), pp.14–28. Interestingly, the one policy that would seem to confront this, the use of partnership in the administration of the structural funds, has foundered precisely upon its inability to recreate new local or regional centres of administrative power, L. Hooghe and M. Keating, 'The Politics of EU Regional Policy', *Journal of European Public Policy* 3 (1994), p.367.

79. In this respect on financial services and lawyers within the UK, see A. Alcock, 'UK Implementation of European Investment Services Directives', *Company Lawyer* 15 (1994), p.291; C. Hadjiemmanuil, *Banking Regulation and the Bank of England* (London/New York/Hong Kong: LLP 1996), pp.195–225; H. Adamson, *Free Movement of Lawyers* (London: Butterworths, 2nd edn. 1996), pp.72–4.

80. C. O'Leary and D. Goldberg, 'Television without Frontiers', in T. Daintith (ed.), *Implementing EC Law in the United Kingdom* (Chichester: John Wiley 1995), pp.215 and 224–33.

81. N. Burrows and H. Hilam, 'The Official Control of Foodstuffs', in Daintith (ed.), *Implementing EC Law in the United Kingdom.*

82. C. Bellamy, 'The Europeanisation of United Kingdom Competition Law', in N. Green and A. Robertson (eds.), *The Europeanisation of UK Competition Law* (Oxford: Hart 1999); S. Eyre and M. Lodge, 'National Tunes and a European Melody? Competition Law Reform in the United Kingdom and Germany', *Journal of European Public Policy* 7 (2000), p.63.

83. A. Weale, 'Environmental Regulation and Administrative Reform in Britain', in G. Majone (ed.) *Regulating Europe* (London: Routledge 1997).

84. B. Hebenton and T. Thomas, *Policing Europe* (Basingstoke: Macmillan 1995), pp.25–37.

85. A survey of 419 constitutions between 1870 and 1970 found that both administrative jurisdiction over social life and mechanisms of implementation doubled during the period, see J. Boli, 'World Polity Sources of Expanding State Authority and Organization, 1870–1970', in J. Thomas *et al.* (eds.), *Institutional Structures: Constituting State, Society and the Individual* (Thousand Oaks, CA: Sage 1994), p.72.

86. C. Offe, *Modernity and the State* (Cambridge: Polity 1996), pp.60–64.

87. The most wide-ranging study that this supports is F. Duina, *Harmonizing Europe: Nation-States within the Common Market* (Albany, NY: State University of New York Press 1999). See also T. Börzel, 'Towards Convergence in Europe? Institutional Adaptation to Europeanization in Germany and Spain', *Journal of Common Market Studies* 37 (1999), p.573; C. Knill and A. Lenschow, 'Coping with Europe: The Impact of British and German Administrations on the Implementation of EU Environmental Policy', *Journal of European Public Policy* 5 (1998), p.595; C. Spanou, 'European Integration in Administrative Terms: A Framework for Analysis and the Greek Case', *Journal of European Public Policy* 5 (1998), p.467.

88. Even in the implementation of structural funds the influence of central government is strong, I. Bache, 'The Extended Gatekeeper: Central Government and the Implementation of EC Regional Policy in the UK', *Journal of European Public Policy* 6 (1999), p.28.

89. Tensions have arisen between the House of Lords and the Department of Environment, Transport and the Regions about the 'semi-legislative' role of the EU Network for the Implementation and Enforcement of Environmental Law (IMPEL). House of Lords Select Committee on the European Communities, *Community Environmental Law: Making It Work* (Session 1997–98, 2nd Report, HMSO), para. 77.

90. On advanced liberalism, see N. Rose, *Power and Freedom* (Oxford: Oxford University Press 1999), pp.138–47.

91. There is considerable anecdotal evidence that the Environmental Impact Assessment Directive has provoked both high-level and low-level resistance. R. Williams, 'The European Commission and the Enforcement of Environmental Law', *YBEL* 14 (1994), p.351; A. Brown, 'Filtering EU Environment Policies through the Government Layers: The EIA Directive in Scotland and Bavaria', *Environmental Politics* 8 (1999), p.66.

92. Lord Chancellor's Department, *Judicial Statistics: Annual Report 1998* (London: Government Statistical Service 1999) Table 7.1.

93. Ibid., Table 7.1 and Table 7.5.

94. Appeals come from the Employment Tribunals and Commissioners of Customs and Excise respectively. There are no statistics available for how many decisions these bodies make.

95. Case C-188/89 *Foster v. British Gas* [1990] ECR I-3313. C. Davies, '£8m payout for gas women forced to retire', *Daily Telegraph*, 14 June 1996.

96. Case 222/84 *Johnston v. Chief Constable of the RUC* [1986] ECR 1651. D. Hearst, 'RUC women officers win £1 million sex bias award', *The Guardian*, 10 Nov. 1988, p.9.

97. Case C-271/91 *Marshall v. Southampton and South-West Area Health Authority* [1993] ECR I-4367. Bellamy, 'The £100 million babies: Everyone in the armed forces knew the rules: get pregnant and you are fired. But the MoD says it didn't know the rules were against the law. Now they are paying the price', *The Independent*, 13 July 1994.

98. The average rose from £6,481 in 1995 to £18,732 in 1996. B. Clement, 'Middle-class woment boost sex bias claims', *The Independent*, 20 June 1997, p.7.

99. Case C-57/93 *Vroege v. NCIV. Instituut* [1994] ECR I-4541. The basis for this is that as far more women are part-timers, a distinction between full-timers and part-timers breached Article 141 EC, the provision on equal pay for work of equal value.

100. Initial estimates put the cost to pension firms if these were successful at £95 million, C. Dyer, 'Pensions test cases may net £95m for part-timers: Tribunal ruling will cover 60,000 workers after Euro judgment on sex bias', *The Guardian*, 15 Nov. 1995, p.6. Many of these actions were withdrawn following a 1997 decision that a claim must be brought within six months of cessation of employment, *Preston v. Woverhampton Health Care Trust* [1997] EuR 386. The matter has been referred. See Case C-78/98 *Preston v. Wolverhampton Health Care Trust*, Opinion of Advocate General Lüger of 14 Sept. 1999.

101. Case C-262/88 *Barber v. Guardian Royal Exchange Assurance Group* [1990] ECR I-1889. The submissions of the Attorney General, Sir Nicholas Lyell, to the ECJ in the *Coloroll* judgment. See J. Carvel, 'Backdated pension rights for men of 60 "would cost 50 billion pounds"', *The Guardian*, 27 Jan. 1993, p.43.

102. Burley and Mattli, 'Europe Before the Court', p.41.

103. *Atkins v. Wrekin* (1994). 1.58 million men would have benefited from this decision. See R. Ford, 'Bus pass verdict could prompt huge pay-out', *The Times*, 1 May 1996.

104. In this sense, to examine the UK case may be atypical as during the Major administration there were unsuccessful attempts to curb the powers of the ECJ both by the administration at the 1996 Intergovernmental Conference and, more unilaterally, through a 1996 Private Members Bill before the House of Commons. For discussion of both of these see D. Chalmers, 'The Application of EC Law in the United Kingdom 1994–1999', *Common Market Law Review* 37 (2000), p.83. Judicial application of EC law therefore enjoys a salience in British political discourse not found in some other member states. Notwithstanding this, some generalisable conclusions are possible.

105. The papers used were *The Independent, The Independent on Sunday, The Guardian, The Daily Mirror, The Sunday Mirror, The Daily Mail, The Mail Upon Sunday, The Times, The Sunday Times, The Daily Telegraph, The Sunday Telegraph*. Deliberately omitted from the survey was the *Financial Times* on the grounds of its reasonably specialised readership. The papers were chosen on account of the spread of ownership, spread of style – four were tabloid, seven broadsheet – and spread on general attitudes to European integration – five are broadly positive, six are broadly negative.

106. P. Bourdieu, 'Rethinking the State: Genesis and Structure of the Bureaucratic Field', *Sociological Theory* 12 (1994), p.7.

107. Directive 77/388 sets out what can be taxed and who bears the tax, OJ 1977, L 145/1. The principles under where VAT is levied and floors for the level of VAT that member states must charge were first set out in the amending Directives, Directive 91/690/EEC, OJ 1991, L 376/1 and Directive 92/111, OJ 1992, L384/47.

108. The matter has proved sufficiently contentious to be discussed first at the Vienna European Council, Conclusions of the Presidency, EU Bulletin 12-1998, I.5 11 and then at the Cologne European Council, Conclusions of the Presidency, EU Bulletin 6-1999, I.7.

109. On the difference between these see D. Chalmers, *EU Law: Law and EU Government* (Ashgate: Dartmouth 1998), ch. 7.

110. The legal debate about the 'judicial activism' of the ECJ suggests there may be something in this. Although how far it, *per se*, has provoked national resistance is doubtful.

111. In the period 1994–99, 22 of 104 references stemmed from either judicial review proceedings brought by non-commercial interests or from private disputes sponsored by a quango or non-governmental organisation. This was lower than the other main category, judicial review and tax proceedings brought by commercial actors, which accounted for a further 47 references. Yet as the interests affected were intentionally generalisable, the impacts of individual judgments were more broadly felt. For more detailed analysis, see D. Chalmers, 'The Much Ado about Judicial Politics in the United Kingdom: A Statistical Analysis of Reported Decisions of United Kingdom Courts Invoking EU Law 1973–1998', *Harvard Jean Monnet Working Paper 2000/1*.

112. Application of this form of analysis to EC law and politics can first be found in M. Anderson and D. Liefferink (eds.), *European Environmental Policy – The Pioneers* (Manchester: Manchester University Press 1997), pp.10–35.

113. A perennial criticism of TUPE it that it is a piece of employment protection legislation. Its merits are more apparent in the case of transfer of reasonably successfully undertakings with a relatively immobile labour force than in the case of transfer of undertakings which are either bankrupt or where the employees are highly mobile. In the case of the former it endangers the transfer and therefore the employment of the workers and in the case of the latter it damages wage flexibility. See B. Hepple, *Main Shortcomings and Proposals for Revision of Directive 77/187* (Commission: OOPEC 1990), pp.6–8; P. Inman, 'Unions and Bosses Unite to Bash Law: When a company takes over another business, what protection is there for the employer and employee', *Guardian*, 5 Dec. 1998, p.18.

114. The first of these was Case C-392/92 *Schmidt v. Spar- und Leihkasse der früheren Ämter Bordesholm, Kiel and Cronshagen* [1994] ECR I-1311. By holding that transfer of assets was not central to transfer of an undertaking but rather all that was necessary was a continuation of similar activity and and re-employment of the workers it extended the protection of the directive to all contracting-out services and embroiled the directive centrally in the debate about privatisation in the early 1990s. On this and reaction to the judgment in the UK and France, see G. More, 'The Concept of "Undertaking" in the Acquired Rights Directive: The Court of Justice under Pressure (Again)', *Yearbook of European Law* 15 (1995), p.135. The other was Case C-13/95 *Szen v. Zehnacker Gebaüdereingum* [1997] ECR I-1255 where the ECJ refused to apply to extend the directive to where a service contract with one undertaking was terminated and transferred to a competing undertaking.

115. M. Pollack, 'Delegation, Agency and Agenda Setting in the European Community', *International Organization* 51 (1997), pp.99 and 119–21.

116. *Wren v. Eastbourne* [1993] ICR 955. See J. Wolf, 'UK fails to ease contract-out law', *The Guardian*, 4 June 1994.

117. Of the five Directives mentioned earlier, only Directive 89/104/EEC was adopted by qualified majority vote.

118. In the case of Maastricht Case C-159/90 *SPUC v. Grogan* [1991] ECR I-4685; Case C-262/88 *Barber v. GRE* [1990] ECR I-1889. In the case of Amsterdam see Case C-233/94

Germany v. Parliament and Council [1997] ECR I-2405 and Case C-450/93 Kalanke v. Freie Hansestadt Bremen [1995] ECR I-3051.

119. See most recently Directive 1999/59 as regards value added taxation on telecommunications services, OJ 1999, L 162/63. This has been shown to be more generally true in Golub's pioneering piece which shows the limited encumbrance placed on decision-making by the veto. See J. Golub, 'In the Shadow of the Vote? Decision-Making in the European Community', International Organization 53 (1999), p.733.

120. Cf D. Goodhart, 'Britain Close to Victory on Contracting Out Services', Financial Times, 31 May 1994, p.1; J. Wolf and S. Milne, 'Get Britain on the Other Side to Win in Brussels-UK Trade Unions find way to Gain Support on the European Stage', The Guardian, 28 Feb. 1996, p.16. See also More, 'The Concept of "Undertaking" in the Acquired Rights Directive', pp.149–50.

121. The Directive was eventually amended by Directive 98/50, OJ 1998, L 201/88. On the history to the revision see J. Hunt, 'Success at Last? The Amendment of the Acquired Rights Directive', European Law Review 24 (1999), p.215.

122. C. Hoskyns, Integrating Gender: Women, Law and Politics in the European Union (London: Verso 1996), pp.202–7.

123. T. Moe, 'The Politics of Structural Choice: Towards a Theory of Public Bureaucracy', in O. Williamson (ed.), Organization Theory: From Chester Barnard to the Present (Oxford: Oxford University Press 1995).

124. D. Chalmers, 'Judicial Preferences and the Community Legal Order', Modern Law Review (1997), p.164. More recently, see Alter, 'Where, When and How does the European Legal System Influence Domestic Policy'.

125. Conant, 'Europeanization and the Courts'.

126. W. Scott, 'Symbols and Organizations: From Barnard to the Institutionalists' in Williamson (ed.), Organization Theory, pp.38 and 46.

127. Haughton v. Olau Line (UK) [1986] 1 CMLR 730; Kuikka v. CCE [1991] 3 CMLR 161; Duke v. GEC Reliance [1988] AC 618; Bell Concord Educational Trust v. CCE [1989] 1 CMLR 845; Finnegan v. Clowney [1990] AC 407; Wychavon District Council v. Secretary of the Environment [1994] 6 Journal of Environmental Law 351; Bhudi v. IMI Refiners [1994] ICR 307; Macmillan v. Edinburgh Voluntary Organisations Council [1995] IRLR 536.

128. S. Moscovici, The Invention of Society (Cambridge: Polity 1993), p.84.

129. Ibid., p.87.

130. On this, see B. Wright, 'Quiescent Leviathan? Citizenship and National Security Measures in Late Modernity', Journal of Law and Society 25 (1998), pp.226–7.

131. Moscovici, The Invention of Society, pp.87–8.

132. Ibid., pp.87–93. Moscovici is influenced here heavily by the work of Durkheim, most notably E. Durkheim, The Division of Labour in Society, trans. W. Halls (Basingstoke: Macmillan 1984). A not dissimilar dichotomy is present in other traditions. See the dichotomy between sovereignty and governmentality in Foucault's work, M. Foucault, 'Governmentality', in G. Burchill, C. Gordon and P. Miller (eds.), The Foucault Effect: Studies in Governmentality (Hemel Hempstead: Harvester Wheatsheaf 1991).

133. See, most notably, Re Colgan [1997] 1 CMLR 53 where the Northern Irish High Court took a 'communautaire' interpretation of Article 39(4) EC which deals with the circumstances in which EC nationals have right to access civil service jobs.

134. The earlier ones have been critiqued in Golub, 'The Politics of Judicial Discretion', p.36. More recently see R v. National Rivers Authority ex parte Moreton [1996] Environmental Law Reports 234 and Berkeley v. Secretary of State for the Environment [1999] 1 CMLR 945.

135. For example, the comments of the Legal Adviser to the Council who argued that nothing in the 'political debate' should not or would not prevent 'the improvement of the existing constitutional features'. J.-C. Piris, 'Does the European Union Have a Constitution?', European Law Review 24 (1999), pp.557 and 585.

136. The average delay for a case before the ECJ at the end of 1998 before judgment was given was 21 months. The backlog was 748 cases. EC Commission, *Reform of the Community Courts* COM (2000) 109 final, p.3.

137. This is currently the situation for matters that fall within Title IV. of the EC Treaty on Visas, Immigration and Other Policies related to Free Movement of Persons, Article 68(1) EC. Member states accepting ECJ jurisdiction to give preliminary rulings on matters that fall under Title VI of the Treaty on European Union on Police and Judicial Cooperation on Criminal Matters can also make it a condition of that acceptance, Article 35(3)(a) TEU. The proposal here is that practice should be extended generally. The Commission proposals involve the opposite. It proposes that national courts should only refer where the point of EC law is particularly problematic. This might limit the number of cases referred to the ECJ but would seem to confine references to test cases, thereby exacerbating existing tensions, EC Commission, *Reform of the Community Courts*, COM (2000) 109 final.

European Integration and National Executives: A Cause in Search of an Effect?

KLAUS H. GOETZ

EXECUTIVE EUROPEANISATION IN MEMBER STATES: LINKAGE,
IMPLEMENTATION AND ECOLOGY

The impact of European integration on national executives – here
understood as national central administrations, comprising both the political
and the administrative parts of the ministerial executive – has received
growing attention since the early 1990s. This interest in European
integration as a (potential) source of change in the ministerial executives of
the member states is, in itself, scarcely surprising. Most contemporary
writing in the field of comparative executive studies is explicitly oriented
towards describing and explaining change, and the literature is replete with
references to fundamental reform and transformation. For political and
administrative scientists, European integration provides a welcome addition
to the already long list of challenges to the 'old-time religion' of traditional
public administration.[1] As Edward Page and Linda Wouters note, 'Almost
all discussions of administrative change in Europe in the wake of the
development of closer European integration are couched in terms of a
potential',[2] yet few scholars in search of the European effect seem deterred
by their sceptical conclusion that 'there is no strong reason to believe that
… "Europeanization" necessarily brings with it any substantial change in
the national administrative structure of member states'.[3]

In common with much writing on Western executive systems, the
Europeanisation debate tends to focus on fairly short time horizons,
although there are some studies that seek to trace back the European impact
to the beginnings of the integration process[4] and offer a longitudinal
analysis that covers several decades.[5] Both the founding members of the
Communities and the most recent accession countries, including Austria,[6]
Finland and Sweden,[7] have attracted scholarly attention. The impact on
member states' executive systems is, of course, at the heart of the

discussion; but current Western non-member states seem not immune to Europeanisation effects, as the Norwegian and Swiss cases bear out.[8] Single country studies predominate, although there are also some noteworthy attempts at cross-country comparison, centring, for example, on small European states;[9] France and The Netherlands;[10] or Germany and France,[11] plus the UK.[12]

If one seeks to characterise the state of the debate in terms of substantive emphases, one may distinguish three broad categories, concerned with linkage, implementation and executive ecology, respectively.

Linkage

The majority of contributions to the Europeanisation debate focus on linkage issues, notably the institutional arrangements that link national executives and EU authorities and the institutional practices that have evolved at the national level to support national–EU connections. The underlying assumption of this type of investigation is that as national executives are more and more drawn into the EU decision-making process[13] they come under growing adaptive pressure. Transformation at the national level need not be sudden; it may evolve 'incrementally and creeps into the political and administrative normality at the national level without causing dramatic structural changes there'.[14] Examples of linkage studies include analyses of the role of the member states' permanent representations to the EU and their ties with the national ministries;[15] studies of the structural adaptation of the central ministerial bureaucracy to the dynamics of EU policy-making, both in structural terms,[16] but also in terms of working rhythms;[17] and detailed examinations of the role played by different ministries and centres of government in EU-related policy formulation.[18] A good deal has been written on how national governments co-ordinate their stance on European policies,[19] and diverging national co-ordinating traditions have been identified.[20] Recent studies on national co-ordination practices suggest that the EU impact is by no means unambiguous. Thus, it has been argued that while the EU Commission encourages sectoral, dehierarchical forms of co-ordination at the national level, 'the Council structure works according to a geographical and territorial logic … and encourages geographical, hierarchical forms of co-ordination'.[21]

The linkage perspective also informs a diverse range of studies that have examined, for example, national administrative arrangements for negotiating accession to the EU; national executive infrastructures for the preparation of European summits and intergovernmental conferences; or the manner in which member states administer the European presidency. In the main, the linkage perspective highlights the importance of structures and procedures. But some authors have also examined the impact of integration on personnel, notably the roles and role perceptions of officials in national bureaucracies[22] and the recruitment and career patterns of officials in national ministries that are exposed to EU business.[23] One interesting argument to emerge in this context is that there has been a strengthening of the administrative part of the executive at the expense of the formative influence of executive politicians,[24] not least because EU policy making appears to reinforce trends towards departmentalism and sectorisation in national administrations.[25]

Implementation

Contributions in this category revolve around the question of how national executives implement European policies and to what extent national administrative traditions help to explain, and may themselves be transformed by, the manner in which European policies are implemented. For the most part, such analyses treat implementation as their dependent variable and the nature of the policies to be implemented as the main explanatory variable.[26] The analytical status of national administrative practice is not always clear: it is sometimes treated as part of the independent variable, sometimes as part of the dependent variable (or, confusingly, as both). One of the earliest contributions from an implementation perspective that systematically examined national administrative implementation practice was the two-volume study edited by Heinrich Siedentopf and Jacques Ziller.[27] As the policy *acquis* of the EU has widened, its policy instruments diversified, and its interventions in national policy regimes intensified, the range of polices and implementation arrangements studied has rapidly broadened. Perhaps the most intensively researched field has been regional economic policy and cohesion policy, not least because it has allowed analysts to extend the implementation perspective to the regional and local levels, and, thus, focus attention on multi-level intergovernmental and interadministrative interactions.[28] Other policy areas in which the administrative preconditions and consequences of implementing EU policies have attracted attention include, in particular, environmental policy; telecommunications policy; and technology policy

Administrative Ecology

In contrast to the linkage and implementation perspectives, which centre on the study of differentiation, specialisation, and co-operation *within* the executive, the ecological perspective is interested in the relations between the executive and its constitutive environment. Two relational dimensions are of special importance: the executive–society nexus; and the executive–economy nexus. Analyses of the relations between national executives and society were, for a long time, dominated by the controversy between pluralist, corporatist and statist accounts.[29] While this debate continues (albeit with less vigour than a decade ago), attention has to some extent shifted to new forms of public–private interaction in the policy process, whether in the form of policy networks, policy communities or public–private partnerships. Much of this discussion takes place under the banner of (new) governance, understood 'as a new mode of governing that is distinct from the hierarchical control model, a more co-operative mode where state and non-state actors participate in mixed public/private networks'.[30] In Germany, for example, scholars have talked of the rise of a 'co-operative public administration', engaged in negotiation and bargaining.[31] To what extent European integration re-moulds national co-operative arrangements seems uncertain and the literature arrives at seemingly contradictory conclusions. For example, with reference to the relations between interests groups and the executive, it has been suggested that the vertical extension of the policy-making framework to the EU level might undermine the material bases of corporatist-style arrangements in the national context. Others have argued that, on the contrary, national executive-interest group ties will be strengthened, as national interest representatives seek to persuade governments to champion their demands at the European level.

Finally, it is widely debated whether European integration might fundamentally alter the role of executive institutions in economic regulation and management. It is generally accepted that the role of 'the state' in the economies of western Europe has undergone fundamental changes since the 1970s.[32] As part of this development, member states have had to share more and more of their traditional regulatory and promotional functions with the EU. Accordingly, national economic administration has had to develop new forms of co-operation with external authorities. The best example is, perhaps, the rapidly evolving relationship between national regulatory and competition authorities and the European Commission.

THE NATIONAL IMPACT IN THE WEST: MUCH ADO ABOUT NOT VERY MUCH?

Empirical assessments of the executive impact of European integration certainly differ; but if a general consensus can be discerned it is that there is no straightforward connection between adaptive pressures and adaptive reactions. A brief look at key institutional building blocs of national executive systems serves to underline this point. If we turn, first, to executive structures and procedures, we find examples of unexpected discrepancy between apparent national adaptation requirements and observed empirical outcomes. The manner in which the UK central ministerial machinery has coped with European policy-making provides a case in point. Comparative analyses of European administration regularly emphasise profound differences between continental Roman-law models and the English common-law tradition. Moreover, EU administration itself has been strongly influenced by the administrative practices of the founder states, notably France and Germany, and, to a lesser extent, Italy. Yet what could have been expected to provoke a clash of administrative traditions does, in practice, appear to have caused little more than a small ripple. Thus, Simon Bulmer and Martin Burch argue in their longitudinal study of Whitehall's adaptation to the EU (and its predecessors) that 'the British machinery of government has revealed itself able smoothly to adapt to EU membership, adjusting incrementally to an organizational response already established during entry negotiations'.[33] 'What is remarkable about British central government's adaptation to the EU ... is the extent to which, while change has been substantial, it has been more or less wholly in keeping with British traditions.'[34]

That these traditions may themselves be rather less fixed than tends to be assumed is argued by Christoph Knill and Andrea Lenschow in their Anglo-German comparison of the implementation of EU environmental policy. Where, as in the UK, the 'structural potential for dynamic developments of the institutional core is comparatively high',[35] 'tradition' may be malleable. Thus,

> the study of British implementation records suggests that general national dynamics may result in modifications to the overall state and legal tradition loosening the traditional administrative core in specific policy areas. Consequently, adaptation requirements that previously have been considered as core challenges are now perceived as acceptable reforms "within a moved core".[36]

Personnel policy offers further illustration for the gap between expected adaptive reactions and the often rather modest effects that empirical analyses uncover. A study of the impact of European integration and the New Public Management (NPM) on the recruitment and training of senior officials in the UK central administration has found that, in general, the impact of NPM has outweighed the influence of European integration.[37] Of the three departments studied – Transport, Health, and Agriculture – it is only in Agriculture that personnel policy has been more heavily influenced by European pressures than by NPM. In general, the national context appears to matter more than external adaptive pressures. Research on the identity and role perceptions of ministerial officials would seem to bolster this conclusion. Thus, Morten Egeberg's[38] study of transport ministry officials in Denmark, Finland, Ireland, Portugal and Sweden found that although officials who participate intensively in EU-level structures and are frequently separated from their home institutions develop a sense of allegiance to the supranational level, 'the identity evoked in EU level settings does not replace the identity evoked in national institutions; it is, rather, complementary and secondary'.[39]

Other recent cross-country comparisons of administrative adaptation also tend to stress both the importance of national context and the capacity of national administrative traditions to modify, accommodate, internalise and, perhaps, even neutralise European pressures. For example, Kenneth Hanf and Ben Soetendorp[40] conclude their survey of institutional adaptation to the EU in ten smaller west European states (including two non-member countries) by noting that 'governmental adjustments were made in an incremental way, building upon traditions and arrangements that were already in place'.[41] Thus, 'governmental adaptation was a series of *ad hoc* responses to emerging problems and demands' and 'none of the smaller member-states considered major organizational adjustments at the level of central government to meet the new challenges'.[42] In a similar vein, Hussein Kassim's survey of national co-ordination arrangements for dealing with EU business concludes that 'the way in which member states have responded to the demands made of them by participation in the EU has been shaped by the structural features of national political systems over which the Union can exercise little influence. In this context, it may make more sense to speak of domestication than of Europeanisation'.[43] The importance of pre-existing national context is also underlined by Robert Harmsen in his comparison of the Europeanisation of the central administrations in France and the Netherlands. Thus, he highlights that

> The French and the Dutch states have exhibited markedly different patterns of adaptation to the process of European integration. The differences may, moreover, be linked readily to identifiable differences in both the existing institutional structures and the broader matrices of values which characterize the two polities ... Existing national institutional structures, intellectual constructs, and prior paths

of historical development do not simply disappear when the concept of integration is invoked. Any full account of the integration process must, in some way, account for the persistence of these distinctive and defining national characteristics.[44]

Even where, as in another recent contribution on the Europeanisation of the French polity, it is argued that 'National state traditions ... are inevitably weakened in the melting-pot of the EU policy process',[45] this statement is later qualified by the observation that 'national traditions were reinforced at the implementation stage and French governments demonstrated the capacity to innovate and recodify in accordance with national traditions'.[46]

In line with such a stress on the power of national institutional traditions, European integration tends to be credited with modifying, rather than transforming, national executive arrangements. Moreover, as these modifications are shaped by diverse national contexts, European integration is unlikely to lead to convergence in the executive systems of the member states. For example, Wolfgang Wessels's comprehensive study of the 'opening' of the west German state in the process of European integration notes that

> a fundamental structural reform or even revolution of state administration, which might have been expected or at least considered possible as a result of, or in connection with, the creation of interstate administrative linkages, has not taken place. Even without far-reaching institutional changes, public administrations were able to adjust to differentiated processes of problem-solving'.[47]

Given this emphasis on national 'path dependency' and the accommodating capacity of pre-existing institutional arrangements, a 'differential' executive impact of European integration is only to be expected.[48]

Such cautious evaluations of the transformative potential of European integration can be read as evidence for the extraordinary resilience of national institutions. Yet a more sceptical reading of the evidence may suggest that the differential nature of the European effect in different member state contexts may have more to do with the relative weakness of European integration as an independent source of domestic institutional change than with the strength of national 'institutional cores'. In such a critical reading, empirical work on executive Europeanisation signals that European integration may, at best, be a trigger for, or an intervening variable in, domestic institutional development, but not a major driving force.

WAITING FOR EUROPE: ANTICIPATORY AND ANTICIPATED EFFECTS

Turning from Western-style Europeanisation to developments in the post-Communist countries of central and eastern Europe (CEE),[49] one sees important similarities in the substantive focus of much writing on the EU effect. For example, there are already several surveys of linkage arrangements in the EU applicant states.[50] These set out the domestic arrangements for negotiating accession and chart the adjustments made in anticipation of entry to the EU. There is also a great deal of comment on the administrative preconditions for the effective implementation of the EU's *acquis communautaire,* that is, the anticipated institutional consequences of accession.

The similarities in substantive emphases should not, however, mask important differences in concerns and approach. First, Europeanisation research eastern-style is, at present, largely concerned with predicting the effects of eventual EU membership on the CEE applicant countries; by necessity, the mapping of preparatory and anticipatory adjustments still concentrates almost exclusively on formal organisational measures. More importantly, the debate on the Europeanisation of CEE executives is almost exclusively dominated by an eminently practical concern with preparing the post-Communist executives for what has become known as the 'European administrative space'.[51] Accordingly, most of what we currently know about the state of executive development in the region, in general, and the actual and potential effects of EU integration, in particular, stems from the work carried out by international organisations and academics with whom they co-operate. Typically, they map the administrative requirements of EU membership in more or less detail; assess the applicant countries' current state of development; and, on that basis, spell out a reform agenda that needs to be adopted if the countries concerned are to meet the administrative preconditions for full EU membership.

The analyses of adaptive requirements that have been produced from a practitioners' perspective are, in some cases, considerably more comprehensive and detailed than the more narrowly focused accounts of western administrations. Thus, a study produced for the EU's Technical Assistance Exchange Office (TAIEX) on the administrative implications of integration into the internal market of the EU provides a very detailed account of the institutional preconditions across the range of policies covered by the *acquis.*[52] Similarly, the annual reports of the EU Commission on the applicant states' progress towards accession, although much less detailed, establish the basic administrative requirements for the capacity to apply the *acquis* and provide an evaluation of the progress made in meeting these criteria. The conceptually most sophisticated analysis of the administrative capacities for EU membership is currently being developed by the World Bank.[53] In this exercise, the focus is on human resources management, policy formulation and implementation, and accession management. Under each of these three headings, detailed 'good governance' criteria are developed, performance indicators and benchmark information are stipulated, and detailed information is collected on whether the key indicators and benchmarks are fulfilled.

On the whole, assessments of administrative capacity for EU accession in CEE tend to be fairly critical; calls for further far-reaching reform are the norm. The most recent accession progress reports by the Commission were, in some respects, more critical of administrative conditions in CEE than the initial Commission opinions on the applications for EU membership. Attila Ágh's observation that 'The Europeanization of polity in ECE [east-central Europe] has basically been accomplished'[54] is very much a minority opinion. The prevailing sceptical assessment of the applicant states' EU-related executive capacities is in line with the more general evaluations of executive development in post-Communist Europe. For example, a recent World Bank-initiated comparative survey of post-Communist administrative development, including, *inter alia*, Poland, Romania and Hungary, arrived at very critical conclusions, noting that 'countries frequently have favoured purely legal-formal fixes to institutional problems'.[55] Similarly, a comparative exercise led by Tony Verheijen and David Coombes[56] has highlighted severe performance deficits, not least in the co-ordination and implementation of public policies, and points to political, economic and cultural obstacles to fundamental reform.

In the case of CEE, it is not just the necessarily tentative and, in part, speculative nature of much writing on the anticipated domestic institutional effects of accession that qualifies the Europeanisation thesis. Rather, it is important to stress that European integration is part of a comprehensive process of liberalisation, pluralisation and democratisation, which challenges most, if not all, of the established features of the inherited institutional framework, commonly referred to as 'democratic centralism'. A root-and-branch reform of the executive is, therefore, an essential part of the modernisation logic that underlies change in the political, economic and social spheres[57] and is not specifically tied to the European integration process. A decontextualised focus on the transformative power of the latter alone is, therefore, unlikely to generate a realistic account of the dynamics of executive change in post-Communist settings.

EUROPEAN INTEGRATION: FROM CAUSE TO EFFECT

The preceding brief review of the findings of Europeanisation research in west and east casts some doubt over the explanatory power of 'European integration' as major force driving domestic executive change. To be sure, research on the Europeanisation of national polities has not yet reached a stage where it is possible to set out a widely accepted 'standard version' of executive Europeanisation, not least because of differences in research methods, empirical foci, the interpretation of empirical data and, perhaps most importantly, approach (although much recent writing in the field is informed by neo-institutionalist thinking). However, these doubts also stem from three more general problems that beset much contemporary writing on executive development.

First, comparative executive studies are only rarely informed by a systemic understanding of the executive. This contention may appear surprising, perhaps even misleading. After all, perhaps the most widely employed comparative typology of democratic regimes – the distinction between presidential, semi-presidential and parliamentary forms of government – builds principally on the position of the executive in the political system and the nature of its relationships with other political institutions, notably parliament.[58] Other influential classifications of 'patterns of democracy', such as Arendt Lijphart's account of majoritarian and consensus democracy,[59] though less executive-centred, likewise give prominence to the location of the executive within the political system as a key definitional criterion. Moreover, when it comes to dissecting the internal life of the executive, there is, again, no shortage of concepts to aid comparative efforts. At the political level of the executive, one only need refer to the traditional opposition between prime ministerial and cabinet systems[60] or, more recently, inquiries into the nature of the 'partyness' of European governments.[61] At the administrative level, one finds, for example, a long-standing interest in comparative conceptualisations of the political and administrative roles of civil servants,[62] whilst cross-national analyses of 'core executives'[63] and executive co-ordination[64] provide useful conceptual reference points for studying the political–administrative nexus.

If, despite such efforts to develop conceptual maps of executive systems or subsystems, Europeanisation research can be said to lack a systemic understanding of the executive, this is for several reasons. First, existing accounts of Europeanisation rarely engage with comparative typologies or concepts of the type just mentioned. Second, and more importantly, with the exception of macro-level frameworks that seek to locate the executive in the political system, most conceptual thinking on executives takes place at the meso-level and deals with discrete building blocs of executive capacity, such as organisation, procedures or personnel. By contrast, attempts to understand the interaction between these building blocs are, perhaps surprisingly, still at a fairly early stage, which is probably the key reason why little progress has been made in establishing clear links between particular configurations of executive arrangements and performance.[65] In other words, in the study of the executive, it is generally held that 'institutions matter', but how they matter for executive performance has scarcely been tested. Finally, most comparative conceptualisations are constructed inductively rather than deductively and, in their majority, are little more than stylised and generalised descriptions of existing systems, with little attempt to distinguish between constitutive and incidental features.

What flows from this for the study of executive Europeanisation? Two points deserve highlighting. It can be difficult to assess the magnitude and, in particular, the quality of the changes observed. As regards the latter, there have, of course, been some attempts to distinguish between 'core' and 'peripheral' change[66] or, to give another recent example, between changes at the systemic, organisational, regulative, procedural and cultural levels of central government.[67] But what is core or peripheral, or systemic and non-systemic change may appear the result of fairly arbitrary decisions by researchers, in the absence of agreement in the executive literature on the key definitional components of executive *systems*. Moreover, the tendency in the literature to study discrete institutional building blocs of the executive encourages the neglect of 'spill-over' effects. Put more concretely, it is, at present, difficult to address in anything but an *ad hoc* manner the implications of, say, Europeanisation effects in the ministerial personnel system for the procedural or structural organisation of ministries. Both factors put together mean that the generalisability of empirical findings both cross-nationally and across different components of the executive is limited.

A second limitation of executive studies that has direct implications for Europeanisation research is that it tends to be predominantly interested in outlining the substantive content of change, rather than in its modes and procedural features. There is certainly no lack of 'dynamic' accounts that seek to trace the trajectories of executive development over time; in fact, as was noted at the outset, the literature on comparative government and public administration is saturated with change-oriented analyses. However, these revolve around identifying the substance of change, say, in ministerial organisation or the relationships between politicians and administrators in the process of executive policy-making, but pay little attention to modes and processes of change. As a consequence, theoretically informed hypotheses that help to reconstruct the link between pressures for change and perceived substantive adaptations are rare.

This problem of the 'missing link' is also reflected in the Europeanisation debate. Thus, existing explanations on Europeanisation tend to focus on 'adaptive pressures', on the one hand, and their interaction with national conditions, on the other. Adaptive pressures result from the lack of fit between EU-level institutional and policy arrangements and existing national practice. More reflective accounts certainly do not posit a direct correlation between pressure for change and adaptation. For example, Adrienne Héritier has argued

> Where the established policy of a member state diverges from a clearly specified European policy mandate, there will be an expectation to adjust, which in turn constitutes a precondition for change. Assuming the existence of a need for change, the ability to adapt will depend on the policy preferences of key actors, and the institutional reform capacity to realise policy change and to administratively adjust to European requirements.[68]

A similar point, though put in less actor-centred terms, is made by Calliope Spanou in her discussion of the Greek administrative response to European integration. She notes that

> Responsiveness to European integration is conditioned by a point of departure that does not fully correspond to the implicit assumptions of European policies. Furthermore, adjustment cannot but follow pre-established paths within the Greek political-administrative system, in line with its pre-existing features, and be shaped accordingly.[69]

Perhaps the fullest account of relevant institutional features is given by Knill and Lenschow,[70] who identify national administrative traditions, the 'degree of embeddedness' of national institutional arrangements, policy context, and the national capacity for institutional reform as the decisive factors determining the extent and quality of administrative adaptation. Yet, whilst these examples show that the need for robust causal accounts bridging pressure for change and institutional effects is clearly recognised, the study of Europeansation as a *process* is, perhaps surprisingly, still at a fairly early stage.

Third, in common with executive studies more generally, Europeanisation research is, in the main, single-variable research, in the sense that the explanatory status of European integration as a source of institutional development is not systematically compared with the influence of complementary or rival explanations of change. Thus, it is difficult to arrive at assessments of the *relative* impact and importance of European integration compared to other potential sources of national institutional development. The case for multi-variable explanations in obvious in the central and eastern European context, but, as will be argued in the next section, it also holds in the institutionally more stable settings of western Europe.

EXECUTIVE EUROPEANISATION: MODES, PROCESSES AND CONTEXT

It flows from the above remarks that if the analysis of executive Europeanisation is to advance, scholars will need to cast their analytical net more widely than hitherto. The following comments provide some brief pointers as to how the theoretical underpinnings of Europeanisation research might be shored up. In particular, it is desirable to get a better understanding of the temporality of Europeanisation; the spread of institutional innovations; and the interaction between European integration and other forces of institutional change.

Temporality

Europeanisation is a process, not an event, and there is widespread agreement in the literature that to the extent that change in national executive practice can be attributed to the European integration process, this change has been gradual and cumulative, rather than sudden and dichotomous. Yet, although existing research may allow us to draw up basic chronologies of adaptive steps taken at national level, explicit consideration of the time factor is rare. In this connection, Philippe Schmitter's and Juan Santiso's[71] recent discussion of the temporal dimension in democratic transition and consolidation is pertinent, for they, too, are interested in explaining dynamic processes of change over time. Their distinction between the time, timing and tempo of reform measures should prove useful for achieving a better understanding of the temporality of the Europeanisation process, in particular in order to understand how national decision-makers may manipulate time, that is, 'turn it from an inexorably limited, linear and perishable constraint into something that could be scheduled, anticipated, delayed, accelerated, deadlined, circumvented, prolonged, deferred, compressed, parcelled out, standardized, diversified, staged, staggered, and even wasted'.[72] In their account, time refers to when a decision is made; timing to the sequencing of decisions; and tempo to speed.

Applied to the study of executive Europeanisation, sensitivity to time, timing and tempo should yield important comparative insights into how the process works. Is it possible to distinguish periods of intensive Europeanisation activity from lulls and how can these patterns be explained? Do Europeanisation measures follow a common chronological pattern across the member states or is there no common sequence? For example, do Europeanisation effects first manifest themselves in linkage arrangements, then in implementation practice and then in the relational patterns between the executive and non-executive political actors? Do some countries follow a gradualist path (this might be expected in the case of the founder members of the Communities), while others adapt by leaps and bounds (this might apply, in particular, to the future post-Communist member states)? And, perhaps most importantly, to what extent do national decision-makers control the time, timing and tempo of Europeanisation?

The Transfer and Spread of Institutional Innovations

Whilst temporality refers to a procedural characteristic of Europeanisation, the manner in which innovations are brought about and spread concerns the mode of Europeanisation. In recent years, comparative public administration and comparative government have become increasingly interested in the modalities of cross-border institutional transfer and the cross-national spread of governmental-administrative innovations.[73] Much recent writing underlines that while the international spread of innovations in government and administration is fairly common, coercive adaptation, provoked by the requirement to conform to externally set requirements, is, in fact, fairly rare, at least among the Western industrialised nations. Rather, there is evidence of policy diffusion, where 'transfer arises as a consequence of structural forces', and policy learning, where 'the emphasis is on cognition and the redefinition of interests on the basis of new knowledge which affects fundamental beliefs and ideas behind policy approaches'.[74] In contrast to the existing Europeanisation literature, the debate on policy diffusion and, especially, policy learning does not operate primarily with assumptions about adaptive pressure-and-response. Instead, the emphasis is on voluntaristic changes to national practice, with international organisations and international or transnational policy networks and communities typically acting as channels for the cross-national communication of institutional experiences.

Of course, the EU has rather more extensive powers *vis-à-vis* its member states than most other types of international organisations; its power to mandate change in member states is considerable (as is the power of member states to resist is). However, it seems at least worth exploring whether executive Europeanisation does not owe much more to a *horizontal logic* of cross-border learning, imitation and lesson-drawing encouraged by EU-wide policy networks and communities than existing conflict-oriented accounts, stressing a *vertical logic* of EU-induced adaptive pressure, suggest.[75]

Contexualising European Integration

As the preceding discussion suggests, investing analytical and empirical effort into the procedural and modal aspects of Europeanisation should allow the formulation of more robust causal hypotheses about European integration and executive development than we possess at the moment. This will enable political and administrative scientists to be rather more positive about linking specific effects to particular causes than at present. In short, theory should help to disentangle the European impact.

Trying to identify the European influence does not, however, mean that it ought to be considered in isolation, for Europeanisation is but one of several 'drivers of change' discussed in contemporary comparative government and public administration. There are many different ways in which the story about the decline of the classical public bureaucracy can be told, including, *inter alia*, economic, managerialist, technological, postmodernist and political variants. While some of these accounts would appear to tie in quite closely with arguments about the innovative capacity of European integration, others have little affinity, at least at first glance.

The *economic version* of change identifies shifts in the global economy and their effects on the role of the state in economic management as the main driving force behind governmental-administrative change. The globalisation thesis suggests that capitalism is largely unbound from the nation-state context. To the extent that the public sector retains economic regulatory functions, these are largely delegated to independent regulatory agencies, both at national, but in particular at international and transnational levels. This development is accompanied by a progressive redefinition of the welfare state, which aims at the drastic reduction of public service provision. The de-etatisation of the economy and society points to a 'minimal state'. From this perspective, the massive quantitative and qualitative expansion of west European governments and public bureaucracies during the post-war period will turn out to have been a transient phenomenon.

Whereas in the economic version institutional change is provoked by the transformation of the economic environment in which national state institutions operate, the *managerialist version* focuses on internal change agents. Managerialist accounts revolve around the concept of the New Public Management (NPM). According to Christopher Hood,[76] the core components of NPM include 'hands on professional management' in the public sector; explicit standards and measures of performance; an emphasis on output controls; a shift towards the disaggregation of units and greater competition in the public sector; a stress on private-sector styles of management; and an emphasis on greater discipline and parsimony in resource use. NPM could then be described as a trend towards the internal economisation of the public sector, in which administrative 'enterprises' operate according to a market rationality.

In the *technological version,* advances in information and communication technologies challenge traditional models of bureaucratic organisation.[77] Within government, developments such as the growing reliance on electronic communication, the use of intranets and the internet appear to run counter to traditional principles of a hierarchical organisation of communication and the flow of information. At the same time, the internet has the potential to revolutionise the way in which citizens and the government communicate.

Whereas economic, managerialist and technological accounts belong to the mainstream of the comparative discourse, the theory of *postmodernisation* has been less influential in the Anglo-Saxon discussion,[78] although it has met with considerable interest in some continental European countries, such as The Netherlands. The concept of post-modernity and, by implication, of post-modernisation is certainly ambiguous and has, up to now, defied a commonly accepted definition. If post-modernity is understood as a historical-empirical phenomenon – rather than an epistemology – it describes, in the first instance, the historical conclusion of the age of modernity. The latter's axial developmental principles are either reversed or, in less radical analyses, modified to an extent that suggests a historical discontinuity. Whereas modernisation stands for progressive functional-institutional differentiation, specialisation and rationalisation – the classical features of a bureaucratic ministerial organisation – post-modernisation is associated with de-differentiation, de-specialisation and the growing porosity, if not breakdown, of systemic boundaries and the interpenetrating of value spheres. As part of the process of postmodernisation, the specific internal characteristics of public bureaucracy become less pronounced, the boundaries to the administrative environments less distinct, bureaucratic rationality is supplemented and increasingly supplanted by entrepreneurial rationality and the rationality of the market. Internal de-bureaucratisation and the de-hierarchisation of the relations between the state and its environment are seen as expressions of a post-modern public administration.

Finally, *political versions* emphasise the transformation of the contemporary state as the main force propelling a recasting of government and administration. The literature on the recomposition of the state in western Europe revolves around three major themes: the challenge 'from above', in particular through European integration; the challenge 'from below', through federalisation, regionalisation and decentralisation; and what might be called the horizontal challenge, as the boundaries of the state are 'pushed back' through privatisation and deregulation. The implications of the reshaping of the state for the executive are ambiguous.[79] On the whole, they do, however, point to a contraction of central government and administration; growing internal functional and institutional differentiation, along the horizontal and the vertical axes; and a far-reaching redefinition of the executive task profile.

How might the European integration process fit into, and interact with, these stories of institutional development? The economic and political versions both possess a clear affinity to the Europeanisation argument in that they revolve around the two major pillars of the European project, that is, economic and political integration. For example, Giandomenico Majone's discussion of the regulatory state explicitly engages with the integration process, and much of what is being written about the decline of the European nation state refers back to the impact of the European project. Analytical and empirical connections with the integration process are much less evident when it comes to the impact of NPM, technological change and postmodernisation. Thus, the influence of NPM is felt in many countries outside the Europe, and EU membership in itself does appear to have little discernible effect on the likelihood of the adoption of NPM-inspired reforms. The same observation applies in the case of technological change. As far as the postmodernisation thesis is concerned, it traces the decline of the public bureaucracy paradigm to secular societal forces rather than economic or political integration dynamics.

These brief remarks suggest caution in treating European integration as a major independent source of executive change. This is not to suggest that European integration does not matter; but it might matter in a rather less straightforward manner than the Europeanisation literature tends to assume. Evidently, the *relative* importance of European integration as a source of executive change can only be assessed if it is systematically compared with rival or complementary explanations. Put differently, having 'disentangled' the European effect, Europeanisation research needs to contextualise it and explore its interactions with other sources of change. Political science and public administration have some way to go towards meeting this challenge.

NOTES

1. B.G. Peters, *The Future of Governing: Four Emerging Models* (Lawrence: University of Kansas Press 1996); see also B.G. Peters and V. Wright, 'Public Policy and Administration, Old and New', in R.E. Goodin and H.-D. Klingemann (eds.), *A New Handbook of Political Science* (Oxford: Oxford University Press 1996), pp.628–41.
2. E.C. Page and L. Wouters, 'The Europeanization of National Bureaucracies', in J. Pierre (ed.), *Bureaucracy in the Modern State* (Cheltenham: Edward Elgar 1995), pp.185–204 at 185.
3. Page and Wouters, 'The Europeanization of National Bureaucracies', p.203.
4. *Yearbook of European Administrative History*, 1992, Vol. 4, on 'Early European Community Administration'.
5. S. Bulmer and M. Burch, 'Organizing for Europe: Whitehall, the British State and European Union', *Public Administration* 76 (1998), pp.601–28; W. Wessels, *Die Öffnung des Staates. Modelle und Wirklichkeit grenzüberschreitender Verwaltungspraxis 1960–1995* (Opladen: Leske & Budrich 2000).
6. G. Falkner *et al.*, 'The Impact of EU Membership on Policy Networks in Austria: Creeping Change Beneath the Surface', *Journal of European Public Policy* 6 (1999), pp.496–516; P. Luif, 'Austria: Adaptation Through Anticipation', in K. Hanf and B. Soetendorp (eds.), *Adapting to European Integration: Small States and the European Union* (London: Longman 1998), pp.116–30; P. Pernthaler, 'EU-Mitgliedschaft, Bundesstaatsreform und Verwaltungs-entlastung', *Zeitschrift für Öffentliches Recht*, 53 (1998), pp.1–22.
7. M. Ekengren and B. Sundelius, 'Sweden: The State Joins the European Union', in Hanf and Soetendorp (eds.), *Adapting to European Integration*, pp.131–48; J. Olsson, 'Senvsk statsfoervaltning och EG-integrationen', *Statsvetenskaplig tidskrift* 96 (1993), pp.332–58; M. Sjölund, 'Den svenska foervaltningsmodellen i Europaintegrationen', *Statsvetenskaplig tidskrift* 97 (1994), pp.383–92.
8. S. Kux, 'Switzerland: Adjustment Despite Deadlock', in Hanf and Soetendorp (eds.), *Adapting to European Integration*, pp.167–185; U. Sverdrup, 'Norway: An Adaptive Non-Member', in Hanf and Soetendorp (eds.), *Adapting to European Integration,* pp.149–66; J. Trondal, *Europeisering av sentraladministrative organer. Om tilknytningsformer til EU og departmentale koordineringsformer* (Oslo: ARENA Working Papers WP 97/27, 1997).
9. K. Hanf and B. Soetendorp, 'Conclusion: The Nature of National Adaptation to European Integration', in idem (eds.), *Adapting to European Integration,* pp.186–94; U. Kloeti and S. von Dosenrode, 'Adaptation to European Integration: Changes in the Administration of Four Small States', *Australian Journal of Public Administration* 54 (1995), pp.273–81.
10. R. Harmsen, 'The Europeanization of National Administrations: A Comparative Study of France and the Netherlands', *Governance* 12 (1999), pp.81–113.
11. C. Knill and A. Lenschow, 'Coping with Europe: The Impact of British and German Administrations on the Implementation of EU Environmental Policy', *Journal of European Public Policy* 5 (1998), pp.595–614.
12. A. Héritier, C. Knill and S. Mingers, *Ringing the Changes in Europe: Regulatory Competition and the Transformation of the State* (Berlin: de Gruyter 1996); C. Knill, 'European Policies: The Impact of National Administrative Traditions', *Journal of Public Policy* 18 (1998), pp.1–28.
13. See, in particular, W. Wessels and D. Rometsch (eds.), *The European Union and the Member States: Towards Institutional Fusion?* (Manchester: Manchester UP 1996); idem, 'German Administrative Interaction and European Union: The Fusion of Public Policies', in Y. Mény *et al.* (eds.), *Adjusting to Europe* (London: Routledge 1996), pp.73–109; W. Wessels,

'Comitology: Fusion in Action. Politico-administrative Trends in the EU System', *Journal of European Public Policy* 5 (1998), pp.209–34.

14. Ibid., p.228.

15. F. Hayes-Renshaw *et al.*, 'The Permanent Representations of the Member States to the European Communities', *Journal of Common Market Studies* 28 (1989), pp.19–37.

16. C. Lequesne, *Paris-Bruxelles: comment se fait la politique européenne de la France* (Paris: Presses de la Fondation nationale des sciences politiques 1993); idem, 'French Central Government and the European Political System: Change and Adaptation Since the Single Act', in Mény *et al.* (eds.), *Adjusting to Europe*; H. Wallace, 'Relations between the European Union and the British Administration', in Mény *et al.* (eds.), *Adjusting to Europe*, pp.61–92.

17. M. Ekengren, 'The Europeanization of State Administration: Adding the Time Dimension', *Cooperation and Conflict* 31 (1996), pp.387–415; idem, 'The Temporality of European Governance', in K.E. Jorgensen (ed.), *Reflective Approaches to European Governance* (Basingstoke: Macmillan 1997).

18. A. Jordan, 'National Ministries: Managers or Ciphers of European Integration?' (Paper for the Panel on 'Politicians, Bureaucrats and Institutional Reform', ECPR Joint Sessions of Workshops, Mannheim, 26–31 March 1999).

19. V. Wright, 'The National Co-ordination of European Policy-Making: Negotiating the Quagmire', in J. Richardson (ed.), *European Union: Power and Policy-Making* (London: Routledge 1996), pp.148–69; H.-U. Derlien and A. Murswick, 'Der Politikzyklus zwischen Bonn und Brüssel: Multifunktionalität der Akteure, Iterativität der Prozesse, Informalität der Verfahren', in idem (eds.), *Der Politikzyklus zwischen Bonn und Brüssel* (Opladen: Leske & Budrich 1999), pp.7–19.

20. H. Kassim *et al.* (eds.), *The National Co-ordination of EU Policy* (Oxford: Oxford University Press 2000).

21. Trondal, *Europeisering av sentraladministrative organer*, p.1.

22. J. Burnham and M. Maor, 'Converging Administrative Systems: Recruitment and Training in EU Member States', *Journal of European Public Policy* 2 (1995), pp.185–204; M. Egeberg, 'Transcending Intergovernmentalism? Identity and Role Perceptions of National Officials in EU Decision-Making', *Journal of European Public Policy* 6 (1999), pp.456–74.

23. M. Maor and H. Stevens, 'Measuring the Impact of New Public Management and European Integration on Recruitment and Training in the UK Civil Service', *Public Administration* 75 (1997), pp.531–51. See also M. Maor and G.W. Jones, 'Varieties of Administrative Convergence', *International Journal of Public Sector Management* 12 (1999), pp.49–62.

24. K. Dyson, 'La France, l'Union economique et monetaire et la construction européenne: Renforcer l'executif, transformer l'état', *Revue politiques et management public* 15 (1997), pp.57–77; J. Beyers, 'De verhouding fussen politiek en bestuur in het belgisch Europees beleid', *Res Publica* 39 (1997), pp.399–422.

25. R. Dehousse, 'European Integration and the Nation-State', in M. Rhodes *et al.* (eds.), *Developments in West European Politics* (Basingstoke: Macmillan 1997), pp.37–54.

26. See, e.g., Héritier *et al.*, *Ringing the Changes in Europe*; Knill, 'European Policies'; Knill and Lenschow, 'Coping with Europe'.

27. H. Siedentopf and J. Ziller (eds.), *Making European Policies Work: The Implementation of Community Legislation in the Member States, 2 vols.* (London: Sage 1988).

28. For a recent example T.A. Börzel, 'Towards Convergence in Europe? Institutional Adaptation to Europeanisation in Germany and Spain', *Journal of Common Market Studies*, 37 (1999), pp.573–96.

29. See Falkner in this volume.

30. R. Mayntz, *New Challenges to Governance Theory* (Florence: Robert Schuman Centre at the European University Institute, Jean Monnet Chair Papers No 50 1998).

31. A. Benz and K.H. Goetz, 'The German Public Sector: National Priorities and the International Reform Agenda', in idem (eds.), *A New German Public Sector* (Aldershot: Dartmouth 1996), pp.1–26.

32. For a review of the discussion see W. Müller and V. Wright (eds.), *The State in Western Europe* (London: Frank Cass 1994).

33. Bulmer and Burch, 'Organizing for Europe', p.601.
34. Ibid., p.603.
35. Knill and Lenschow, 'Coping with Europe', p.607.
36. Ibid. p.611; see also Knill, 'European Policies'.
37. Maor and Stevens, 'Measuring the Impact of New Public Management'.
38. Egeberg, 'Transcending Intergovernmentalism?'.
39. Ibid. pp.470–71.
40. Hanf and Soetendorp (eds.), *Adapting to European Integration*, p.186.
41. Ibid., p.186.
42. Ibid., p.187.
43. H. Kassim, 'The National Co-ordination of EU Policy: Must Europeanisation Mean Convergence?' (Paper presented at the PSA Conference, London, April 2000), p.21.
44. Harmsen, 'The Europeanization of National Administrations', pp.105–6.
45. A. Cole and H. Drake, 'The Europeanization of the French Polity: Continuity, Change and Adaptation', *Journal of European Public Policy* 7 (2000), pp.26–43 at 30.
46. Ibid., p.40.
47. Wessels, *Die Öffnung des Staates*, p.433 (my translation, KHG).
48. A. Héritier, 'Differential Europe: National Administrative Responses to Community Policy' (Manuscript, EUI, Florence, 1998).
49. The comments on central and eastern European countries are informed by a research project on 'Executive Capacity in Post-Communist Europe', which is led by V. Dimitrov (LSE), H. Wollmann (Humboldt Universität Berlin) and the author. It is funded by the Volkswagen Foundation.
50. B. Lippert and B. Becker (eds.), *Towards EU Membership: Transformation and Integration in Poland* (Bonn: Europa Union Verlag 1998); M.A. Rupp, 'The Pre-accession Strategy and the Governmental Structures of the Visegrad Countries', in K. Henderson (ed.), *Back to Europe: Central and Eastern Europe and the European Union)* (London: UCL Press 1999), pp.89–105.
51. SIGMA (ed.), *Preparing Public Administrations for the European Administrative Space* (Paris: SIGMA Papers No 23, 1998).
52. V. Diakov, *Study & Analysis of Administrative Infrastructures (On the Basis of the Annex to the White Paper on the Preparation of the Associated Countries of Central and Eastern Europe for Integration into the Internal Market of the Union* (Brussels: Technical Assistance Information Exchange Office (TAIEX); no year given).
53. B. Nunberg, *Public Administration Development in the EU Accession Context* (internal document, The World Bank, 1999).
54. A. Ágh, 'Europeanization of Policy-Making in East Central Europe: The Hungarian Approach to EU Accession', *Journal of European Public Policy* 6 (1999), pp.839–854 at 842.
55. B. Nunberg, *The State After Communism: Administrative Transitions in Central and Eastern Europe* (Washington, DC: The World Bank 1999), p.266.
56. T. Verheijen, and D. Coombes (eds.), *Innovations in Public Management: Perspectives from East and West Europe* (Cheltenham: Elgar 1998).
57. K.H. Goetz, 'Ein neuer Verwaltungstyp in Mittel- und Osteuropa? Zur Entwicklung der post-kommunistischen öffentlichen Verwaltung', in H. Wollmann *et al.* (eds.), *Transformation sozialistischer Gesellschaften: Am Ende des Anfanges* (*Leviathan* Special Issue No 15) (Opladen: Westdeutscher Verlag 1995), pp.538–53; K.H. Goetz and H.Z. Margetts, 'The Solitary Center: The Core Executive in Central and Eastern Europe', *Governance* 12 (1999), pp.425–53.
58. The literature on this topic is enormous. For two recent reviews see K. von Beyme, *Die Parlamentarische Demokratie* (Opladen: Westdeutscher Verlag, 3rd rev. edn. 1999); R. Elgie (ed.), *Semi-Presidentialism in Europe* (Oxford: Oxford University Press 1999).
59. A. Lijphart, *Patterns of Democracy: Government Forms and Performance in Thirty-Six Countries* (New Haven, CT: Yale University Press 1999).
60. See, for example, J. Blondel and F. Müller-Rommel (eds.), *Governing Together: The Extent and Limits of Joint Decision-Making in Western European Cabinets* (Basingstoke:

Macmillan 1993); idem (eds.), *Cabinets in Western Europe* (Basingstoke: Macmillan, 2nd edn. 1997).

61. J. Blondel and M. Cotta (eds.), *Party and Government: An Inquiry into the Relationship between Governments and Supporting Parties in Liberal Democracies* (Basingstoke: Macmillan 1996); W. Müller and K. Strom (eds.), *Koalitionsregierungen in Westeuropa* (Vienna: Signum 1997).

62. J.D. Aberbach *et al.*, *Bureaucrats and Politicians in Western Democracies* (Cambridge, MA: Harvard University Press 1981); E. Page and V. Wright (eds.), *Bureaucratic Elites in Western European States* (Oxford: Oxford University Press 1999).

63. P. Weller *et al.* (eds.), *The Hollow Crown: Countervailing Trends in Core Executives* (Basingstoke: Macmillan 1997); B.G. Peters *et al.* (eds.), *Administering the Summit: Administration of the Core Executive in Developed Countries* (Basingstoke: Macmillan 1999).

64. P.G. Peters, 'Managing Horizontal Government: The Politics of Co-ordination', *Public Administration* 76 (1998), pp.295–311.

65. See M. Egeberg, 'The Impact of Bureaucratic Structure on Policy Making', *Public Administration* 77 (1999), pp.155–70.

66. For example, Knill, 'European Policies'.

67. S. Bulmer and M. Burch, 'The "Europeanisation" of Central Government: The UK and Germany in Historical Institutionalist Perspective', in M.D. Aspinwall and G. Schneider (eds.), *The Rules of Integration* (Manchester: Manchester University Press forthcoming).

68. Héritier, 'Differential Europe', p.1.

69. C. Spanou, 'European Integration in Administrative Terms: A Framework for Analysis and the Greek Case', *Journal of European Public Policy* 5 (1998), pp.467–84 at 481.

70. Knill and Lenschow, 'Coping with Europe'; Knill, 'European Policies'.

71. P.C. Schmitter and J. Santiso, 'Three Temporal Dimensions to the Consolidation of Democracy', *International Political Science Review* 19 (1998), pp.69–92.

72. Ibid., p.71.

73. C.J. Bennett, 'Understanding Ripple Effects: The Cross-National Adoption of Policy Instruments for Bureaucratic Accountability', *Governance* 10 (1997), pp.213–33; P.G. Peters, 'Policy Transfers Between Governments: The Case of Administrative Reforms', *West European Politics* 20 (1997), pp.71–88.

74. D. Stone, 'Learning Lessons and Transferring Policy Across Time, Space and Disciplines', *Politics* 19 (1999), pp.51–9.

75. This point has recently also been emphasised by E. Bomberg and J. Peterson, 'Policy Transfer and Europeanization' (Paper for the Political Studies Association-UK 50th Annual Conference, London, 10–13 April 2000).

76. C. Hood, 'A Public Management for All Seasons', *Public Administration* 69 (1991), pp.3–19.

77. For a critical review of the literature, see H. Margetts, *Information Technology and Central Government* (London: Routledge 1999).

78. R. Rhodes, *Understanding Governance: Policy Networks, Governance, Reflexivity and Accountability* (Buckingham: Open University Press 1997).

79. V. Wright, 'Reshaping the State: Implications for Public Administration', *West European Politics* 17 (1994), pp.102–34.

Abstracts

Introduction: European Integration and National Political Systems
SIMON HIX AND KLAUS H. GOETZ

European integration as a (potential) force of change in domestic polities and politics is attracting growing scholarly attention. European integration comprises two interrelated processes: the delegation of policy competences and the establishment of a new set of political institutions. Most existing studies of how these processes affect domestic institutional and political orders approach the subject from an institutionalist perspective. While such an approach helps to clarify the links between pressures for change and patterns of national adaptation, European integration as a source of change cannot be considered in isolation from other (potential) sources of domestic institutional and political change.

The Limited Impact of Europe on National Party Systems
PETER MAIR

A brief overview of the changing format and mechanics of national party systems suggests that the direct impact of European integration has been severely limited. Although the national party systems as constituted within the European electoral arena may show signs of such an impact, this has as yet failed to spill over into the strictly domestic arena. Two major reasons are suggested to account for this seeming imperviousness of the national party systems. First, the absence of an arena in which parties may compete at European level for executive office, an absence which thereby hinders the development of a European party system as such. Second, the misplaced division of competences associated with the national and European electoral arenas, whereby issues concerning the European political system itself are largely excluded from the national political arena to which they properly belong. The study concludes by suggesting that it is through the indirect process of depoliticisation that Europe may exert its greatest impact on national party systems.

European Integration, Voters and National Politics
MATTHEW GABEL

This study considers how and whether EU membership shapes voting behaviour in national elections. It starts by surveying claims about the relationship between EP elections and national elections. Because voters use EP elections as markers for the electoral prospects of national governing parties, the later an EP election follows a national general election, the greater the impact of the EP election on the governing parties' fortunes in the subsequent national election. It goes on to explore whether and how issues of European integration have influenced voting behaviour in national elections. Building on previous studies, the discussion shows that for most of the EU member states, voters' support for EU membership provides the basis for a new electoral cleavage. However, a variety of questions remains to be addressed regarding the extent and character of this electoral cleavage and how this cleavage may develop with further economic integration. The analysis consequently develops a research agenda and several theoretical hypotheses about how the link between macroeconomic performance and support for governing parties may change as economic integration deepens.

Political Contention in a Europeanising Polity
DOUG IMIG AND SIDNEY TARROW

European-level government presents new opportunities and constraints for domestic social actors. But barriers remain to contentious action in the transnational realm. Most individuals have difficulty ascribing the sources of their grievances to the EU, transaction costs impede their efforts to co-ordinate collective action across national boundaries, and traditional routines of collective action attach citizens to their national systems. Nevertheless, some actors are able to mobilise at the European level. Using reports from Reuters, the study finds that most protests are made by occupational groups, such as farmers or workers, with little mobilisation of non-occupational groups (such as environmental or women's NGOs). Also, rather than a direct displacement of contentious politics to the supranational level, one sees a range of mobilising styles: transnational co-operation against domestic actors, collective European protests, and the domestication of European issues within national politics. The authors speculate that these outcomes will allow the EU Commission to keep such protests at a distance, and that activists whose careers are in Brussels-based NGOs will be deprived of the weapons they need to back up their claims.

Policy Networks in a Multi-Level System: Converging Towards Moderate Diversity?
GERDA FALKNER

Researchers have put forward seemingly contradictory hypotheses on how European integration might impact on national interest intermediation. This study proposes to include the meso-level in the analysis – in other words, to look systematically at policy- and sector-specific characteristics in European governance. From such a perspective, it seems the impact of EU-level politics could be much more diverse (in the sense of being differentiated between policy areas) than hitherto expected. In addition, attention needs to be paid to the existence, and limits, of different types of impact potentials of Euro-level patterns on the national systems. Although no uniform systems of interest politics can be expected, even in the longer run, persisting or even growing intra-system diversity of public-private interaction might increasingly be accompanied by a trend towards inter-system convergence of policy-specific networks due to the process of European integration.

Europeanised Politics – Europeanised Media? European Integration and Political Communication
HOLLI A. SEMETKO, CLAES H. DE VREESE AND JOCHEN PETER

A comprehensive framework for analysis of the impact of European integration on political communication needs to take account of developments in four areas: media and political systems, media and political organisations, media content and potential effects, and media audiences and audience characteristics. In this study, the focus is, first, on changes in media systems, and, second, on media organisations and journalists' role orientations. Third, what is known about news concerning 'Europe' is summarised and the impact of 'Europeanisation' on news content discussed. The authors identify the conceptual, theoretical and empirical challenges facing students and scholars of political communication in understanding the impact of European integration in member states. It is argued that it is important to consider both the historical, institutional and media system contexts and patterns in news content. The discussion concludes by proposing new avenues for research on the link between media coverage of politics and potential effects on audiences.

Backbenchers Learn to Fight Back: European Integration and Parliamentary Government

TAPIO RAUNIO AND SIMON HIX

The ability of parliaments to control executives has declined since the 1950s, and most existing research claims that European integration has contributed a great deal to this decline, by providing executives with an arena away from domestic parliamentary scrutiny and a monopoly on information in an ever-larger portfolio of public policies. However, when looking empirically at the impact of the European integration on parliamentary government, one finds that in the 1990s most parliaments in Europe established institutions and mechanisms that forced governments to explain their policies and actions in the European arena to national legislatures. Also, since EU policy choices adopted constrain member states' domestic choices, parliamentary scrutiny of EU issues has contributed to greater supervision of executives on other domestic matters. It is argued that the driving force behind this partial assertion is the desire by non-governing parties and backbench parliamentarians to redress the 'information gap' between governing elites and the parliamentary rank-and-file.

The Positioning of EU Judicial Politics within the United Kingdom

DAMIAN CHALMERS

This study proceeds from the observation that any analysis of the depth and contribution of judicial politics to EU integration must use national courts as its principal laboratory. In its empirical part, the analysis is based on an examination of all reported judgments in the UK between 1971 and 1998 in which EC law was addressed by national judges. In substantive terms, there is no evidence that the UK judiciary has been concerned to protect particular central spheres of British political and legal life from EU intrusion. Resistance has, however, been marked where EC law restricts domestic institutions' capacity to secure conformity in British society whether that conformity takes the form of securing those conditions that sustain and stabilise private relationships and private autonomy or whether it takes the form of protecting those institutions, such as criminal and immigration law, which are taken to sustain a common collective consciousness.

European Integration and National Executives: A Cause in Search of an Effect?

KLAUS H. GOETZ

The impact of European integration on the executives of current EU member states has been studied from three perspectives: linkage, implementation and executive ecology. A review of research and writing about executive Europeanisation in both western and eastern Europe raises doubts about the explanatory status of 'European integration' as a major variable driving domestic institutional change. If knowledge in the field is to advance, the analytical scope of Europeanisation research needs to be extended. First, more attention must be paid to the modes and processes of Europeanisation (as opposed to the substance of institutional adaptation). Second, it is necessary to examine more systematically the manner in which European integration interacts with other (potential) sources of institutional development.

About the Contributors

Damian Chalmers is Senior Lecturer in Law, Law Department, London School of Economics and Political Science.

Gerda Falkner is Professor in the Department of Government, University of Vienna, and at the Max-Planck Institute for the Study of Societies, Cologne.

Matthew J. Gabel is Associate Professor, Department of Political Science and Martin School of Public Administration, University of Kentucky.

Klaus H. Goetz is Senior Lecturer in Government, Department of Government, London School of Economics and Political Science.

Simon Hix is Senior Lecturer in European Union Politics and Policy, Department of Government and European Institute, London School of Economics and Political Science.

Doug Imig is Associate Professor, Department of Political Science, University of Memphis.

Peter Mair is Professor of Comparative Politics, Department of Political Science, Leiden University.

Jochen Peter is Ph.D. candidate in the international Ph.D. programme at the Amsterdam School of Communications Research, University of Amsterdam.

Tapio Raunio is a Researcher in the Department of Political Science, University of Helsinki.

Holli A. Semetko is Professor and Chair of Audience and Public Opinion Research, Amsterdam School of Communications Research, University of Amsterdam.

Sidney Tarrow is the Maxwell Upson Professor of Government, Departments of Government and Sociology, Cornell University.

Claes H. de Vreese is Ph.D. candidate in the international Ph.D. programme at the Amsterdam School of Communications Research, University of Amsterdam.

Index

agenda-setting 135–7, 143, 153
agriculture 144, 180, 198, 216
'aid shopping' 73
American Congress system *see* United States
Amsterdam Summit 75, 131–2
Amsterdam Treaty 7, 44–5, 85, 144
Andersen, S.S. 148, 149
Anderson, C. 65
Anderson, K.A. 96
animal rights 90
anti-nuclear action 90
anti-racist movements 90
ARD (Channel 1 German television) 127, 133
Asian stock markets, Euro, the and 133
'Audio-visual Eureka' 125
Austria 17, 59; corporatism and 96, 99, 106; decision-making 149; EAC 156–8; effect of Europeanisation 211; effect of Maastricht convergence criteria 110; elections in 32–4; environmental policy 106; Freedom Party 34; likelihood ratio (LR) test 61; Nationalrat (parliament) 157; referendum on European integration 48
autoworkers, cross-border actions 89

Barber judgment, pension entitlements 188
Basque country 82
Belgium 59; EAC 156–7; elections 32–4; federal state (1993) 150–51; likelihood-ratio (LR) test 61; Renault and 74, 77
Berlusconi (Fininvest) 125
'best practice' 104
bi-cameralism 13
blockades of roads and ports 85
Blondel, J. 147
Bomberg, E. 96, 106
Britain *see* UK
Britain's Channel 5 news programme, news bureau 128
British Broadcasting Corporation (BBC) 127
British Cabinet office, guidelines on directives 184
British Conservative Party 35, 55–8
British constitutional settlement, judicial revisiting 173–8
British Gas, Equal Treatment (Directive 76/207/EEC) 187

British government, EC law and 183, 187; TUPE Directive and 193
British House of Commons 148, 151, 153, 155, 163
British Labour Party 57–8
British Liberal Democratic Party 58
British political scientists, policy network ideal types 100
British Trade Union Congress, TAUPE Directive and 193
British trade union movement, European level and 13
broadcasting 123–8, 186
Brussels 8, 75, 90, 155
Bulmer, S. 16–17, 19, 215
Burch, M. 16, 19, 215
bureaucracy 148
Burns, T. 148–9

CAP 5, 7, 44, 52, 85, 88
capitalism 5, 18, 76, 174, 225
Carrubba, C. 56, 68
'catnets' 80
CEE 17, 21, 89, 159, 218–19
central and eastern Europe post-Communist states *see* CEE
CFDT (Confédération Française Démocratic du Travail) 74–5
CFSP 152, 155
CGT (Confédération Générale du Travail) 75
Chalmers, D. 2
changing world of European contention 81–2; domestication and transnationalisation 85–6; euro-protest 84–5; instrumentation and sampling 82–3; types of transnational protest 86–7; who protests? 87–9
Channel Islands courts 178
'Checklist for the Transposition of European Legislation' 184
Chirac, Jacques 74
civil codes 174
civil servants 144–5, 155, 220
Clark, W. 66–7
cleavages 15, 38, 58, 68
'co-decision procedure' 7, 105, 144
co-ordinated domestic protest 78
coalition government 13, 37
Cohen, B. 136

collective European Protest 87
Commission, the 6, 8, 44, 74, 90; applicant
    states and accession 218–19; British
    government and 184; domestic legislation
    and 153–4; European culture and 125;
    national political leadership and 45;
    resolution of contentious actions 77; role
    of 7; role of 'the state' and 214; sectoral
    dehierarchical co-ordination 212; TUPE
    Directive amendment and 193;
    withholding tax on savings 190
Common Agricultural Policy *see* CAP
Common Foreign and Security Policy *see*
    CFSP
common law 175, 177, 215
competence transfers, macro-corporatism and
    108
competences 110
competition 4, 15, 180, 186, 192, 198
Conference of the European Affairs
    Committees (COSACs) 154
Conservative parties, flexible exchange rates
    67
construction workers, protest and 89
consumer groups 109
consumer law 144, 175, 179, 181
contentious events analysis, data and 81
contract law 175, 197
contracting-out 89
Coombes, D. 219
'core executives', executive co-ordination
    220
Coreper, EACs and 157
corporatism 8, 12, 95, 95–6
corporatist policy community 102–3, 105–7
corporatist systems 98–9, 101–2, 110, 113,
    160, 214
Council of Economic and Finance Ministers
    (EcoFin) 5
Council, the 6, 8, 44, 55, 144–5, 154, 200;
    Cabinet ministers and 152; domestic
    legislation and 153–5, 160; geographical
    and hierachical co-ordination 212
Court of appeal (England and Wales) 174,
    178–9
criminal law 173, 180, 196
cross-border crime 6
cross-national research, political
    communication and 122

Dalton, R. 69
Danish Folketinget (1986) 142, 157
Danish public service broadcasting
    organisation 127
De Gaulle, President 52
de Vreese, C.H. 2

decision trap 193
decision-making 149, 152, 155, 164, 212;
    council 144; electoral access to European
    44; judicial 195; process 153; sovereign
    90; structures in Brussels 194; trickle
    down of EU-level 105, 111; voters and 47
Dehaene, Jean-Luc (Belgium P.M.) 73
'democratic centralism' 219
'democratic deficit' 17, 142
Democratic Party of the Left (Italy) 62–3
democratisation 21, 219
demonstrations 74, 85
Denmark 5, 48, 59–60; Brussels office 155;
    decision-making 149; EAC 156–7; EP
    1999 election turnout 127; the euro and
    135; executive–legislative relations 151;
    likelihood ratio (LR) test 61; national
    elections 32–4; news coverage of 1998
    election 130–31; People's Movement
    against EU 31; SEA rejected by
    Folketinget 142; TAUPE Directive 193;
    transport ministry officials 216
'deparliamentarisation' thesis 143, 147
depoliticisation 28, 47–8
deregulation 4, 13, 126, 227
Désir, Harlem 75
'desk-top journalism' 128
different arenas, different competencies 41–7
'direct effect', meaning 7
direct impacts, definition 10
Directives 107–8, 124, 153, 176–9, 181, 184,
    186–7
Directorate-generals 100–101, 146
division of labour 46
domestication, changing role of states and
    89–90; European contention 77;
    Europeanisation and 216; protests and
    85–6
Duisenberg, Wim 131
Duncan-Smith, I. 176
Dutch Christian parties 36

EACs 152–3, 155, 157–8, 161–3, 167
East-central Europe, subcontracting and
    contracting-out 89
EC agricultural reforms, protest and 87
EC law, administration of legal institutions of
    civil society 174–5; application of 182,
    195; bureaucratic rents 186–7; conflict
    with UK parliamentary statute 176–7;
    constitutional resettlement of
    administrative power 178–83; direct or
    indirect source of rights 190; domestic
    institutions and 173; imposition of private
    duties and costs 190–91; individual and
    state 173–4; institutional capabilities for

conformity as constraint on 195–9;
integration and expectations 171; internal
judicial hierarchies and 174; national law
and 197–9; normativity and 184–5, 199;
precedence of 176, 196; rent-seeking
versus other arms of government 170;
structural constraints 194–5
'EC Membership Evaluated Series' 17
EC policy community, automobile sector 106
ECJ 7–8, 8, 13, 170, 177–8; case law 191–4;
German Federal Constitutional Court 16;
national courts 16, 171; normative
qualities and 185; 'outsider' elites and
172; part-time workers and pensions 188;
Private Member's Bill curbing powers of
176; resolution of contentious actions 77;
sex discrimination 193–4, 198
Economic and Monetary Union see EMU
economic version of change 225
ECOSOC (Economic and Social Council)
100
Egeberg, M. 216
electoral cleavage 68
electoral disempowerment, parties in
competition 28
Eliassen, K.A. 96
Employment Appeal Tribunal 178–9, 187,
193
employment tribunals 172, 178
EMU 2, 5, 10, 33, 146; EP and 44; French
and British voters and 58; macro-
economic choices and 10; members
participating (January 1999) 132; neo-
Keynesian demand-management policies
5–6
Entman, R. 123
Environment Agency 186
Environmental, law 144, 199; policy 12, 56,
106, 108, 175, 179–80, 198–9; protection
4, 186
environmentalists 14, 90
EP 7, 36, 100; 1979 and 1999 elections 129;
basket of parties 39; competences 43–4;
decision-making 164; environmental
concerns 56; European Commission and
41; implications of direct elections 11, 29,
67; legislation 154–5; national
parliaments and 143; petitions re Renault
74; policy independence of committees
146; resolution of contentious actions 77;
TAUPE Directive 193; Treaty of
Amsterdam and 45; voting behaviour in
national elections 53
ETUC (European Trade Union Council), EU
and 89, 193
EU, acquis communautaire 17, 52, 213,
218–19; arguments over fishing
regulations 87; citizens' welfare and
political interests 55; contentious events
motivated by 83; countries with right
ideology 60; decision-making and
national parliaments 155;
departmentalism and sectorisation 213;
direct redistributional capacity 5; EMU
and member states 67; enlargement
debate 130; European legislation 106–7;
European Works Council 73–4;
governance 94; how it might be
'democratised' 17; impact on national
interest intermediation 95;
intergovernmental bodies 43–4; macro-
economic stabilisation 5; market
regulation 4; membership and vote choice
61, 63–5; national courts and Brussels
policies 79; newspaper stories on
institutions 121; officials and Renault 74;
parliamentary control over office holders
142; press coverage of European news
129–30; public–private co-operation 104;
'regulatory state' 9, 146–7; 'supremacy'
of law 7; trickle down of decision-making
105, 111; voter choice on EU issues 56
EU regional funds 5
EU summits 75, 130–32, 152, 212
EU Treaty, national budget deficits 5
EU-based Schengen agreement 131
Eurikon experiment (1982) 126
Euro, the 6, 35, 55, 68, 132, 137; Britain and
Germany and 122; effects of 67–9, 75;
news and 132–5
Euro-Disney 86
Eurobarometer mega-survey (January–March
1996) 58, 62, 68, 70
Eurocritical MPs, European questions and
163
'Euroimages' 125
Euronews (1993) 126
'Europa TV' (1985) 126
Europarties 38, 40
Europe 84–5, 131
Europe and national party systems 29–30;
format and 29, 30–31; mechanics 31–7
European Affairs Committees see EACs
European arena 28–30, 42–3, 45–7
European Broadcasting Union (EBU) 126
European Central Bank 5, 131
European cleavage system 38
European Communities Act (1972) 176
European contentious events, conservative
operationalisation 83
European Court of Justice (Luxembourg) see
ECJ

European Economic Area (EEA) 159
European effect, contextualising 20–23;
    determining 14–17; explaining 17–20
European elections, issue of Europe 47;
    national political issues and 53–4;
    national politics rehearsed 38
European electoral arena 41, 43
European Federation of Metalworkers
    (Brussels) 74, 78
European integration 101, 196; 490 protest
    events over 14 years 84; arena of direct
    democracy and 48; British judicial
    contribution 171; constraints on national
    policy-making 66; direct impacts 10, 12,
    28; domestic impact 9–10; domestic
    parliamentary government 151–60;
    domestic political consequences 2–3, 23;
    electoral cleavage in national electorates
    58; electoral dealignment and
    disengagement 49; elite-led project 14;
    Europeanisation of domestic politics 90;
    executive change and 227; from cause to
    effect 220–23; impact on parliamentary
    government 143–4; indirect impact
    10–11, 12, 78; influence on broadcasting
    systems 123; internal party conflict and
    competition 56; issue-voting in national
    elections 55–65, 68–9; macro-institutional
    accounts 18; material consequences and
    modalities 14; 'moderate diversity' 94,
    111–12; modifying national executive
    217; national policy delegation and
    European-level political outcomes 3–6;
    national political systems and 1, 29;
    national voting behaviour 52, 62; new
    exit, veto and information opportunities
    12–14; news organisations and 128; non-
    member countries and 21; political news
    coverage and 121; requirements 137;
    source of change 22; strengthening
    executives 160–61; study on and NPM
    215–16; supranational institution-building
    6–9; top-down and bottom-up process
    138; traditional left–right divide and 11
European integration and national executives
    211–12; administrative ecology 213–14;
    implementation 213; linkage 212–13;
    national impact in the west 214–19
European integration and national
    public–private relations 95; definitions of
    'Corporatism ' and 'Pluralism' 95–7;
    models and expectations concerning the
    EU 97–8
European integration and political
    communication 121–2; broadcasting 124;
    cultural products 125–7; media systems

123–4; ownership 125
European Journalism Centre 128
European Monetary System (EMS) 66
European multi-level system, 'uniform
    pluriformism' 112
European Parliament see EP
European parliamentary–government model,
    party competition and information
    160–63
European parliaments, decline of 143,
    147–51, 162
European party system, limits of spillover
    and absence of 37–41
European policies, Channel 4 productions
    and 127
European presidency, member states and 212
European project 17, 19
European trade unionists 75
European Works Councils (EWCs) 73–6
European-level party system 28
Europeanisation 3, 16–20, 48–9, 85, 94; CEE
    applicant countries 218; debate 16, 18,
    23, 211–12, 222; direct impact 31, 33, 35,
    47; domestic 15, 23, 90, 111; economic
    and political integration 227; effect 14,
    17, 22, 211, 221; effect of direct elections
    to EP 29; effects on national interest
    intermediation 104, 109, 111; format and
    mechanics of party systems 36; impact on
    executive systems 211; labour law and
    103; literature 15, 17, 20–21, 224;
    national party systems 27; news content
    and 122, 129; number of parties in
    domestic elections 30; policy-making and
    86; of politicians 137; research 20,
    220–23, 228; voluntaristic patterns 21,
    101
Eurosceptic position, 'outsider' party 34, 163
Eurosport (Sky and EBU 1989) 126
Eurostrike 73–6, 77
Evans, G. 55–60, 64
exchange function of contract, EC
    competition law and 175, 203
exchange-rate menchanism (ERM) 56, 66
executive Europeanisation, contextualising
    European integration 225–8; temporality
    223–4; transfer and spread of Institutional
    innovations 224–5
executive policy-making 222
executive studies 220–21
executive–economy nexus 214
executive–legislature relationship 158
executives 144, 149–50, 153, 160–61, 163,
    220–21; national and EU decision-making
    212
exit opportunity, veto on domestic actions
    and 13

external relations 180
external trade 144
extreme right parties 31

Fabius, L. 73
Factortame saga 177
Falkner, G. 2
farmers 8, 52, 79, 85–90
Federal Republic of Germany 21
federalism 13, 227
FGTB (General Trade Union of Belgium) 76
Financial Services Authority 186
Finland 17; decision-making 149, 152; EAC
    156–7; Eduskunta (parliament) 155;
    left–right self-placement 59; likelihood-
    ratio (LR) test 61; national elections 32,
    34; new constitution (2000) 151; office in
    Brussels 155; study of Europeanisation
    211; transport ministry officials 216
fisheries 144, 180, 198
fishermen 87, 89
Fligstein, N. 185
Forza Italia party 62–3
Foster case, Directive 76/207/EEC and 187
Foucault, M. 185
fragmentation 30, 37, 100, 163, 186, 199
framing analysis, agenda-setting research and
    137
France 19, 212; amendment of Constitution
    158–9; cross-media ownership 125; EAC
    156–7; European monetary unification
    and 64; Europeanisation 216–17; farm
    protests 79, 85; farmers and CAP 8, 52;
    influence on EU 215; likelihood ratio
    (LR) 61; National Assembly 142, 148,
    163; national elections 32–4, 48, 57, 59;
    National Front 34, 53; office in Brussels
    155; Renault and 74, 77; statism 11, 96,
    98; TUPE Directive 193; voting in
    presidential elections (1995) 58
Frankfurt/Main 134
Franklin, M. 53–4
free movement of goods 178–80, 183, 198
free movement of persons 178, 180, 183,
    197–8
freedom of establishment 180, 198
freedom to Provide Services 198
French fishermen, Spanish fishermen 87
French Gaullists 36
French National Assembly (1954), European
    Defence Community and 142
'From National Corporatism to Transnational
    Pluralism' 97

Gabel, M. 2
'gain from exchange' 162

General Agreement of Tariffs and Trade
    (GATT) 126
genetically modified organisms 81, 85, 87,
    90
Germany 19, 21, 212; 'co-operative public
    administration' 214; Basic Law 16, 158;
    broadcasting 125, 127; Bundestag 148,
    150, 153, 158; centre-right government
    13; corporatism and 96; decision-making
    149; EAC 156–7; EU membership and
    59; the euro and 133–5; European
    integration and news coverage 122;
    farmers and CAP 8; Free Citizen's
    Alliance 31; Green Party and European
    elections 53; influence on EU 215;
    likelihood ratio (LR) test 61; miners and
    pit closures 79, 83; national elections 32,
    34; news coverage of 1990 and 1998
    elections 130–31; TAUPE Directive 193
globalisation 22–3, 79, 86, 225
Goetz, K.H. 2, 123
Greece 21, 30; EAC 156–7; EU membership
    and vote choice 62, 65; left–right self-
    placement 59–60; likelihood ratio (LR)
    test 61–2; national elections 32, 34
Green Cowles, M. 97
Green Papers on telecommunications and
    satellite communication (1987 and 1990)
    124
Green parties 12, 31, 36–7, 53, 163
Growth and Stability Pact 5
'guerrilla actions' 74
Guyomarch, A. 17

Haas, Ernst. 1
Hallerberg, M. 66–7
Hanf, K. 216
'harmonisation', national standards and 4
harmonisation of excise duties (Directive
    92/12/EC) 181
harmonisation of trademarks (Directive
    89/104/EEC) 181
Harmsen, R. 216–17
HDTV (high definition television) 125
Health 216
health and safety law 175
Hegeland, H. 153
Héritier, A. 112, 222
High Court of England and Wales 174,
    178–9
Hix, S. 2, 123
Hoffmann-Riem, W. 126
Holland 127, 130–32, 135, 148, 157
Hood, C. 226
House of Lords (England and Wales) 174,
    178–9

Hue, Robert 75
Humphreys, P. 124
Hungary 219

Imig, D. 2
immigration 6, 180, 196, 198
immigration adjudicators 172–3
Immigration Appeals Tribunal 178
immigration and refugees, 'Europe-related
    issues 131
Independent Television (ITV) 126–7, 133
individualisation 37
industrial tribunals 177
Industry Federations, EU and 89
inflation, right-wing parties and 66
'information' 161–3
'information gap' 164
informational advantage, European-level
    governance and 13
institutional congruence, 'snugness of fit' 19
institutional environment, patterning of
    judicial behaviour 194–5
institutional politics, judicial politics and 170
'institutions matter' 221
intellectual property 174, 178, 180, 188,
    190–91, 198
inter-sectoral diversity 112
inter-systemic diversity 112
interest-group politics, judicial politics and
    170
intergovernmental bodies 154
intergovernmental conferences (ICGs) 6, 193,
    199, 212
'intergovernmentalist' school of integration
    theorising 145
internal market 144
international co-operation, protest campaigns
    86
international conflict 87
Ireland 32–4, 59, 61, 156, 216
Irish Oireachtas 148, 159
Isle of Man courts 178
issue network 102, 105–6, 111
Italy 12, 21; broadcasting 123, 125; Camera
    dei Deputati (parliament) 148, 150;
    centre-right government 13; Communist
    Party 36; EAC 156–7; EMU and 152; EU
    fines for milk overproduction 79; EU
    membership and vote choice 62–3; EU
    influence on EU 215; left–right self-
    placement 59; likelihood ratio (LR) test
    61–2; National Alliance Party 34, 63;
    national elections 32–4; statism 11, 96;
    TUPE Directive 193
ITN (Independent Television news) 133

JCFA committee 159
JHA (Justice and Home Affairs) 155
Johnson case, Royal Ulster Constabulary 187
Jordan, A.G. 100
Jospin, Lionel 75
journalism, media organisations and 127–9
Jupeé, Alain 74, 76

Kassim, H. 216
Katzenstein, P.J. 19
King, A. 149
Kirch (Germany) 125
KKE (Communist Party of Greece) 62, 65
Knill, C. 215, 222
Kohl government, target of protests 83, 93
Kohler-Koch, B. 96, 98
Kosovo War, common foreign policy and 137
Krehbiel, K. 161–2

labour and immigration 171, 174
labour law 179
Lafontaine, Oskar 134
Lamizet, B. 124
law, role of 196–7
laws on blasphemy and obscenity 196
left–right self-placement, voter choice and
    59–60, 62
left-wing parties, unemployment and 66
Lehmbruch, G. 99
Lenschow, A. 215, 222
liberalisation 4, 10, 13, 21, 79, 86, 219
Lijphart, A. 220
likelihood ratio (LR) test, EU membership
    and vote choice 61
lobbying 154
London 134
Luxembourg, broadcasting 123; EAC 156;
    left–right self-placement 59; likelihood
    ratio (LR) test 61–2; national election
    votes 32, 34; trade unionists (1997)
    protest 87

Maastricht Treaty 7, 35, 44, 85, 106, 152,
    158; convergence criteria and EMU 109
McAdam, D. 85, 88
McCombs, M.E. 136
McDonald's restaurants 86
'mad cow' disease 85, 130
magistrates 178
Magone, J. 152
Mair, P. 2, 19, 123
Majone, G. 227
Major government (1992–96) 176
majoritarian redistribution 9
managerialist version of change, internal
    change agents 226

Mara-Drita, I. 185
marches 75, 85–6
marker elections 54, 68
'market failures', European re-regulation and
    4
Marks, G. 88
Marsh, D. 100–101
Marsh, M. 53–4
Marshall (No.2) case, Ministry of Defence
    187–8
'MEDIA' programme 125
media systems 123–4; broadcasting 124;
    content 129–32; cultural products 125–7;
    ownership 125
media, the, public opinion and European
    integration 135–8
Members of the European Parliament
    (MEPs) 154
Mezey, M. 147, 163
Miert, Karel Van (European Competition
    Commissioner) 73
migrant workers, social entitlements
    (Regulation 1408/71 EEC) 179, 197
miners 79, 83, 89
'minimal state' 225
'moderate diversity' 94, 111–12
modernisation 21, 148–9, 226
Moe, T. 194
Monde, Le 76
Monitoring Euromedia reports 130
Moravcsik, Andrew 1, 9, 145
Mueller (German Minister of the Economy)
    135
multi-national firms 13–14, 77
multinominal logit (MNL) model of vote
    choice 60–62
Murdock, Rupert (Australia) 125

nation-state, citizens' claims and 83
nation-state context, capitalism 225
National Alliance party (Italy) 63
national arena 41–6, 90
national courts 16, 171
national elections 32–6, 46–7, 53–5, 130–31
national interest intermediation, competence
    transfers 108–9; EU decision patterns
    104–6; impact of European integration
    98–103; positive integration measures
    106–8; role of mediating factors 109–11;
    types of potential impact 103
national monopolies 4, 10–11
national newspapers, protest event analysis
    81–2
national parliaments 15, 144–5, 150–53,
    159–60, 164
national party systems, Europeanisation

27–8, 38, 43; format and mechanics
    29–36; government and 148; indirect
    impact of European integration 48;
    membership 37
'nested game', politics at domestic level 12
Netherlands 212; broadcasting regulations
    125; corporatism and 96; EAC 156;
    Europeanisation of administration 216;
    left–right self-placement 59; likelihood
    ratio (LR) test 61; national elections
    32–4; news coverage of 1998 election
    130
'New Approach to Harmonisation' 185
New Democracy Party (Greece) 62, 65
New Public Management *see* NPM
Newman, M. 154
News at Ten 123
NGOs 5, 7–8, 89–90, 192
Nine o'Clock News 123, 128
Nollet, Michel 76
non-governmental organisations *see* NGOs
non-member states, Europeanisation effects
    21, 212
non-occupational groups, protests and 88
Nordic countries 155
normativity 184–5
Norris, P. 130
Northern Ireland courts 178
Northern League Party (Italy) 62–3
Norton, P. 148–9
Norway 17, 21, 212
Notat, Nicole 74–5
NPM 215–16, 226–7

occupational groups, protests and 87–9
occupations of factories and public buildings
    85
Offe, C. 186
O'Halpin, E. 159
'organisation', 'mobilisation model' 80
OSCE (Organisation for Security and Co-
    operation in Europe) 200
outcomes of contentious politics 77

Page, E.C. 211
Palmer, H. 67–8
parental leave directive (OJ 98/L 14/9) 107–8
pareto-efficient EU policies 4, 9
part-time work directives (OJ 96/L 145/4)
    107
particularisation of voting choice 37
PASOK (Panhellenic Socialist Movement of
    Greece) 62, 65
Pasqua, Charles 74
Paterson, W. 17
Pedersen, M. 39–40

pensioners' parties 31
People's Movement Against the EU
(Denmark) 31
People's Party (Spain) 62, 64
Peter, J. 2
pharmaceuticals 180, 198
Pierens, Willy 76
pluralism 8, 94–9, 101, 111, 186, 214, 219
Poland 219
policing 186
policy community 8, 106
policy competencies, European level and 142
political cleavages 15
political communication, research 122
political parties, media coverage 69, 127
political versions of change 227
political world, indifference and
disengagement 37
Pollack, M. 192
Portugal 21, 30; EAC 156–7;
executive–legislative relations 151–2;
left–right self-placement 59; legislature
148; likelihood-ratio (LR) test 61;
Maastricht and 158; national elections 32,
34; transport ministry officials 216
posting of workers directive (OJ 97/L 18/1,
Art.3.3) 107
postmodernism 22–3, 226–7
Powell, G.B. 65
Prime Minister 152
private property rights 174, 197, 199
privatisation 4, 10, 21, 146, 227
Privy Council 178
pro- *vs.* anti-European alignment 33, 35
pro-European parties, votes and 33
processes of contentious politics 76–7
professional associations 197
proportional representation 13
protection of young people at work directive
(OJ 94/L 216/12 Art. 17.4) 107
protests 78–89
proto-Europarties 38
public procurement 180, 198
public–private co-operation 103–6, 108–12,
214
public–private networks in a multi-level
system 94–5; 'corporatism' and
'pluralism' 95–7; differing models and
expectations concerning EU 97–8; EU
level 100–101, 111; national level
99–100; typology connecting two strands
of literature 101–3; varying networks
98–9
public–private relationships 95, 102

qualified majority voting 7, 142, 144–5, 159

quangos, ECJ and 192
quotas, broadcasting and 124–6

'rational myths' 195
Raunio, T. 2, 56, 123
Ray, L. 31, 34–5
referendums 48
refugee and asylum policies 6
regulation of food stuffs 186
Reif, K. 38
Renault affair, contentious politics 76, 89
Renault plant (Douai) 75
Renault plant (Vilvoorde) 73–4
responsibility, social problems and 132
Reuters World News Service 82
Rhodes, R.A.W. 100–101
Richardson, J.J. 100
Roederer, C. 79, 85
Romania 219
Rometsch, D. 146
RTL (Radiotelevision Luxembourg) 127,
133, 135

Santer, Jacques (European Commission
President) 74
Santiso, J. 223
Sartori, G. 40
SAT 1 (German television) 127
Scandinavian countries 125, 131, 148
Scharpf, F. 185
Scheve, K. 58, 64, 69
Schmidt, V.A. 95, 97–8, 153–4
Schmitt, H. 38
Schmitter, P.C. 21, 97, 109, 223
Schröder, Chancellor Gerhard 134
Schweitzer, L 73, 75
Scottish courts 178
Scottish farmers, Irish beef and 87
Seguin, Philippe 74
Semetko, H.A. 2
Sewell, W. 85
sex discrimination 178, 180, 187–91, 193,
196–8
sex discriminatory effects of social security
schemes (Directive 79/7/EEC) 179
Shaw, D.L. 136
Siedentoph, H. 213
single currency *see* Euro, The
Single European Act (1992) 7
Single Market (1992) 2, 67, 124–5, 146, 154,
158, 179, 181
sixth VAT Directive (77/388/EEC) 189–90,
193
Smith, G. 36
'snugness of fit', institutional congruence 19
'social dialogue', employers and trade
unions 8

'social pacts', Maastricht convergence criteria and 110
social security 171, 180, 198
social security commissioners 172, 178–9
Socialist Party (Spain) 62, 64
Soetendorp, B. 216
sources of contentious politics 76
sovereignty 144, 158, 174–6, 185
Spain 11–12, 21, 30; broadcasting regulations 125; decision-making 149; EAC 156–7; EU membership and vote choice 62, 64, 151; left–right self-placement 59; legislature 148; likelihood ratio (LR) test 61–2; national elections 32–4; statism and 96
Spanou, C. 222
specialised agents 148
spillover 28, 37–41, 151, 159, 221
Springer & Bertelsmann (German) 125
statism 95, 97–9, 101–2, 105–6, 111, 214
Status Report on European telecommunications (1997) 124
Strasbourg 38
Streeck, W. 97, 109
student action 90
subcontracting 89
Sun, The 134
'supremacy', meaning 7
Sweden 17, 48; decision-making 149; EAC 156–7; Left Party 34; left–right self-placement 59–60; likelihood ratio (LR) test 61; media and 129; MPs and EP 164; national elections 32–4; Riksdag 153, 163; study of Europeanisation 211; TAUPE Directive and 193; transport ministry officials 216
Switzerland 17, 21, 212
Szen judgment 193

Taggart, P. 34–5
Tarrow, S. 2
tax/taxation 171, 174, 178, 180, 189–91, 198
Technical Assistance Exchange Office (TAIEX) 218
technological version of change 226
television Directive (1989) 124
'Television without Frontiers' 124, 126
Thatcher, Margaret 4, 13
Tilly, C. 80
Timpone, R. 56, 68
tort law 175
trade unions 14, 109
traditional policy community 102–3, 105, 111
trans-European social movement organisations 77

transfer of ownership of undertakings *see* TUPE
transnational activity, judicial politics and 170
transnational contention and its obstacles 77–9, 89; collective identities 80; political opportunities 81; social networks 79–80
transnational media 79
transport 180, 198, 216
TUPE 180–81, 187–93, 197–8
Turner, L. 87
typical domestic protest 78–9, 82–3

UK 4, 12, 16, 19, 97, 212; decision-making 149; devolution 151; EAC 156–7; EC law and private relationships 190; the Euro and 122, 133–5; European integration and voting behaviour 53, 64; European monetary unification and 64; European policy-making and 215; implementation of EC law 183–7; likelihood ratio (LR) test 61–2; media 123, 125–8, 130–31; national elections 32, 34, 48, 57, 59; parliamentary election (1997) 35, 57; political reaction to judicial politics 187–90; positioning of EU judicial politics 169–73; pro- *vs.* anti-European divide 35–6; TUPE Directive 193
UN bodies 200
unemployment 66, 75, 86–7
UNICE 193
UNICITRAL (United Nations Commission of International Trade Law) 183
UNIDROIT (1995 Convention on Stolen or Illegally Exported Cultural Objects) 183
'uniform pluriformism' 112
UNISON trade union 188
United Left Party (Spain) 62, 64
United States 162; Congress 40; EU concessions and 86; the Euro and 133; judges and policy-making 171; labelling of GM products 85–6; media 123, 125–6; perceptions of news media 127; pluralism and 97
University of Amsterdam, cross-national research on EP elections 129

Valladolid plant (Spain) 73
van der Eijk, C. 53–4
VAT tribunals 172, 179, 187–8
Verheijen, T. 219
veto strategies, advantages of governing forces and 14
Viannet, Louis 75
Vilvoorde plant (Belgium) 73–6, 81, 90; events 78–9; lessons of 76–7

Von Beyme, K. 160
voters 15; alternatives for 49; apathy in
    European elections 12; choice and EU
    issues 56, 60–61, 63–5, 68; choice and
    left–right self-placement 59–60; decision-
    making and 47; environmental policy in
    European elections 56; EU policies and
    52; French and British and EMU 58; two
    channels for access to Europe 43, 45
voting behaviour, economic voting 65–7;
    Euro and 68–9; European and national
    elections 53–5, 67; instructions from
    EACs 157; issue voting in national
    elections 55–65

Weiler, J.H.H. 144

welfare state, redefinition of 225
Wessels, W. 146, 217
western Europe, changes in role of 'the state'
    214
Weymouth, A. 124
Whitten, G. 65, 67–8
Working Time Directive (OJ 93/L 307/18
    Art. 17.3) 107
World Bank, EU membership and 219
World Trade Organisation (WTO) 154
Wouters, L. 211

ZDF (channel 2 German television network)
    127, 133, 135
Ziller, J. 213